Inquisition in Eden

Inquisition
in Eden

ALVAH BESSIE

The Macmillan Company, New York

First Printing

The Macmillan Company, New York

Collier-Macmillan Canada, Ltd., Toronto, Ontario

Library of Congress Catalog Card Number: 65–15558

DESIGNED BY RONALD FARBER

Printed in the United States of America

The author wishes to thank the following for permission to reprint previously copyrighted material, which first appeared in substantially different form:

Masses & Mainstream, for "July 4, 1950," July, 1951 issue; *Contact: The San Francisco Collection of New Writing, Art and Ideas,* for "The Non-Existent Man," October, 1960 issue, and "Dissolve To," July, 1964 issue; *Das Magazin,* for "Leonhard Frank in Hollywood," August, 1962 issue; *The Realist,* for "Sneak Preview of a Hollywood Flashback," June, 1964 issue. Nazim Hikmet's poem, "Advice to a Fellow Prisoner," is reprinted from *Masses & Mainstream.*

for Sylviane, who heard the guns

although she was 120 miles and 21 years away . . .

We are a rebellious nation. Our whole history is treason; our blood was attainted before we were born; our creeds are infidelity to the mother church; our Constitution, treason to our fatherland. What of that? Though all the governors in the world bid us commit treason against man, and set an example, let us never submit.

—THEODORE PARKER

Inquisition in Eden

Strip away the phony tinsel of Hollywood and you find the real tinsel underneath.

—OSCAR LEVANT

cast of characters

(Not necessarily in the order of their appearance or importance)

THE NARRATOR . . . A bald man of fifty-nine who has spent most of his adult life trying to make a living as a writer but has been other things: lecturer in natural history, assistant bookstore manager, incompetent actor, newspaper and magazine editor and writer, combat soldier, translator, private pilot, teacher of short-story and novel technique, publishers' consultant and editor, screenwriter and convict, trade-union editor and PR man, nightclub stage manager, light man, and announcer. He has had three marriages and two divorces; has three children, four grandchildren, and a host of other troubles. He may be slightly bitter around the edges.

HELEN CLARE . . . His second wife and mother of his only daughter; short-story writer, editor, teacher and putative dramatist; of Swedish-American lineage, blond, blue-eyed, and somewhat *fey;* she has described herself (since she was twenty-seven) as looking "like an old chorus girl."

HIS CHILDREN . . . Daniel, David, and Eva.

MR. MCDONALD . . . Ageless Scot, about sixty, warden of U.S. Federal Correctional Institution, Texarkana, Texas, during The Narrator's visit (1950–1951). He has the deadest pan ever seen on a man's head but, underneath, is quite human.

WRITERS . . . Dick, Dan Fuchs, Howard Koch, Jo Pagano, Thomas Mann, John Howard Lawson, Dalton Trumbo, William Faulkner, Al, Robert Rossen, Bertolt Brecht, Norman Corwin, Clifford Odets, Leonhard Frank, Albert Maltz, and others.

PRODUCERS . . . Jack, Jerry Wald, Mark Hellinger, Lou, Adrian Scott, Dore Schary, Wolfgang Reinhardt, A. and/or S. Lyons, Milton Sperling, and others.

DIRECTORS . . . Delmer Daves, Raoul Walsh, Vince, Edward

[1]

Dmytryk, Mikhail Kalatazov, Herbert Biberman, and others.

ACTORS . . . Walter Huston, Monte Blue, Eleanor Parker, Constance Bennett, Walter Hampden, John Garfield, Bette Davis, Adolph Menjou, Charles Chaplin, Gene Kelly, Gary Cooper, Errol Flynn, Katina Paxinou, Lee J. Cobb, Helmut Dantine, Edward G. Robinson, and others.

BIT PLAYERS . . . Various prison officials, guards, inmates, Earl Browder, lawyers, military and Civil Air Patrol personnel, Major General Evans Carlson, Vincent Sheean, Ernest Hemingway, agents, messenger girls, Glenn Anders, extra players, cops, crooks, secretaries, Bennett Cerf, goons, men's room attendants, finks, Jack L. Warner, bartenders, fairies, Big Bill Tilden, Stark Young, various varieties of ass-kissers, Winston Burdett, amateur whores, Richard M. Nixon, art directors, Boris Moros, publicity men, Ayn Rand, editors, Eric Johnston, opportunists, talent scouts, probation officers, FBI men, investigators, the Most Powerful Man in the United States Today, judges, Congressmen, and other actors.

LOCATIONS . . . Hollywood; Beverly Hills; Washington, D.C.; Spain; the San Fernando Valley; Chicago; New York; the *Santa Fe Chief*; a Mercury sedan traveling from Washington to Texas; Washington District Jail; Burbank, California; county jails in Roanoke, Virginia, and Memphis, Tennessee; Washington District Court; Federal Correctional Institution, Texarkana, Texas; San Francisco.

FEDERAL CORRECTIONAL INSTITUTION. Texarkana, Texas. July, 1950. The pastel-green two-story building looks like a modern high school. It stands on a wide lawn that is shaded by some stately old trees, and it has an exercise yard (like a high-school athletic field) with a baseball diamond and bleachers, a basketball court, horseshoe pits, and a few weights.

While it is true that there is a ten-foot cyclone fence around the acreage and there are three guard towers (two of which are manned at all times) and the grounds around the cellblocks are floodlighted at night, the atmosphere is by no means oppressive.

The installation was built during the first administration of Franklin Delano Roosevelt and was one of the fruits of a program he initiated to reform the Federal prison system and reclassify inmates according to their offenses, length of sentence, and incidence of recidivism.

Thus, this type of institution receives first offenders, short-time prisoners, and others not classified as habitual criminals. A good fifty percent are Negroes; a large percentage of whites are from the South; and the prison population is composed mainly of moonshiners, wetbacks, narcotic addicts, men who have sold alcohol without a license or have been convicted of other Federal offenses such as transporting cars or women that did not belong to them across state lines (Dyer and Mann Acts), robbing the mails, forging money orders, and income-tax evasion.

INTERIOR. QUARANTINE CELLBLOCK. DAY

—on the ground floor of one wing of the main building. It consists of a corridor locked at both ends by grilles made of steel bars. There are twenty cells facing one another, and there is one man in each cell.

In one of these cells stands the NARRATOR, an inmate. He is a bald man of forty-six, in reasonably good physical condition. He had worn a moustache for twenty-two years preceding his admission to the institution (probably because his father wore one, though if you questioned him he would insist that he did not like his father). Unfortunately, the screw on duty ordered him to "Shave that thing off!" the day he arrived, and when he feels his upper lip—as he is doing now—it feels obscenely bare.

At the moment, the NARRATOR is rather nervous. He is awaiting a "call-out" for an important interview, and with considerable effort he is resisting the temptation to do what he has seen any number of other prisoners do (at least in the movies), that is, pace back and forth. To steady himself, he has taken up position in one corner of his cell; his eye, like the eye of a camera, PANS his surroundings. He is not very happy at what he sees.

The cell has a solid steel door with a small window inset. It may be locked by the guard but not, unfortunately, by the inmate. The room measures only ten by twenty feet (the NARRATOR has paced it out); in it are an Army cot (hard), with a steel drawer underneath that has a combination lock; a steel chair; a small steel table, on which there are a few books that he has borrowed from the prison library; a washbowl on the wall, with two push buttons for hot and cold water; and a toilet bowl (without a wooden seat), also operated by a button—an odd thing to find right in your bedroom.

A small shelf, built in the corner of the cell near the window and set about seven feet from the concrete floor, holds the inmate's extra blue-denim shirt, trousers, and two extra pairs of shorts and T-shirts. There are a radiator and a steam pipe. No pictures on the wall (*verboten*). There are no bars on the window, but it is made of solid panes of thick glass set in solid steel frames

[4]

and may be opened from the top, at a diagonal angle, to let in fresh air. On the floor there is a pair of wooden clogs that the inmate uses when he goes to the end of the cellblock to take a shower—which is just about all the NARRATOR is allowed to do, for at the moment he is "in quarantine."

When you go to Federal prison, you spend the first thirty days segregated from the rest of the population, during which time you are subjected to a battery of tests designed to evaluate your health, intelligence, achievement, personality, and aptitude for work (for you will work eight hours a day). They fill you with shots to protect you from disease; if your teeth need fixing, they will fix them free; if you need dentures (or eyeglasses or a wooden leg), you will get them.

In addition to these fringe benefits, each inmate, shortly after his arrival, is granted an interview with his parole officer, a man who is supposed to assist him in applying for parole by the end of the first third of his sentence. In the Federal Correctional Institution in Texarkana, Texas, where I served a year's sentence in 1950–1951 for a misdemeanor called contempt of Congress, there were two parole officials. The one I drew (because I had an odd number—5853-TT) was named Huber. This was the gentleman I had been anxiously waiting to see; and when we finally met, he proved to be reasonably intelligent, if not widely educated. He was also reasonably sympathetic, if unutterably bored.

CUT TO

MED. TWO SHOT. HUBER AND NARRATOR
—in the former's office on the second floor.
HUBER
(seated behind desk)
This is where I get *your* side of the story; why you think you're here.
HUBER PAUSES, LIGHTS a cigarette, NODS when the INMATE GESTURES toward the pocket of his blue-denim shirt. INMATE, seated in a chair across from HUBER, LIGHTS his own cigarette.

[5]

HUBER
(continuing)
But before you start, let me tell you that in twenty years of custodial work, I have yet to meet an inmate who wasn't here on a bum rap.

NARRATOR
(all officers are "sir")
Sir, in my opinion I'm a political prisoner.

HUBER
(deadpan)
Bessie, we don't have any political prisoners in the United States.
(glances at dossier on his desk, points with finger)
You're here for violation of Section 192, Title 2, U.S. Code, which means refusal to testify before a duly constituted committee of Congress. . . .

Neither I nor the nine other writers, directors, and producers who were first called "The Unfriendly Ten" (and later "The Hollywood Ten") had exactly refused to testify before the House Committee on Un-American Activities when, in October 1947, it "probed" the motion-picture industry for evidence of Communist infiltration. Our names: Herbert Biberman, Lester Cole, Edward Dmytryk, Ring Lardner, Jr., John Howard Lawson, Albert Maltz, Samuel Ornitz, Adrian Scott, Dalton Trumbo, and the Narrator.

We had been more than willing to talk, but the Committee was not interested in the sort of testimony we were anxious to adduce. Our point was that the Committee itself was unconstitutional, since it could not legislate in the field of ideas, opinions, or associations.*

So, after consultation with our attorneys, we had individually refused to answer the only questions the Committee cared to ask,

* First Amendment: "Congress shall make no law respecting an establishment of religion, or prohibiting the free exercise thereof; or abridging the freedom of speech or of the press; or the right of the people peaceably to assemble and to petition the Government for a redress of grievances."

[6]

questions to which, incidentally, it claimed to have the answers in advance: What were our trade-union affiliations? What were our political affiliations?

The Committee's point was simple: it had announced in advance—and it presented a number of "friendly" witnesses to buttress its contention—that the Screen Writers' Guild was dominated by Communists.

It had announced in advance that it had "found" that the Communist Party was not a political party in the accepted sense of the word, but an international conspiracy directed by Moscow and designed to overthrow the United States government by force and violence. (There were friendly witnesses to testify to that as well.)

When I think back today, it occurs to me (as it has many times in the last seventeen years) that very few people in the United States understood the position we took before that Committee, despite the endless statements we issued during the years 1947–1950, the countless speeches we made all over the country, and the international publicity attendant on the inquisition. The assertion has often been made, for example: "Any American should be proud to stand up and say what he believes in," and the assertion has a certain specious cogency. Yet our position was even simpler than the one that the Committee itself advanced:

Some of the original nineteen who were subpoenaed (only eleven * got to testify) could have said, "Sure, I belong to the Screen Writers' Guild," or, "I belong to the Communist Party— so what?" Or some could have said, "No, I don't, and what the hell do *you* care?"

But we had decided to challenge, for the first time in its sordid history, the very basis of the Committtee's existence and the validity of its mandate; an answer either way would therefore have been an answer to an impertinent question.

Ring Lardner, Jr., an excellent comedy writer, gave the most cogent reply. He said, "I could answer it, but if I did, I would

---

* The late, great German dramatist Bertolt Brecht was the eleventh, but since he was an alien he was forced—reluctantly—to take a different position vis-à-vis the Committee.

hate myself in the morning." (The hand he got from the audience was spectacular and heartening, but the answer availed him not at all.)

What the Committee wanted was simple enough: all it wanted was for us to say, "Yes, I am." Then it could say, "Just like we said, the Reds are infiltrating the motion-picture industry. Who are the *others*?"

Or, it wanted us to say, "No, we're not," so that it could produce a witness who would swear that we had lied, and perjury is a felony worth five years, while Contempt carries a maximum of one; and nobody in history, as far as we could discover, had ever been jailed for that misdemeanor—up to that point.

The real point, which never emerged despite our expensive efforts to publicize it, was this: the Committee was not in the least interested in *anything* we had to say. It was interested in intimidating—and controlling—the motion-picture industry, and it succeeded. It was not interested in the truth, but to this day you will find millions of Americans who simply cannot be convinced that a committee of our Congress (or, for that matter, any elected official or administration) can talk one way and act another.

For example, the Committee's trained seals spent five days on the stand insisting that American motion pictures were infiltrated with Communist propaganda.* (This was the ostensible reason for the investigation.) And this is an accusation that could easily have been answered, had anyone actually wanted to answer it—or even to investigate.

The producers, for example, who momentarily bucked the Committee, until they were told where to head in by the Wall Street gentlemen who actually own The Industry, offered to screen any American motion picture ever made and let the Committee point out the subversion. The offer was refused.

Dalton Trumbo, novelist and screenwriter, offered to put into the record twenty screenplays he had written and let the Com-

* *Hearing Before the Committee on Un-American Activities, House of Representatives, Eightieth Congress,* October 20, 21, 22, 23, 24, 27, 28, 29, and 30, 1947.

[8]

mittee indicate what he had done to subvert the American mind.

"May I ask how long one of these scripts may be?" said Chairman J. Parnell Thomas, *né* Feeney (R., N.J.).

"They average from 115 to 160 or 170 pages," Trumbo said, reaching for a neatly tied bundle of scripts, about three feet tall, that stood on the floor next to his chair.

"Too many pages," said the chairman.

I explained all these things to Mr. Huber as we sat smoking in his office, and he listened courteously and even agreed to read the transcript of our testimony; but since ten of us had landed in a variety of Federal institutions by arguing our case with the Committee and the judges, and in spite of a number of resounding Supreme Court decisions in parallel cases * that supported our arguments, I saw no particular point in litigating it with my parole officer. Besides, he couldn't have done anything about it even if he really became convinced that I *was* in on a bum rap.

So I went back to my cell in the quarantine block (next door to director Herbert Biberman, who had accompanied me to this joint in Texas). The temperature in that cell in July, 1950, was well over one hundred degrees Fahrenheit, and the air-conditioning system, which had been installed when the joint was built, had never worked.

In a temperature of over one hundred degrees Fahrenheit, it is easy to luxuriate in recollection, fantasy, or flashback as you sit in a metal chair or lie on a hard cot and let the perspiration run off your nose and ribs, and two actual scenes from the past rose before my inner eye: (1) A night under an *avellano* tree in Aragon, Spain, in 1938, when my company commander, a young man of twenty-four named Aaron Lopoff, said to me, "You started something, baby, when you came to Spain." (I was ten

* The most resounding was the majority opinion, written by Mr. Justice Jackson in *West Virginia* v. *Barnett*, 1943: "If there is one fixed star in our Constitutional constellation, it is that no official, high or petty, can prescribe what shall be orthodox in politics, nationalism, religion or other matters of opinion or force citizens to confess by word or act their faith therein." In 1950, the Supreme Court sidestepped this opinion by simply refusing to review our case.

years his senior.) At the time, I thought he meant I wouldn't get out alive, but that isn't what he meant at all. (2) An evening before we went to trial, when I met a cultural attaché of the Polish government at a party in Hollywood. He said, "Your task is to develop as much support for your case as you possibly can. And if you succeed, your first prison term will be of great benefit to your fellow Americans."

"*First* prison term?"

He looked at me. "I am a man," he said, "who in my time has spent fifteen years in prison. I assume that I am speaking to an honest man."

DISSOLVE TO

EXTERIOR. FRENCH LINE PIER. New York. December, 1938.

It is a bitterly cold day, but for many hours since dawn, some THREE THOUSAND MEN, WOMEN, and CHILDREN have been gathered in the streets outside the pier to await the arrival of the S.S. *France,* which is carrying one hundred American veterans of the Spanish Civil War. They bear American and Spanish Republican flags, placards reading: WELCOME HOME; LIFT THE EMBARGO!; MADRID WILL BE THE TOMB OF FASCISM. Others carry handmade posters with blown-up photographs of men in the haphazard "uniform" of the Lincoln Battalion (or studio portraits) with such inscriptions as: "Joe Comiskey, last seen at Jarama. *Alive?*" or, "Has anyone seen Ben Blau?" or, more simple and affecting, "Bob O'Hara?"

Before he got a machine-gun bullet through his eye on Hill 666 in the Sierra Pandóls (Catalonia), Aaron Lopoff had more than ordinary prescience. He was only twenty-four, but he was—in some ways—far more of a man than I was at thirty-four. I was aware that he was trying to prove himself as a man and a commander of men, and his gruff manner and daily insults were only a mask for a basic insecurity he was determined to overcome—in action.

Of course, he knew little of my past. He came straight out of the Jewish working class; I out of the Jewish upper middle class;

[10]

but we had both arrived at the same point at the same time in history and with the same purpose—to fight and, if necessary, to die in defense of human decency.

Put that way, it sounds pompous and self-righteous, but we had both been incensed by the rise of Hitlerism; we had both been insulted (in our very flesh) by the cynical attack on the Spanish Republic, the obscene bombing of unarmed civilian populations, the demolition of a harmless town called Guernica (and all its people)—for the purpose of testing the Nazi Stukas and the Fascist policy of atrocity.

And since I was ten years older than Aaron, I had a backlog of indignation and outrage of which he could not have been aware, for I never got a chance to tell him about it. I could remember—even under that *avellano* bush in Aragon—that time during the first Great Depression, when my first wife and I were gracefully starving to death in Vermont and putting what food we had into the belly of our first son.

There was no market for the short stories I turned out with admirable regularity, and at one point one of my old professors at Columbia College, John Erskine, offered a helping hand. He induced one of the biggest literary agents in New York to write to me and suggest a theme for an article that they both thought would have a surefire sale, and I still don't know whether the idea was Erskine's or the agent's.

The title: "Extenuations of Sudden Poverty."

Being in my twenties and rather naïve (or perhaps, without knowing it, I was a budding subversive even then), I indignantly refused the assignment and received a hot letter from Professor Erskine that said, "How *dare* you tell Mr. X that there is *anything* you cannot or will not write! I was trying to get you a chance."

With some cogency, I tried to explain to my old professor that I could see *no* extenuations in poverty, sudden or gradual, but relations between us were strained from that time on. My development into a dangerous radical was no doubt accelerated by five years on the submarginal soil of the Green Mountain State, where I tried with some success to grow chickens, lettuce, cabbage, and peas and with no success to sell stories to the New York magazines.

There was a time when I hired myself out to one of our neighbors, Mr. Richardson, whose ten sons and daughters were still considered foreigners because the old man and his wife had come from Boston twenty years before.

The year before I went to work for him, Mr. Richardson had invested in a mechanical potato digger and chemical fertilizer, and he planted about twenty acres to potatoes. The crop was enormous, and I worked alongside the Richardson brood for a week and took my hire out in trade.

That fall when the A & P truck came around, the produce man offered to buy a thousand bushels from Richardson at fifty cents a bushel.

"Why," said the old man, "it cost me more than that to grow them!"

"Too bad," said A & P.

"Before I'd sell 'em for fifty cents a bushel, I'll let 'em rot in the cellar!" Richardson shouted. And that is precisely what he did.

The next summer, he decided that he would plant just enough potatoes to feed his family, and when the A & P truck drove up that fall, the buyer offered him $1.10 a bushel—and he had none to sell.

The A & P puzzled me, and I embarked on a self-imposed, lifetime reading course in history, political economy, classical and Marxist economics, philosophy: idealist, mechanical materialist, and dialectical materialist—and other forbidden subjects.

And the "sudden poverty" of Vermont was only extenuated once, in 1935, when the Guggenheim Foundation granted me the sum of $2,000 for a novel I had submitted—for the third year running. The novel was finally completed (and published) that year—and then the extenuation ran out.

A friend named Edward Cushing created a job for me as his assistant on the Brooklyn *Daily Eagle*, and I got along well until the Spanish war began and Cushing sent me out to interview Ralph Bates and André Malraux. What I wrote outraged the hierarchy of the Roman Catholic Church in Brooklyn, which insisted on having equal space to answer what I had printed—and got three times as much. I quit the *Eagle* in disgust to work as a publicity man for the Spanish Republican government in New York and then left their information bureau to volunteer to fight for Spain.

And when we returned to New York, I was met at the French Line pier by two newspapermen, who actually wore press cards in their hat bands (like in the movies).

One of them was Winston Burdett, who had become a close friend of mine when we worked on the *Eagle* together. He was motion-picture critic for the paper. Now he took me to his apartment in Brooklyn Heights and literally kept me for a month until I could find work.

The other was a legman for the *World Telegram*, who said that his managing editor wanted to see me about a possible series of stories on the American volunteers in Spain.

This was a shocking surprise, for in spite of the fact that public opinion polls had demonstrated that the majority of the American people—in fact, the majority of the people of the world—were on the side of the legally elected Republic of Spain, many of the papers (and the Hearst press in particular) had been describing the volunteers for Spain as international revolutionary gangsters, assassins, and minions of Moscow. The power of the press and of the Catholic hierarchy was so great that even Franklin Delano Roosevelt could not reveal his known partisanship or lift the embargo on Republican Spain.

But I began to think that the truth about Spain had finally got through to the people when David McKelvey White, secretary of the Friends of the Abraham Lincoln Brigade, told me that he had received a message for me to call Bennett Cerf of Random House! It could not *be!* A place to stay, a newspaper series to write, a possible book on Spain—all in ten minutes!

The legman advised me to work up one sample story before I saw his editor; and in Burdett's apartment, I got to work on his portable and tore off a passionate piece that described our all-night hike across the Pyrenees in dead of night (and winter), avoiding the French nonintervention patrols, and our arrival in Figueras to join the International Brigades. (I also wrote outlines for four more articles.)

When I took the piece over to the *World-Telegram*, the managing editor shook his head in admiration.

CAMERA COMES TO
CLOSE TWO SHOT. MANAGING EDITOR and NARRATOR
—as the EDITOR TAPS the manuscript he has laid respectfully on his desk.

EDITOR

Good copy. But not exactly what we're looking for.

NARRATOR
(suspiciously)

What exactly are you looking for?

EDITOR
(deprecatory smile)

You know. The romance. The adventure. Beautiful dark-eyed *señoritas* in lace mantillas. Color stuff.

NARRATOR
(somewhat bitter)

I never saw a mantilla in the year I was in Spain. And we weren't adventurers.

(getting hot)

We were there because we believed in what we were doing, because we—

EDITOR
(interrupting)

Look, brother, I'm on *your* side. I admire what you guys did. I'm just telling you what the paper wants. Maybe you can fancy it up a little.

NARRATOR
(rising)

If I could have fancied it up, I wouldn't have gone to Spain in the first place.

EDITOR
(rising, extending hand)

No hard feelings.

[*14*]

So, I peddled the sample article and the outlines of the other four all around the city—and got exactly nowhere. Then I visited Bennett Cerf. We had had a tenuous acquaintance in the past. He had been a fraternity brother of my own brother at Columbia College, and he had once offered me a royalty (but no cash) to translate a book on the Borgias (which I refused).

He lived in a fine apartment off Central Park, and when I got there he gave me a snifter of cognac, a cast-off overcoat (the one the French workers had provided on our way home was rather odd-looking for New York), a dark fedora hat that was too large, and said he wanted to publish a history of the Lincoln Battalion.

When I told him that I wasn't a historian but that I did want to write a book, he asked, "What kind of book?"

"A personal history," I said, "of my own participation in the war."

"That's not the kind of book I want," said Cerf, so I told him that the one man to write the book he did want was the poet Edwin Rolfe, who had been in Spain from the beginning of the war as a soldier, a writer for our frontline newspaper, *Volunteer for Liberty*, and a correspondent for the *Daily Worker*. (Cerf later commissioned Rolfe and published his book *The Lincoln Battalion*.)

With the newspaper series down the drain and the book teetering on the brim, I then called on a slick New York agent named Carol Hill. I was somewhat worried about her, because Vincent Sheean, whom I had met in Spain, recommended her but cautioned me that she thought that *he* was a Red (which was a laugh). Apparently she was not only friendly to Sheean but was an astute businesswoman as well, for she made an appointment for me with Maxwell Perkins of Charles Scribner's Sons.

Perkins listened to my description of the book and said that he would think about it. So, that was that. Another bum steer, another delay in finding a source of income. But the hand of God intervened at this point in the person of Ernest Hemingway (whom I had also met in Spain), for Carol Hill phoned a couple of days later and told me to call on Perkins to discuss a contract.

Hemingway, he said, had visited him the day after our interview and he had told him about the book I wanted to write. "Grab it," he quoted Hemingway as saying; "it'll be the best book written by any of the guys."

This was a rash statement by Hemingstein (as he liked to call himself, with a slight, self-deprecatory touch), but the book was published under the title *Men in Battle*, and despite a full-page review by Sheean in The *New York Herald Tribune* and the *only* review I ever got in *Time*, it never sold. For it appeared the week that Hitler invaded Poland, and people had other things to read—the newspapers.

The series of articles never sold, either, but when I offered it to Joe North, who had preceded Edwin Rolfe as *Worker* correspondent in Spain and was then editor of *New Masses*, he offered me a job at $30 a week.

"Didn't you used to be an actor?" he said.

"Sort of."

"We need a drama critic," North said.

"I was never a very good actor."

"What's that got to do with it? How many plays were you in?"

"Maybe a dozen. But I never played any big parts. Only bits and understudies."

"You know what Shaw said," said Joe. "You sound admirably equipped to criticize other actors—"

"There's more to it than that."

What am I doing, I asked myself, talking myself out of a job? So I started that week and spent my first night in the theater (we never got first-night tickets, only second) reviewing a revival of Sidney Howard's *They Knew What They Wanted*, in which I had appeared as an extra and bit player with Richard Bennett and Pauline Lord in 1925.

Having always been a frustrated ham (I can read lines beautifully but never learned what to do with my hands or body once I was standing up), I thoroughly enjoyed evaluating other actors (and the plays in which they appeared). But despite Rex Stout's telling Brooks Atkinson that I was the best drama critic in New York (or perhaps because of it), the *New Masses* reviewer was never admitted to the New York Drama Critics' Circle. (It might have had something to do with the magazine's political stance, at that.)

My reviewing improved immensely after I met a beautiful young woman of Swedish-American extraction, at a party given in honor of returned veterans of the Lincoln Brigade, and followed her home.

Her name was Helen Clare, and she was too much of a lady to put me out of her house immediately, though she soon made it plain that she could not take me seriously. I aided and abetted her in this opinion by knocking at her door and calling her on the phone at all hours of the day and night. I sat on her front steps, waiting for her to come home from the McGraw-Hill Book Company, where she edited technical manuscripts, and occasionally I even went up to the roof of her apartment house on West Eighth Street, came down the fire escape, and let myself in through her window so that she could "discover" me sitting in the armchair when she got home.

In an effort to improve her opinion of me—this was in the spring of 1939—I took her to a dance that the VALB held and introduced her to the man who had supplanted Aaron Lopoff in my heart—Joe Hecht. I had known him for years, first meeting him during the 1936 seamen's strike, when my first wife organized a soup kitchen for the striking sailors, and then again in Spain.

Joe was so ugly that he was positively beautiful, and he survived Spain only to be killed in his first action in World War II. At the dance, he took me aside and said, "She's a bleached blond, and she looks like a—"

"She's *not*," I said, "and she doesn't," and I continued to pursue her and pester her for more than a year, until she married me out of sheer desperation (she *said* it was because her lease was up and she needed a place to live). The marriage lasted fourteen years, but she has long since admitted it was a sad mistake.

And during our courtship and early marriage, before he was shipped out to Germany, Joe learned that she *was* a natural Swedish blond (with the bluest eyes I have ever seen), and he

[*17*]

came to love her. The three of us would sit around our West Tenth Street apartment fortifying ourselves with a huge salami and a bottle of Courvoisier, and Joe would roar with laughter when Helen Clare told him the stories about her hair: how she had been fired from her first teaching job in her native state of Washington because the school board also thought that she was bleached and adamantly refused to change its mind, even when her mother appeared indignantly on the scene—with identical Swedish blond hair—to protest the dismissal.

In addition to her physical attributes, my wife was a putative playwright who knew a good deal more about dramatic construction than I had ever learned, and her taste in the theater was impeccable. She accompanied me to most of the plays I saw, and as I rarely reviewed a play without holding a conference with her, the *New Masses* drama reviews got better and better.

And during the four years I remained on the staff of *New Masses* as drama, book, and movie critic and feature writer, we had what is called a running gag in our ménage.

My wife was slowly being driven to drink by the nine-to-five routine of editing manuscripts on hydrodynamics, electrical engineering, and chemistry, and I had induced her to persuade McGraw-Hill to let her work on a free-lance basis at home.

This way she could get up when she wanted to—and it was as difficult for her to wake up as it always has been for me—and go to work when she wanted, and make even more money. (Actually, she made even less money, because she never felt like working till afternoon, which meant that to earn the same amount of money she had to work late every night.)

And every day that I was at the office of *New Masses*, I would call home at least once and say, "Any telephone calls? Any Hollywood contracts?"

For Hollywood had always been a goal of mine, because I loved the films and had the misbegotten idea that I could make a contribution to the medium. Through my closest friend for many years, the late Kyle Crichton, I even had contact for a while with a Hollywood agent named James Geller, who reported (pre-Spain) that he couldn't get me a job because I was considered a highbrow writer and (post-Spain) because I was considered a Red.

DISSOLVE TO

CLOSE SHOT. NARRATOR. IN BED. January, 1943.
He has his semiannual case of flu and is flowing from the nose, SNEEZING, and COUGHING. There is a box of Kleenex and a telephone on a bed table and a wastepaper basket next to the bed. The NARRATOR is trying to read Thomas Mann's *Joseph in Egypt* and is having an even worse time with it than with the cold. The phone RINGS.

NARRATOR
(stuffed up)

Yeh?

MALE VOICE
(over phone)

Alvah Bessie?

NARRATOR

Yeh.

MALE VOICE
This is Jake Wilk of Warner Brothers pictures.

NARRATOR
(suddenly angry)

Cut out the crap!
HE HANGS UP, PICKS UP his book, and tries to find the page, when THE PHONE RINGS AGAIN. He lets it RING three or four times before he PICKS IT UP again.

NARRATOR
(shouting)
What the hell d'you want *now*!

It *was* Jake Wilk of Warner Brothers (whoever *he* was), and he wanted to know whether I would like to come to his office to discuss a contract for writing films.

I told him I was in bed with flu, and he said, "Well, come in when you're *well*," and hung up as unceremoniously as I had done a few moments earlier.

That was on a Friday night, and flu or no flu, I had to review a

[19]

play at the Guild Theater. My wife and I discussed this new twist in our running gag on the subway. Who could be responsible for so unlikely an eventuality? Certainly not James Geller, whom I had not heard from in more than a year. Certainly not my college friend Guy Endore, who had not written from Hollywood in years. Certainly not Kyle Crichton at *Collier's* or he would have warned us. Who else did we know in Hollywood?

Well, there was Daniel Fuchs, whose novel *Low Company* I had reviewed enthusiastically when I was Sunday-magazine editor of the Brooklyn *Eagle* before I went to Spain. He used to write once in a while, but we had not heard from him either.

In the lobby of the Guild Theater, where I had worked more than fourteen years before in such plays as *Marco Millions, Faust,* and *Volpone* (as an extra and understudy), we ran into a University of Washington classmate of my wife named Sophie Rosenstein.

We had not known she was in town, and we had not even recalled that she worked at Warner Brothers studio in Burbank as a drama coach and talent scout, but we immediately accused her of being responsible for the offer.

She protested that she knew nothing about it and introduced us to a man she had run into in the lobby, a handsome and obviously homosexual gentleman, who, she said, was a Hollywood agent.

"If Warners actually wants you on a contract," said Sophie, "you'd better let Billy here represent you or you'll be screwed."

Billy said that he was registered in a midtown hotel; he advised me to see Wilk on Monday and, "Listen to what he has to offer, but don't commit yourself. Then, when you're through, come to my hotel and we'll have lunch."

DISSOLVE TO

MED. TWO SHOT. WILK AND NARRATOR

—in Wilk's office in New York. WILK is irascible (it seems to be his permanent condition). He GESTURES the NARRATOR to a chair.

WILK

(abruptly)

You want to go to Hollywood or don't you?

NARRATOR

(containing his excitement)

What do they want me for? A single picture or a contract?

WILK

I told you, a contract. Look—

(hot gesture)

—I want to assure you, I don't know you from a hole in the ground. I never heard of you in my life.

NARRATOR

(to himself)

I never heard of you either, Wilk.

WILK

I had a hell of a time finding you.

NARRATOR

(containing his curiosity)

How *did* you find me?

WILK

(lighting cigar)

Look, every day of the week, I get wires from the Coast asking me to dig up this or that dead body. You're just another one.

NARRATOR

You could have found me in the phone book.

WILK

I didn't. I called up the biggest agent in New York, figgering they'd know who the hell you are, but they said they didn't represent you and told me to try Carol Hill.

NARRATOR

She *used* to be my agent, but I—

(catching himself, not wanting to say they had had a political argument and he had quit her)

WILK

Yeh. She said, "No, I don't represent him. Try the *Daily Worker*." So I tried the *Daily Worker*—

(looks apoplectic)

They said, no, you didn't work there, try the *New Masses*. So I tried the *New Masses*.

(pause)

You want to go to Hollywood or don't you?

NARRATOR

(cautious)

Well, Mr. Wilk, I don't know anything about Hollywood, and maybe you'd better talk to my agent.

WILK

(growing furious)

I don't want to talk to any agent! You don't *need* an agent; they want you on a contract. They don't want you, *then* you need an agent. How much you want?

NARRATOR

(more cautious)

I have no idea what these jobs pay, Mr. Wilk, and my agent—

WILK

We're offering $150.

NARRATOR

(doggedly)

My agent's at the—

He took the agent's name and address, and I knew I was dismissed. So I dashed to Billy's hotel. It was noon and he was still in bed, but he ordered coffee for us and lay in bed in his silk pajamas and listened to my description of the interview.

"It so happens," he said, "that Jack Warner's in town, and I'll talk to *him*."

He reached for the phone, gave the operator a number, and it was promptly answered by Mrs. Jack Warner.

Said Billy, "Annie, what kind of a shit you got working in your New York office, anyhow? . . . He offered a writer of mine a lousy $150 on a contract. . . . What's that? . . . All right, I'll talk to him."

He hung up the phone and said, "Jack's out, but they'll be at the Stork tonight, so I'll talk to him there. Tell me something about yourself."

I told him something about myself. I told him that I was the drama critic for *New Masses* and broadcast for the magazine for fifteen minutes every Sunday morning on Station WQXR (for free). I told him that I had had a novel published a year earlier (that would make a good movie) and had just received an offer to go on a one-month speaking tour for the International Workers Order, which was a mutual benefit insurance society and fraternal order—subject: the war. This would have paid about $50 a week and expenses. And that is all I told him, because that was all there was to tell. And I doubt that Sophie Rosenstein told him anything more, because I had met her for the first time the night I met him, and she had turned right around—after scouting the Broadway plays—and gone straight back to Burbank.

Billy called the next noon and told me to drop in on him at two and then go to Wilk's office to sign a contract. When we met, he reported a conversation that I would not have believed even if I had heard it myself, though in light of what went on in Hollywood those days and what happened to me when I got there, it might very well have taken place. The conversation at the Stork went like this:

BILLY (to Warner): What kind of a shit you got working for you in your New York office, anyhow?

WARNER: Why, what's wrong with him?

BILLY: He offered my writer, Bessie, a lousy $150 a week.

WARNER: That's what I told him to offer.

BILLY (hot): Bessie don't have to work for you for a lousy $150. He's the drama critic for a national magazine. He's got a house in the country. He's got his own radio program. He's got a best-selling novel on the stands that would make a great picture. He's going on a nationwide speaking tour.

WARNER: Well, I don't know that I want him, anyhow. I hear he's a Red.

BILLY (pitching): Warner, you guys make me sick. The Reds are saving your goddamn moving-picture business on the Stalingrad front tonight!

[23]

WARNER (enthusiastically): You're *right!* I'll give him $300.

Warner and Billy look at each other, do a double take, then laugh loudly.

SLOW DISSOLVE TO

THREE SHOT. WILK, NARRATOR, and SECRETARY
—in Wilk's office. WILK PLACES before the NARRATOR a twenty-three page, legal-sized, mimeographed contract. In addition to requiring the Narrator's signature (twice), it has to be initialed by him on every single page as well. This takes time. WILK PACES UP AND DOWN, CHEWING on his cigar.

NARRATOR
(looking up)
When do you want me in Hollywood?

WILK
Next week.

NARRATOR
That would be difficult. We have a number of—

WILK
When can you get there?

NARRATOR
The week after.

WILK
Look here. Do you belong to any organizations that advocate the overthrow of the government?

NARRATOR
I belong to the Authors' Guild, and when I get to Hollywood I'll join the Screenwriters' Guild.

WILK
(to SECRETARY)
Take that down. He belongs to the Authors' Guild and will join the Screenwriters'.
(to NARRATOR—clairvoyantly)
I don't want some clown to stand up in Congress one of these days and say, "Look what Warner's hiring."

TRUCKING SHOT. THE *Santa Fe Chief*
—as it tools its way from Chicago to Los Angeles in January, 1943. The NARRATOR SITS glued to the window next to his lower berth. He would have liked to go by plane, but in those days only VIP's could get plane reservations ("There's a war on, you know"). He has never been any further west than Detroit and is enchanted by the changing landscape of America. He is accompanied on this momentous journey by BILLY THE AGENT, who, it develops, is not only a patent homosexual and a violent reactionary, but a Southerner as well. He is also accompanied by a man he had noticed in the dining car, an hour after the *Chief* pulled out of Chicago, and to whom he had introduced himself. This is EARL BROWDER, general secretary of the Communist Party of the U.S.A., who is also going to Los Angeles—to address a win-the-war rally. . . .

I had heard Browder speak many times at Madison Square Garden (in fact, my last assignment at *New Masses* had been to cover the Lenin Memorial Meeting a few days earlier). He had never impressed me as much of a speaker or a personality, but after I introduced myself to him he said that he enjoyed my book and film and drama reviews in *Masses* and invited me to his drawing room.

There I expressed my disappointment that the Allies had not yet opened a second front in Europe, and he smiled cynically and said, "What's the matter? Don't you trust our glorious allies?"

I decided then that I did not like him at all and regretted having shared with him a half-pint of Courvoisier my wife had given me for the journey (she was to follow a week later, after subletting our apartment on Tenth Street and packing various articles to be sent by Railway Express).

"Don't set Hollywood on fire," was the last thing Browder said to me the night before we pulled into Los Angeles—and it didn't seem a particularly prophetic statement at the time—but there were other things and people aboard that train that were more depressing, interesting, or exciting.

Item: A short piece in the weekly *Variety* that read, in effect,

"Scribblers are so scarce in Hollywood these days—most having gone into the Armed Forces—that anyone who can write a simple declarative English sentence is being inked to long-term pacts." I circled this item, wrote "Me" next to it, and mailed it back to Helen Clare from Chicago.

Item: Billy in the dining car (he had a compartment instead of a lower berth) calling a waiter and then cursing out loud when the overworked man didn't get there in time to suit him. "These goddamned black baboons," he said, "aren't fit to wait on *no*-one!" I felt like flattening him for that remark, but I didn't, and I wondered at myself: Had I become corrupt so *fast* that I did not immediately react the way any decent person (let alone a radical) would react to such vicious contempt for another human being? Was it because Wilk had handed me nearly a thousand dollars in cash—in advance? Because I was afraid that if I alienated my agent, I would be back on *New Masses* in no time at all?

Item: A Marine Corps major who was apparently a heterosexual acquaintance of Billy's and was returning to the Coast to rejoin his outfit in the Pacific. He had a mess of fruit salad on his tunic, was six feet six inches tall, carried a swagger stick and invariably referred to me as Hemingway. (He also had a wife and kids back home.)

Item: A curiously mixed sensation of excitement and depression—excitement over the achievement of a "life ambition": to write for Hollywood, with all that this entailed in terms of prestige, opportunity to contribute to the medium, and, yes— money; together with a growing conviction of being lost (corrupted? sold out?) because I had abandoned my job on *New Masses,* where I could really write what I felt and really felt that what I wrote had some impact on our readers. And that job was a symbol of the attitude I had developed during the Depression; my developing radicalism; and the like-minded friends with whom I associated days and nights; and the men we had left behind in the Spanish earth, who had died for what we all believed in—not radicalism, but simple human decency and human love. Would these be found in Hollywood? And where?

Item: The terms of my contract with Warner Brothers, one item of which has fascinated me to this day and which details precisely the relationship of the writer to the medium. It reads:

"The Author agrees that all material composed, submitted, added and/or interpolated by the Author hereunder shall automatically become the property of the Producer, who, for this purpose, shall be deemed the author thereof." A copy of an affidavit stipulating to this incredible situation was to be executed and turned in with each and every assignment performed by the author.

Item: A screenplay based on a Broadway play called *Brooklyn, U.S.A.,* written by John Bright and Asa Bordages, which Wilk had handed to me the day I signed the contract. He told me my first assignment would be to rewrite it, since the studio was not satisfied with it.

I read this screenplay three times between New York and Pasadena, and it seemed absolutely wonderful—far better than the play itself, which I had reviewed for *New Masses*—and I wondered what in hell I could do to improve it, when I could see nothing in it that I would change for any reason whatsoever.

Item: A voluptuous female creature, about twenty-five years old, who got aboard at Albuquerque and flopped in the seat opposite me and promptly fell asleep. I sat gazing at her magnificent haunches until she woke up half an hour later, yawned like a cat (no, a jaguar), looked at me, and said, "What time is it?"

I told her, and she pulled out an empty cigarette package and held it in front of me. If she had said, as Ginger Rogers did in *Young Man of Manhattan,* "Cigarette me, big boy," I would not have been astonished, but I did it anyhow and lit it for her, and she told me her name, said she had been bumped off a plane in Albuquerque, was married to a soldier in Alaska, had a small daughter, and worked in Lockheed's aircraft factory in Burbank.

She also asked me who I was, and when I told her (and added that I was a writer on my way to Hollywood), she said she had never heard of me.

I invited her to dinner that night in the dining car (it was our

[27]

last night aboard) and engaged in beautiful fantasies (for after all, I was only thirty-eight and two years married). These fantasies lasted only the few minutes that passed before Billy and his Marine major arrived in the dining car.

They took seats at our table without being invited (the Major next to the Jaguar), and from that moment on, I was exactly nowhere and had to fall back on my so-called literary mind for some form of consolation.

The Major bought the Jaguar a number of drinks and insisted on paying for her dinner, referred to me at all times as Hemingway (*that* name the lady knew, but it did not impress her), and a phrase kept running through my head for the next few hours that was no consolation at all: "When six foot six speaks, women listen."

She not only listened, but also laughed loudly, displaying beautiful teeth; and later that night, when I was trying to go to sleep in my lower berth, I heard her and the Major in the aisle, for they were standing right next to me.

They made loud sucking noises and moaned and whispered, and he tried to persuade her to visit his roomette; and at one point, he gently parted the curtains in front of my berth, saying, "Is this bird asleep?" and looked in on me. I guess my eyes were closed, for he dropped the curtains and continued to importune the Jaguar, but she said she was tired and added, seductively, "Tomorrow, honey," and there were more sucking noises, and I heard her giggling as he boosted her into her upper berth across the aisle.

They apparently had what my nineteenth-century father used to call "an understanding," for when I passed the Major's roomette in the morning, on my way to the dining car, his door was open and they were breakfasting on a bottle of whiskey.

Billy was already at table, and we watched the California desert flow by (which excited me enormously). He said that he was staying at something improbably called The Garden of Allah, which I vaguely recalled as the onetime home of Alla Nazimova but which was now, apparently, a hotel.

He did not ask me where I was staying, and I did not tell him, because I did not know, having fondly believed that he and/or Warner Brothers would do something about accommodations for a writer whose way they were paying across the country and with whom they had signed a seven-year contract (with options) that guaranteed no more than six months of employment.

But the four of us left the train together, and when Billy inquired how he could get in touch with me, I told him I would call his office. The three of them hailed a cab and took off, leaving me alone in the monstrous "Spanish" station in downtown Los Angeles.

I gathered my luggage together and looked up Dan Fuchs's number in the phone book. He said that he was about to leave the house to play tennis and that if I would tell him where I was staying, he would have me out to dinner one of these nights.

I must have sounded somewhat miffed, for he said, "I'll see you at the studio on Monday, anyhow."

Then I looked up a comrade from Spain named Luke Hinman, who had been a battalion scout and a close friend during the last weeks that the Lincoln Battalion spent in action in the Sierra Cabálls, when we were both attached to the brigade staff—I as correspondent for *Volunteer for Liberty* and Luke as my personal legman, who was usually so tired that he rarely left his bunk under the olive trees or in the auto park, which meant that I did all my legwork myself.

Luke came for me in less than half an hour in an ancient automobile (I sent a wire to Helen Clare giving his address); and on the way out to his place in the Silver Lake district, he told me that he was married, had a child, and worked for the Watchmakers' Union. (Before he went to Spain, he had been an organizer for the agricultural workers.)

Luke was the ideal American outdoor type, resembling Gary Cooper in height; rangy construction; hard-bitten, deadpan face; blue eyes; and "cracks in the cheeks" (my wife's ideal type too).

His redheaded wife had formerly been associated with the League of American Writers in New York, and we got along famously the two weeks I (and later my wife) stayed with them, except that I began to feel guilty almost immediately, for Luke

[29]

and his family were living on next to nothing, and he obviously considered that I was now a rich man—and about to become even wealthier.

It seemed inappropriate to be going to my first Hollywood job on the streetcar up Sunset and then Hollywood Boulevards, but Luke had to be at work early that morning and said that he could not furnish *transporte*.

But it was no odder than the sights I was eagerly devouring from the car: the palm trees that looked out of place, even in that subtropical climate; the hot-dog stands in the shape of dogs (hot or literally canine); the endless lines of used-car lots and crummy-looking stucco houses built in imitation Spanish or Moorish styles.

At one corner, a strange-looking woman got aboard carrying a mynah bird in a large cage and took the seat directly across the aisle from me. I looked at her, but she looked straight ahead.

The mynah bird, however, turned its head and looked at me and said loudly, "What're*you*doinghere, what're*you*doinghere, what're*you*doinghere?" which was a good question—which I could not answer then and have never been able to answer since.

The question did set me to thinking of all the Hollywood stories I had ever heard: the one about the popular novelist Louis Bromfield, who had been employed at an enormous salary and sat around in his office for weeks doing nothing. He finally sought out his producer and said, "You know, I appreciate the salary you're paying, but I'd really enjoy doing something in return for it," to which the producer replied, "Think nothing of it. It's an honor just to have a man like you around, Mr. Blumberg."

Then there were the stories that had proliferated around the small figure of William Faulkner, one of which concerned his first film assignment. He had flown up from Oxford, Mississippi, in his personal aircraft; after a week, he told his producer that he could not work in the studio atmosphere and asked whether it would be all right to work at home. Permission granted. Three weeks later the producer told his secretary to get Faulkner on the line and, when he had him, said, "How's it coming along, Bill?"

"Fine."

"When can I see some pages?"

"Soon."

"How soon?"

"Oh, in a week or so, I reckon."

"How about coming in for lunch and showing me what you have?"

"Oh, I couldn't do that. You said I could work at home."

"Well, sure I did, but where are you staying, Bill?"

"In Oxford."

It couldn't possibly be that way anymore, I thought; they are surely not as insane here as the stories would have it. If they were, they could never get any work done, nor even make as many fairly decent pictures as they do.

I was thinking of this and of my swan song in *New Masses*, where I had written: "Leaving *New Masses* to work for the motion-picture industry as a writer has not been the easiest thing in the world to do . . . having had the opportunity . . . of sounding off on the products of the film industry, I have sort of put myself on the spot by accepting a chance to show what I can do myself.

"So I want to warn you in advance that if you see any exceptionally bad moving pictures in the future, it will be reasonably certain that I've had a hand in them . . . ."

Then I recalled the script of *Brooklyn, U.S.A.*, which I was carrying under my arm and I was quite literally terrified. For what could I say to the still-unknown-to-me producer (Jerry Wald) when he asked what I thought of it, except (since I *am* an honest man, as the Polish cultural *attaché* assumed), "I think it's wonderful"?

Then I would be given the other half of the round-trip ticket Warner Brothers had purchased and told to go back where I came from, which would have been a deflation the likes of which no one (outside Hollywood) could ever conceive of, for I was probably the only writer ever hired by The Industry off the staff of a radical magazine in the history of either.

There was a bank on the corner of Hollywood and Cahuenga Boulevards, and I did not have to stand there long before Billy came along in a convertible (just as he had promised when I finally reached him on the telephone) and picked me up. He looked dragged out. I asked how he was, and he said he'd had no sleep at all.

"How come?"

"That Major," he replied, steering through Cahuenga Pass. "That morning we arrived, he asked if he could borrow my bungalow at The Garden of Allah, and I said sure; and when I got back late that afternoon, he was still screwing that broad, and I had to practically walk the streets all night—and he's still at it."

There wasn't much time to contemplate my jealousy of the Major's opportunity (and stamina), because the distance between Hollywood and Burbank is relatively short, and we were soon being admitted to the studio.

"I'll introduce you to the story editor," Billy said, "and then I'll take off and get some shut-eye."

"Who's the story editor?"

"Jim Geller."

"Didn't he used to be an agent?"

"The same."

Geller was an owlish-looking man who sat behind a desk on the second floor of the administration building; when I walked up, he smiled sourly at me and said, "You finally made it."

"I don't believe it yet."

"You can thank *me*," he said. "I got you the job. Been working at it ever since I've been here."

"Well, thanks."

"Another thing," he said, smiling his acidulous smile, "you better get yourself another agent."

"What's wrong with him?"

"I'll tell you. While he was pressuring Jack Warner in New York, his office here was calling me. A dame named Mary Baker. You know her?"

"No."

"Well, she called me up and chewed me out. Wanted to know how come we were offering only $150 a week. Said, 'She's worth a lot more than that. She's one of our best writers.'

" 'Oh,' I said, 'you *know* her?'

" 'No,' she said, 'but she's one of our most successful authors.'

" 'Well,' I said, 'she's a *he!*' and hung up on her."

Geller's door opened at that point, and in came Dan Fuchs, who didn't smile any more often than Geller (less, in fact) and, I soon found out, was therefore called Laughing Boy by all the other writers.

Dan and I, Geller said, would be working together on *Brooklyn, U.S.A.* for Jerry Wald, since I knew nothing about screenplay technique and Dan was now an experienced craftsman. It was the usual procedure. So Dan took me down the hall to meet the producer, and on the way he said, "I want you to know I got this job for you; been after Wald and Geller ever since I got here."

"Thanks."

Wald was a fat and apparently jolly character who leaped up from his desk and came around it to shake my hand. "I want you to know," he said, "that I'm the only producer who ever came to Hollywood *with* an ulcer. Now my ulcer's got an ulcer."

Dan didn't laugh, but I did, and Wald said, "How do you like the script?"

I opened my mouth, then swallowed, and said, "I like it."

I looked at Dan, and he was looking at me—piteously—but all he said was, "Come to the writers' building when you're through and we'll have lunch." He left.

"It needs a lot of work," Wald said, after Dan had gone, "and that's the reason I sent for you. I've wanted you out here a long time now. You know about labor conditions on the Brooklyn waterfront. Didn't you work on the Brooklyn *Eagle?*"

"I did," I said, but I did not tell him that I really knew a lot about the longshore situation because I had been involved in the 1936 seamen's strike as a volunteer publicity writer for the National Maritime Union and my first wife had set up a soup kitchen, practically single-handed, for the striking seamen.

"What we want to do," said Wald, and he always talked faster than a typewriter, "is to make a red-hot exposé of what's going on there, and I don't care whose toes get stepped on.

"I like to make topical pictures," he said. "Topical—but not typical. They got a rotten, reactionary union there, the ILA, and there's a war on now and a lot of sabotage is going on by Axis sympathizers—that's not in the original play, of course—and we want to help put a stop to it.

"There's good reason to believe there's a connection between the shipowners and the gangsters who run the ILA—and the U.S. Shipping Board, at that. It's not like the honest union we got out here run by Harry Bridges."

My hair (what hair I had even then) was standing on end, and I kept saying to myself, *This* is a Hollywood producer talking; *this* is a representative of the gigantic capitalist monopoly you've been lambasting in the pages of *New Masses* for the last four years!

"You get together with Dan," he said, "and later we'll have a story conference."

He told me how to find my way out of the administration building and to the writers' building, and there I found Dan's name on the directory. I was pleasantly surprised to find a name on that billboard whose presence made my heart leap, for he was probably the only writer in the United States I had ever wanted to meet, the only one to whom I had ever written a fan letter (there was no answer), and the only one about whom I had ever dreamed: William Faulkner.

I saw another name on the directory that I knew: Richard Aldington, whose *Death of a Hero* had helped to form my own antiwar convictions, and I was feeling pretty good as I walked down the corridor looking for Dan's office. For here were three writers I respected: two of them major novelists, in my opinion, and one, Dan Fuchs, a man whose humanity and warmth and sensitivity I had felt first in his novels *Homage to Blenholt* and *Low Company;* and if Hollywood could hire artists like these, I could shrug off some of the alcoholic and sectarian remarks that had been made to me that night the *New Masses* people (and a lot of other New York friends) had given a farewell party for the man who had sold out to Hollywood.

But when I walked into Dan's office, the first thing he said was, "Don't ever let me hear you make another crack like that."

"Like what?"

"When a producer asks what you think about a script—you said you think it's good."

"It *is*," I said, sitting in a chair opposite his desk.

"Of course it is," he said, deadpan. "But we've been put on the script to rewrite it, so it has to stink."

My mouth was probably open. This time he smiled a little and said, "Listen to me. The first thing you have to learn out here is that you can't make anything good. They won't let you. The original material stinks; but if you play it right, you can be on top of the heap in a couple years and making big money."

I had come three thousand miles, from $30 a week to $300, and this seemed like big money, even though I knew (and the figure jumped in my head day and night) that if they kept me on, I would be earning $1,000 a week in seven years! (What in God's name could anybody *do* with $1,000 a week?)

And big money—or rather the desire for it—was not something I had ever found in Dan's novels (or in the emotion that lay behind his total involvement with the poor and the exploited of the Brooklyn milieu with which he dealt). To the contrary, he had lived for years on the miserable pay of a substitute teacher in the New York school system, and I suppose I expected him to be the same in Hollywood as the sweet and somewhat melancholy man I had known in the Prospect Park section of Brooklyn.

He took me to lunch that day in the Green Room—a lunchroom for stars, starlets, featured players, writers, and other workers who do not rate lunch in the Executive Dining Room. Secretaries, carpenters, juicers, grips, gaffers, and other lower-class people who do not rate the Green Room eat in the cafeteria.

The bedazzlement that had hit me riding up Hollywood Boulevard on the streetcar overwhelmed me again, for sitting in the Green Room I saw Bette Davis, with whom I had fallen in love when I first saw *Of Human Bondage* in 1934. She was writing letters, and to my amazement nobody was paying the slightest attention to her.

And there was Ann Sheridan, whose face and figure I had often commented on, much to Helen Clare's disgust, for she insisted that Miss Sheridan's face looked as though it had come "out of a Jell-O mould." And there were—were they?—*yes*, Paul Henreid and Ida Lupino and Errol Flynn and Humphrey Bogart and John Garfield, whom I had known in New York when he first appeared with the Group Theater and was called Julie Garfinkel.

He waved at me, and I wondered whether he had ever seen that crack I took at him in a *New Masses* review, when I asked, rhetorically, when he was going to stop being a *star* and come back to the New York stage and be an *actor,* but he didn't mention it when I shook his hand.

Dan towed me to the writers' table and introduced me to a score of men and women, some of whose names I knew, who looked at me with some curiosity but then seemed more concerned, throughout the lunch, with topping each other whenever anybody made a wisecrack. This competition was invariably won by a pair known as the Twins (Julius and Philip Epstein), who were almost identical, were always seen together, and were said to spend more time with each other than they spent with their respective wives.

I was thinking of my date for lunch the next day with John Howard Lawson, whom I had known years before in New York, when one of the Twins rose with a glass of water in his hand and said:

"A toast!"

"In *water*?" another writer said with disgust.

"When the Green Room provides it, I will propose the toast in Cordon Rouge," said the Twin—and smiled at me.

"To Alvah Bessie," he said.

The others held up their water glasses.

"Welcome to Warner's Concentration Camp." He waved his glass hand and the water spilled onto another writer, who rose immediately and made a great production out of wiping his tweed jacket with a silk handkerchief. The others laughed.

"Bessie, meet your fellow inmates."

DISSOLVE TO

TRUCKING SHOTS. WASHINGTON, D.C., DISTRICT JAIL to FEDERAL COR-RECTIONAL INSTITUTION, Texarkana, Texas. July–August, 1950.

There are things about "your first prison term" that you can never forget. In addition to the interviews with your parole officer, there are the psychometric and achievement tests, the physical examinations and shots, the "adjustment" to a way of life that is even more inhuman than Army life itself, since you never get so much as a twenty-four-hour pass.

When you arrive in such a place, you are apprehensive, since it *is* your first experience. You have seen too many movies; you have read too many books. None of them corresponds to the reality.

Nor did our distinguished battery of attorneys help to prepare us for the experience, for none of them had ever been in prison— in that way.

Thus, when we entered the Washington District Jail, after trials that lasted half an hour each, we went "prepared" for it: we had each purchased white nylon shirts, undershirts, shorts, and socks (it was very hot in Washington that month, and prisoners, we were told, had to wash their own laundry).

What the other inmates thought when they saw this squad of seven men (Bessie, Biberman, Cole, Dmytryk, Lardner, Maltz, and Ornitz) dressed identically in nylon shirts and underwear, I do not know, because they never told me; but these elegant garments were removed from us the moment we were in the joint, were returned to us when we traveled to our ultimate places of confinement, and then were taken away for the duration of our sentences.

Each of us had a paper bag containing toothbrush, tooth powder, soap, and shaving tackle; we had ball-point pens, notebooks, nail files, and scissors; we had cigarettes and wristwatches. These were confiscated immediately upon our arrival (watches were *verboten*, and the other articles had to be purchased in the commissary).

Each of us was carrying a minimum of $200, for it had been cleverly calculated that we would each remain ten months (except Biberman and Dmytryk, who had drawn another judge, who took a less serious view of our offense and gave them each six months). You are permitted in the Federal joints to spend (you never see the cash) $10 a month at the commissary and another $10 on such luxury items as newspapers, magazines, and books that must be ordered through the institution. The money is deposited to your account, and what is left is returned when you are released. (Prisoners without money—the majority—received an issue of cheap tobacco and cigarette papers, but no candy, cookies, talcum powder, or other minor luxuries that make life bearable in such a place.)

The Washington District Jail looked and felt like a penitentiary—the way they look in the movies. You were locked into a steel-barred cell containing an upper and a lower bunk, except for meals and one hour a day when you went into the yard (if it was not raining) or to the upper tier (if it was) for exercise.

You did no work at all; you sat. A dozen times a day the loudspeaker said, "Now hear this! Now hear this! Attention all units; attention all units; make your count," and the guards paced up and down the range, counting the men in the cages.

Every morning, an inmate who was a trusty passed down the range and shoved into your cell a long-handled brush with the invariable words, "Here's your toothbrush." (You used it to clean the toilet bowl.)

Three times a day the steel-barred doors rolled back; you formed a line (no talking) and marched down the clanging metal range and staircase to the central well, where tables were set up, pausing at steam tables to receive your dreadful food on metal trays.

You marched to the tables in single file and ate (no talking) while guards posted around the walls stood and watched. A Negro inmate with a stainless steel basket hung around his neck passed among the tables chanting, "*Bread*man, *bread*man!" and forked a few slices of bread onto your tray. Then you marched upstairs again, stepped into your cell, and the door rolled shut with a hollow clang.

And then you sat.

Or if you had a cell mate, you talked. I had one during the eleven days we were in Washington, but he was an immigrant from Albania who did not speak a single word of English. We tried to make contact. I used my seven words of German, my rusty college French, my creaking Spanish and four words of Italian—to no avail.

But we drew pictures for each other and played ticktacktoe and the dot game, and that is all we did. We listened to the music on the loudspeaker and the Fourth of July speeches from Capitol Hill, and we could even hear the fireworks on that national holiday; and in the daytime, by standing up and peering across the range and out the narrowly opened clerestory windows, you could catch a three-inch glimpse of actual human beings (girls too!) and automobiles moving on the street.

But mostly we sat, and I wrote a long poem that presented me with a torturous dilemma: how to get it out of there. It was the first alleged poem I had written since college (twenty-six years gone past), and I knew that they would not permit me to mail it (I asked).

So I tried—in vain—to memorize it, and finally I copied it onto toilet paper and folded it till it was the size of a fat postage stamp and kept it in my pocket.

In the yard, those days we were allowed to go there, the Hollywood characters would pace the creaking gravel in pairs and talk about the war in Korea, the world situation, and the prognosis for the future.

There we were cheered by the invariable good humor of director Edward Dmytryk, with whom I had shared a hotel room the last days we were at liberty. (In the better days, in Hollywood, I had also rented one of his apartments.) There we learned from Herbert Biberman that he had a fascinating cell mate—a "typecast Southern gentleman" of sixty, with white hair and a distinguished air.

This man, said Herbert, was courtesy personified, and although he was elderly and Herbert so much younger, he insisted that Herbert have the lower bunk. "You could not find a finer gentleman anywhere," said Herbert, and told us that his cell mate was an alcholic.

[39]

The next morning when the trusty came around with my toothbrush, I said, "I hear my friend Biberman has a marvelous cell mate—a Southern gentleman–alcoholic."

The trusty looked at me openmouthed, then started to laugh until I thought he'd split his pants (he bent over and slapped his thighs).

"He ain't no drunk," he choked.

"What *is* he?"

The man was practically strangling with laughter. "We get him regular," he finally said. "We get him at least one time a year."

"What does he *do*?"

"They catch him in the toilet of movie houses—with little boys."

Call it comedy relief; the rest was tragedy. All night, there were the noises of freedom and confinement, life and death. All day and night, the roar of eight-thousand-horsepower aircraft engines, letting down, gaining altitude, rising to Pittsburgh, sinking from New York or Kansas City, climbing to Los Angeles . . . Los Angeles . . . *El Pueblo de Nuestra Señora, la Reina de los Angeles.*

                    Over in the District Zoo
        the beasts revolve in their cages day and night
        and I, who am a lover of animals, remember them with pity:
        the Bengal tiger with his deadpan stare,
        in geometric pattern, back and forth,
        rubbing his right flank on the bars. The polar bear
        in the heavy heat of Washington's summer
        (stir crazy) who reverses gears, walks backward
        once his snout has touched the opposite wall . . .
            The PA system speaks: "Hear this, now hear this"—
            (through every speaker perched at each small cell)—
            "Attention all units: make your 7:45 count.
            Attention all units: make your 7:45 count."
        This is our day of freedom; this day we said:
        "We hold these truths to be self-evident . . .

All men are created equal . . . they are endowed," we said,
"with life, liberty . . ."
   (The guard counting . . . "12 . . . 14 . . . 16"
as he paces down the range.) That day the bars rolled back
(automatic electric?), the gaol doors swung on rusty hinges,
and ragged mechanics and stocky yeomen stood in the cobbled
   streets
and cheered. ". . . and the pursuit of happiness!"
   All night there were voices in the place . . .
"Attention all units: the count is clear."
That means: all present or accounted for;
each man in place; a place for every man:
   the alcoholic (in for ten days, out for two; in for thirty days
   and out for one; in for sixty days—); the thief:
four counts of armed robbery. "I said,
   'Gimme back my gun an' my false nose;
   they're the tools o' my trade'";
the signers of bad checks, the "lewd molest,"
the statutory rapists, and the peddlers of dope;
the con man from Santa Monica who said:
   "I saw Betsy Grable lots of times";
the derelict who brained the flophouse owner
with a baseball bat: "It's a *good* thing I did," he said;
   "That guy was no damn good at all;
   Took men in and robbed them of their dough
   And threw them out into the wilderness of Ninth Street";
The alien who made the sad mistake
of watching a car for a man and being nabbed
for stealing it; the Mexican (called *amigo* here)
who kissed a girl fourteen (she looking twenty):
"rape," reduced when she was found intact
to "indecent liberties" and deportation (natch).
The Negro lad (called *nigger* here)
condemned to die this morning; only yesterday
I asked if he could play piano, and he said:
   "If I could play piano, man,
   I'd be invulnerable to sorrow."

[*41*]

All night, the Albanian immigrant in the bunk over my head snored and tossed, groaned and spoke out loud in his outlandish tongue. One man coughed all night; another screamed in sleep. The Negro boy moaned softly on his segregated tier, saying, "Sin . . . it's a sin. . . . Everything is sin. . . ." Somebody shouted, "*Shaddup* and go-ta-*sleep!*"

Most of the men confined with me rode to the places where we were to serve our sentences on trains—in chains. Here again, the lawyers were mistaken, for they had said we could exercise a choice of institutions—the Federal prison bureau would cooperate and make it easier for relatives to visit us. So we canvassed our fellow inmates and learned where most of the Federal joints were located.

Lardner and Cole were lucky; they wanted to be near New York and drew Danbury, Connecticut. Maltz and Dmytryk went to West Virginia, and Ornitz, despite medical testimony that confinement could further deteriorate his precarious health, was —considerately—sent to a prison hospital in Missouri. Biberman and I wanted to be near Los Angeles, and there is a joint outside Tucson—and so we drew Texas.

And by chance, a Federal marshal and a detective from Sherman, Texas, had brought a prisoner to Washington and were assigned to carry us to Texarkana in a car.

The marshal was the biggest man I had ever seen. He looked down on us (and he was just as broad as he was tall, and Biberman is more than six feet tall himself) and said, "You-all don't look like you would need leg-irons."

So we rode in the back seat of his 1950 Mercury from Washington to Texarkana, Texas, traveling three days at speeds up to eighty miles an hour—handcuffed to each other. And the marshal, being a decent guy, ignored the regulations. He was not supposed to let us out of the car except to go to the toilet (cuffed together), but he let us eat in restaurants (unshackled) instead of bringing a sandwich and a cup of coffee to us in the car.

The first night of the journey, we were deposited in the county jail at Roanoke, Virginia, and it was a preview of what we feared to find in Texas. It was on the seventh story of an ancient brick building. It was dark and smelled. There were two tiers of cells, and Negro prisoners were on the upper level.

The admitting officer fascinated us on sight. At some time in the past, his long, thin nose had been smashed to one side, so that it literally pointed at his ear, and when he saw anyone looking at it, he quickly turned his head.

We were ushered through the usual grille of bars into an unlighted tier of cells, each containing four men. The bedclothes we were issued consisted of one stinking mattress (bare), one tiny towel (gray with age), no mattress cover, no sheets, or pillowcase, no pillow, no blanket.

"No lights?" you say. A voice in the dark replies, "Whatya want with a light? Ain't nothin' here t'read. You gotta butt?"

Reading was not permitted. The men in the cells sat or sprawled on iron shelves bolted to armor-plated walls that had not been painted or washed down since they were riveted together. Some tried to write letters in the dark. Others talked and talked and talked—about their crimes or their innocence, for half were "innocent" (as Mr. Huber later told me), and the rest pretended to crimes they would not have had the guts to commit. The toilet would not flush, could not be used unless you stood on it. I thought of e. e. cummings' book *The Enormous Room* (*ça pue*).

We were just in time to be fed—through the bars—nameless slops, in baking tins, that looked like black-eyed peas and collard greens (we got a spoon), and then we listened to the talk.

Some slept, some squatted with head in hands. One man had managed to pilfer two spoons, which he used as drumsticks on the edge of his iron shelf—and made what jazz musicians call "a good sound."

One told me that he had been there three months without being charged with anything; one had been there six without a trial. One showed me a snapshot of a pretty girl and said, "I killed her an' I won' deny it. She horsed me all around an' took my dough an' spent it on the other guys she laid. I ain' one bit sorry what I done. I tell you, I'm at peace—the only time since I married her."

He held the photograph under my nose in the dark and said,

"Ain' she purty? She's a knockout, mister." Then, anxiously, "You think I'll burn? You think they'll knock me off? Ain' no one in this rotten town don' know how she done me. I admit I had the huntin' knife when I went up t'see her. I was drunk."

That night it rained. There were windows for ventilation—on the far side of the bars and the narrow corridor and the wire fence and another corridor—and the rain came through the windows all night long, and long before dawn it rippled on the floor a half inch deep.

But we left with the dawn and rode catty-corner through the rest of Virginia and across Tennessee (how beautiful!) into Nashville. And all across Tennessee and the next day across Arkansas and into Texas, the man to whom I was handcuffed by my left wrist talked.

Herbert Biberman is one of the most effective speakers I have ever known, and I have known him since the Theatre Guild production of *Faust* (1926) in which I was an extra in the Walpurgisnacht scene and he was assistant to its imported German director.

It was during that memorable production that I met a girl who gave me gonorrhea and he met his future (and present) wife, the fine actress Gale Sondergaard.

Herbert (and no one would ever dream of calling him Herb or even Bert) is a man who speaks with authority on many subjects, and I can never think of him without remembering a phrase that Vincent Sheean used in Le Havre in December, 1938, when the returning Spanish volunteers were interned by the French government for a week before we sailed. We were drunk on Black & White Scotch that Sheean had smuggled into the joint, and he was trying to impress me with his allegiance to the cause of Spain—and to humanity. Said he, "I would die in pieces for what I believe."

Herbert is a man who *would* die in pieces for what he believes. He is also one of the most brilliant organizers I have ever known, and during the three years that we were waiting for the Supreme Court to hear our case, he headed a committee that raised money for our appeal (thousands upon thousands of dollars) and co-ordinated all the publicity for the cause in which we were engaged. He was both a spark plug and a dynamo, and while it is possible to dislike him (as it is possible to dislike anyone), it is impossible not to respect and admire him.

So, for three days en route to Texas, Herbert talked. No, he did not talk; he lectured. He sat on the edge of his seat and instructed the marshal and the dick from Sherman, Texas, relating to them the history of our case and its importance, from the standpoint of constitutional law. He told them how motion pictures were made and detailed the relationship between the creative artist and the management.

He gave them, in slightly oversimplified but relatively cogent (and generally accurate) terms, the history of the American Revolution of 1776, the French Revolution of 1789, the second American Revolution (1861–1865), and the Russian Revolution of 1917.

I lay back in the seat of the careening car, trying to go to sleep. Every once in a while, the marshal, who was so broad he took up more than half the front seat and so tall he had to hunch his shoulders to see through the windshield, would glance over his shoulder and say, "How you doin', Bessie?" I would open one eye and mumble, "I'm alive."

I pondered on the generosity of the marshal, who allowed us not only to eat decent meals with him and his companion (but drink no alcohol), but also to write letters (that's how I mailed the toilet-paper poem, which had not been taken away from me when we left the Washington District Jail; and my wife must have thought, How *clever* of him to smuggle out this work of art!), and he even allowed me (somewhere in the blue-grass region of Virginia) to buy and mail a small cast-iron horse to my six-year-old daughter in Beverly Hills, who was going through her cowboy period at the time we left.

We stayed overnight in the county jail in Nashville, which was identical in accommodations with the one in Roanoke, except that it was relatively new and impeccably clean and it was possible to borrow a razor and some soap from other inmates.

From Nashville, the marshal phoned ahead to let the warden in Texarkana know the time of our arrival, so we could be processed—and even fed—and then we continued our journey, crossing the Mississippi at Memphis and speeding through Arkansas, arriving at the institution after dark.

There were many men who had arrived just before us, and all were Mexican *mojados*, caught trying to cross the Rio Grande in search of work. They were young (and old beyond their years), and most of them wore their hair long. They were dressed in rags and broken sandals made of leather or cast-off, cut-up rubber tires, and they seemed to be in a hilarious mood. I even caught—and understood—scraps of conversation and was amazed that some boasted of having received sentences of six months to two years—for repeated illegal entry. But after hearing their stories in the days ahead, I understood their glee. In prison, they were fed three times a day and had clean clothes and medical attention; and six months in an American prison, they told me, was heaven compared with life in their native land.

One inmate, a trusty, told me to give him my cigarettes and he would return them later—otherwise I'd have nothing to smoke. (He did.) We were stripped and bathed (our rectums were examined for concealed narcotics) and given clothes. Then, in a reception room, we were lined up and questioned by the staff, and an inmate at a typewriter took down the vital statistics.

Biberman preceded me on the line, and after answering the routine name, address, age, marital status, children, he was asked, "Religion?"

I saw him draw himself up, thrust back his broad shoulders, and heard that voice I knew so well, the deep baritone, resonant and reverberating from the diaphragm, the Voice of Command. "I am a *Jew*," he said.

When they asked my religion, I said, "None," which did not prevent me, the next day, from receiving from the educational supervisor a copy of the Talmud in Hebrew, which I could not read. (No more could Herbert.)

DISSOLVE TO
THE WRITERS' BUILDING. WARNER BROTHERS STUDIO. Burbank, California. January–June, 1943.
Your first option period on a Hollywood term contract bears cer-

tain resemblances to quarantine in prison, but there is a difference —in reverse. For if you don't get a screen credit during the first six months of your contract, there is an excellent chance that you will be sprung: the option will not be exercised, and back you go—out into the population of the *free* world, instead of remaining in the studio (prison) cocoon, where choice, free will, and individual responsibility do not operate and you do precisely what you're told.

It was a gag, of course, but the other inmates of the writers' building always referred to the joint as Warner's Concentration Camp. You were expected to be on time in the morning, and while you did not punch a time clock, the uniformed guard in the office checked your name off his list. You were not expected to leave till five o'clock. And while you had a private office and a private secretary who sat outside your door and would stand guard if you felt like sleeping instead of working (and some would join you on the couch), the atmosphere of the place was oddly oppressive and full of fear.

Within fifteen minutes of my installation in an office of my own on the second floor, I received three visitors. One was an enormously fat man with a huge, beaked nose who welcomed me, assured me he had read me in *Masses,* and said, "That fellow Dan you're working with is a sweet man. But watch out for him; he's just as likely to put a knife in your back."

He put his hand inside his sports-jacket pocket and produced an enormous bundle tied with rubber bands and patted it. "War bonds," he said, "$3,000 worth. Ticket to freedom."

He left (his name was Dick); within a moment, a fellow who introduced himself as Arthur came in, nodded over his shoulder, and said, "Dick's a sweet guy, but you ought to know. Keep an eye on him; he's quite capable of putting a knife in your back."

While Arthur was still there, Al came in, and they kidded around about my being hired off the staff of *New Masses.* When Arthur left, saying, "See you at lunch," Al said, "Arthur's a sweet man, but there's something . . ."

When I walked to the Green Room for lunch that day, I ran into a fellow I had known in New York named Vince. He was a director now, and he promptly told me that he had been responsible for getting me my job. (I thanked him too.)

"You can do good work here," he said. "I've made things like *Underground,* and I'm going to make better. You have to know how to play your cards; you have to learn diplomacy and politics. You can't trust anybody—not even me."

Vince joined me at the writers' table, and he talked far more radically than I even dared to think. He beefed about the failure of the Allies to open a second front in Europe to relieve the pressure on the Soviet Union, and I began to think that Hollywood was not at all what I had been told that it was—and had written that it was—on *New Masses.* For it had been not only the fashion but the conviction in radical circles to believe—since Hollywood was a vast capitalist monopoly—that it was a self-contained community of self-centered people who were so corrupt on every level that they could scarcely be bothered with so small a thing as a world war.

Not that The Industry was not supporting it—it was, and it knew very well that its patriotism would pay off at the box office, for the purchase of tickets during the war was at an all-time high. But the general condemnation of Hollywood extended even to those who were the humblest workers in the place, and a radical writer who "sold out" as I had done was about as low a creature as you were likely to find between the Atlantic and the Pacific coasts: he was a "Hollywood whore."

As things turned out, Dan and I did not write *Brooklyn U.S.A.,* for he was taken off the script and I was teamed with a young fellow of Italian descent named Jo Pagano, who had published a novel called *Golden Wedding,* which had attracted some attention.

Jo (not Joe) was the epitome of the Continental gentleman; he was dressed to the nines at all times, had a fine Renaissance face—and had come from a mining town in Colorado. And though our ideas about the socialist system did not gibe in many respects, he had the natural class consciousness (and hatred of bigotry) that Americans of working-class origin and foreign extraction suck in with their mothers' milk.

He therefore protested violently (and I was delighted to back him up) that the heavies in the picture were all Italians and that he would not work on such a story unless it were changed.

It was a fact, of course, that Murder, Incorporated (on whose activities the play was based), was strictly an Italian-American outfit, run by the notorious Camarda brothers of Red Hook, Brooklyn, and the original play was based on the murder of Pete Panto, a rank-and-file longshoreman of the ILA who was killed by the goons when he tried to develop some democracy in that rotten outfit.

Jerry Wald pointed out to us that the hero of the script was also an Italian-American (we knew it), but Jo felt it necessary to overbalance the heavies by more than one good, democratic, anti-Fascist Italian-American, and it was not too difficult to win Wald's support for his point of view.

I called the research department for some dope on the Brooklyn waterfront and promptly received (from a girl messenger in skintight pants) a photostatic copy of my own *New Masses* review of *Brooklyn, U.S.A.*

But despite my personal knowledge of the situation and this heavy research, we were of no help to the film, for it was shelved— as were twenty-five other properties out of the grand total of twenty-eight on which I worked in the next three years.

Jo and I were reassigned by Wald to write an original story about the Marine Corps. We had worked six weeks on *Brooklyn* before it was shelved; we worked six more on the Marine Corps story, which had its origin in a *Life* magazine story about a fellow named Al Schmidt. This one got made, but not by us. It turned up later in a far different form under the title *Pride of the Marines,* written by Albert Maltz.

Then I worked for three days for another producer, Henry Blanke, on a nonfiction book called *Country Lawyer,* which had been edited by my wife when she worked at the McGraw-Hill Book Company. This brought me to April.

Then I ran into another writer, Robert Rossen, who sat me down in his office in the music building (what he was doing *there,* I never knew, unless he didn't like to work in the writers' building) and talked turkey to me.

[49]

"You got three more months to go on your option," he said, "and you don't have a credit yet."

"You're telling *me*."

"If you don't get a credit—or look as though you're going to get one by June—they'll drop your option."

"So it seems."

"Now," said Rossen, who was always an operator, "I've got an idea. There's a producer here named Jack—and you must understand that producers work on the same terms we do; if they don't get a picture made or it doesn't make money, their options get dropped too."

I nodded.

"Jack came here from MGM, and he's in trouble with this story right now. I think I can con him into taking you on; the picture has a shooting date, and it will guarantee you a credit."

"Who's on it now?"

"Frank Gruber."

"How will *he* feel about having me on it with him?"

"He won't be on it," said Rossen. "He'll be off."

"I don't like that—"

"Listen," he said, "there're ways of doing these things, and Gruber won't be sore about it at all; part of the deal will be that he gets a credit too."

So he took me to Jack's office that afternoon, and Jack, a tall, ugly fellow who had a long, gold key chain, which he continuously twirled (it spelled out J-A-C-K and his second name), talked to me about the story and called Geller's office and got me reassigned to a thing called *Northern Pursuit*, which was to star Errol Flynn.

This was a miserable little adventure-story-magazine yarn that had cost the studio $500. It was about as incredible as any story can be, short of science fiction, but I was stuck with it. It had the Nazis (commanded by Helmut Dantine) surfacing a submarine in Hudson Bay and proceeding overland on skis to an abandoned mine, where—years before—they had been foresighted enough to stash a bomber. After assembling it and rolling it out, they intended to bomb the canal at Sault Ste Marie and thereby fatally disrupt the work of the war factories in Detroit, Michigan.

Naturally, they were foiled by Errol Flynn, who was an officer in the Royal Canadian Mounted Police and, to make the cheese more binding, was under suspicion by his superiors because he was of German descent!

All you can do with a story like this is make the characters more believable and somewhat more complicated, fancy up the action, and create suspense, and this is what I proceeded to do.

The job lasted till my thirty-ninth birthday (June 4) and provided my first fascinating glimpse of the actual making of a film. The first thing that became apparent was that the technical personnel in the studios were geniuses, whereas those who had control of story properties and production generally did not know what they were doing and cared even less, unless . . .

The sequence in the abandoned mine was supposed to run about five minutes. For these scenes, the art department had designed and built the most elaborate and authentic structure ever found—outside of an abandoned mine. It had several galleries, several storage rooms—closed off with heavy oak doors hung on massive iron hinges (which creaked); it had tracks, dump trucks, heavy overhead beams, facings of ore, and what looked like genuine spiders' webs spun in the corners (with what looked like genuine spiders inhabiting them). It was a masterpiece.

When I told Jack that it looked far too big for the sequence that was to be played in it, he gave me a vicious jab in the ribs and yanked me outside.

"You want to get somebody canned?" he said.

"What do you mean?"

"So, the dumb art director built the set too big! The damned thing cost about $50,000, did you know that?"

"No."

"Don't ever say a thing like that again! The art director could get canned—and me too. If you notice something like that again, you zip the lip."

"What'll we do?"

"It's simple," said Jack. "You'll write some more scenes for the mine."

So I wrote some more scenes for the mine, and I had the opportunity to watch them make large portions of the film itself, which was far more interesting than writing it.

The cast included one excellent actor, Gene Lockhart, and a onetime star who was now playing a four-line bit and was genuinely moved when I introduced myself and told him that I would never forget him in a film called *The Perfect Crime*. His name was Monte Blue, and he was a fine man, who seemed to take his fall from stardom with real grace.

There was also the intense young German actor who was generally called Helmut *Dent*ine because he had brilliant white teeth and flashed them at every opportunity (as well as when there was none), and he looked enough like a Nazi to be one.

But the star was Errol Flynn, whose exploits—as reported in the papers—had fascinated me for days on the trip from New York aboard the *Twentieth Century Limited* and the *Chief*. From coast to coast, I had followed his trial and his acquittal on a charge of statutory rape. He was alleged to have taken a minor girl aboard his yacht and induced her, one lovely moonlight night, to watch the moon through a porthole.

My secretary told me that Flynn had cost the studio hundreds of thousands of dollars in little escapades like this, for the girls could generally be bought off, but this one had insisted on going to trial. And all the secretaries in the writers' building and the secretarial pool were busily engaged for weeks after I arrived in January typing hundreds and thousands of individual letters to people who had written to Flynn about his trial.

I saw some of these letters, although they were supposed to be Top Secret, and the secretaries answered them on In-Like-Flynn's personal stationery, with the heading "Mulholland Farm," and signed them—in a multitude of handwriting styles —"Errol Flynn."

Almost invariably, the letters congratulated him on his acquittal, said their writers knew that evil forces were trying to crucify a fine, clean-cut American boy, and offered, "If you're ever in Keokuk, drop in for some good old-fashioned American home cooking."

Yet, the rumor was, Flynn had not been chastened by his narrow squeak. He was said to employ two full-time pimps whose job was to line up young girls for him, and I saw Flynn many times, after work was finished on the set, climb into his convertible in the parking lot and roar off with three or four girls clinging to the chassis of the car—and to him.

People who claimed to have visited Mulholland Farm insisted that the bedroom had the largest bed in creation; that its walls and ceilings were covered with mirrors; and that there were bed tables on which were displayed a variety of contraceptive devices, from "French ticklers" to plain and fancy diaphragms, not to mention any perfume or cosmetic luxury a casual female guest might fancy.

Watching the man, on and off the set, there could be no doubt that he had charm, even though his chest was somewhat concave. (He was alleged to have tuberculosis, which is alleged to increase the libido.) But his charm was not half so compelling as the ingenuity displayed by his director, Raoul Walsh, who was confronted every time he directed Flynn with the problems presented by an actor who cannot act—even in films.

There was one memorable scene in which Flynn and his Mountie buddy John Ridgely were ambushed by Dantine and his Nazi pals and were forced to lay down their arms. Dantine assured the two men that if they surrendered and advanced, they would not be harmed, but as they came forward with arms raised, one of the Nazis shot poor John Ridgely right between the eyes, and he fell dead on the frozen gypsum. This, of course, constitutes a situation: your best friend has been murdered in cold blood before your very eyes—in the most treacherous and cowardly manner possible.

Anyone would react to such a situation. But not Flynn. He stood there looking at his dead pal, his face as dead as the carcass lying in the Hollywood snow. Walsh said: "Errol—he's *dead*! He's your *pal*!"

"I know," Flynn nodded, showing some annoyance on his handsome face.

"Take it again!" cried Walsh. "Silence! This is a take."

So they took it again. In fact, they took it five more times—and not an emotion rippled the surface of that handsome face.

Walsh's solution was as simple as Flynn's repertoire of reactions, but it was also brilliant. He told Flynn to drop to his knees beside Ridgely, feel his body, and then look up at the off-scene Nazis. As he did so, the camera swiftly dollied in, and within a moment the screen was filled by an enormous pair of eyes—eyes that, in the absence of any surrounding face, chilled the preview audience and induced *Daily Variety* and the *Hollywood Reporter* to rhapsodize over the flick:

" 'NORTHERN PURSUIT' TIPTOP/FAST ACTION MELODRAMA" said the *Reporter*, adding, "Jack ———'s First For Warners Smart Job," and, more explicitly, "The feature marks Jack ———'s bow as a producer at Warners and it instantly establishes him as an important contributor to the season's output of money product."

Neither *Variety* nor the *Reporter* deigned to mention either writer (except in the diamond-point credits), but Jack was so impressed by the result and the attendant prestige that I began to believe what Dan had told me when he said, "The original material stinks; but if you play it right, you can be on top of the heap in a couple years and making big money."

The only trouble was, I didn't know *how* to play it right, though Jack certainly stood at my side for a few months and kibitzed. He told me nothing was too good for me. He said, "We'll make pictures together from now on in. We'll go around the world together making pictures. You want to go to Russia? I'll go *with* you."

He invited my wife and me to his lovely house for dinner, and we returned to another dinner on his wedding anniversary. His wife was a former stage beauty, and he had lots of leather-bound books and a pinball machine in the game room, a formal garden, and an autographed picture of Henry A. Wallace. What's more, on the night of his anniversary, there were at least fifty guests who sat down to a dinner table laden with steaks.

Tactlessly, I asked him where he got all the meat, and he replied, "Not on the black market," which left me in the dark, for nobody could get *that* many red points in 1943, and I had a hard enough time getting enough gas coupons to go to the studio and back every day, in spite of the fact that people who worked in films were laughingly alleged to be employed by an essential industry.

But my lack of tact did not prevent Jack from introducing me to every single one of his guests with extremely embarrassing remarks: "This is the best goddamned writer in Hollywood today." (I blushed.) "I'm putting him under personal contract"— (laugh)—"as soon as I have my own studio." Then (serious), "No crap. This guy can write rings around all the most expensive hacks in town."

What the hell, I thought. I've got it made!

At that anniversary party, we met a fellow who said that he was a labor relations expert for the studios, and Helen Clare, who had had one Martini too many, asked him, "What, precisely, does a labor relations expert *do?*"

"My lovely creature," he replied, "it's very simple. The unions come to me and ask for more money. . . . I say no." ("A Red," said that fellow in *The Grapes of Wrath*, "is any son of a bitch who wants thirty cents an hour when we're paying twenty-five.")

This son of a bitch was so taken by my wife that he invited us to dinner two weeks later at *his* house, which was near the beach in Pacific Palisades. Jack and his wife were also present, as well as Ernie Pagano, who was a producer himself (and Jo's elder brother).

Promptly after dinner the party broke up, the men retiring to the "study" to play poker, the women to a sun porch, where (my wife later told me) they discussed nothing but the impossibility of getting good servants so long as the war was going on, because the damned servants preferred to go into a war plant and make more money.

I was terrified to find myself in a poker game with these sharks (who also had the money to play it) and recalled my gambling father's advice (which he had borrowed from a really successful gambler named Titanic Thompson): "Never bet on anything less than a sure thing."

By dint of never betting on anything less than a sure thing (which I never seemed to hold that night), I managed to escape with a trifling loss of only $40, whereas Ernie Pagano and the host won a couple hundred each—mostly from Jack, who was drunk before the game began.

The conversation at that poker table was even more harrowing to a former critic on *New Masses* than the game itself, for with the exception of Jack, who had been a poor boy on New York's Lower East Side and never forgot it, I thought for a moment that I was at a meeting of the America First Committee.

The Labor Relations Expert bemoaned the fact that his two teen-age children were "Reds" (they were reading the Dean of Canterbury's book *The Secret of Soviet Power*), and this despite the excellent education he was giving them, as well as "everything their hearts desire."

He contended that instead of opening a second front in Europe, we ought to let the Russians and the Germans fight it out and kill each other off—an opinion, of course, which had been voiced two years earlier by Senator Harry S. Truman (D., Mo.).

Everyone left after the poker game except the Labor Relations Expert and his wife, Jack and his wife, and the Bessies.

Jack was drunker than I have ever seen most men and lay supine in a chair, mumbling, his long legs stretched into the room. "Alvah," he said carefully, "'s a dirty coward."

"What's that?" said the host.

"Alvah's a cow'rd. Hadda run away t'Spain."

"What was cowardly about that?"

"Besi's," said Jack, "he's a Comm'nis'."

"Cut that out, Jack."

"He's a goddamn Comm'nis'."

"Look here," said the goddamned Fascist Labor Relations Expert, "you can't talk about my guests like that!" He looked at me. "I *like* him," he said. "He's my guest. You can't talk about my guests like that!"

"Goddamn dir'y Comm'nis'," said Jack and passed out.

FEDERAL CORRECTIONAL INSTITUTION. Texarkana, Texas. August, 1950.

The NARRATOR has "come out" of quarantine into the population of the prison. Before he did, he was interviewed by the warden and his top officers and asked what sort of work he would like to do. (So was his "fall partner" Herbert Biberman). The NARRATOR had said that he was equipped to teach English literature and composition or, if necessary, classes in elementary Spanish or French. He could also put on plays for the entertainment of the inmates, type, file, or do any other kind of work that a bachelor of arts degree in English and French literature qualified him for.

Accordingly, he was (1) astonished to be handed a small identification card, to be kept in a green waterproof plastic folder, certifying to the fact that he was a "trusty," and (2) amazed to be told that his job would involve pumping gas in the prison garage, which was outside the gates of the institution and serviced the cars belonging to the officers and the trucks and tractors that were used to work the seven-hundred-acre farm surrounding the main buildings.

The routine was very simple: the whistle woke everyone at seven; breakfast was at seven-thirty; cleanup and cell inspection followed; at eight you formed into lines outside the main building, and the garagemen, truck drivers, and "farmers" proceeded to the main gate (double), where we were sometimes shaken down as we left the joint but more often when we returned from work at four.

We walked twenty feet to the garage, which was presided over by a very human guard with a bald head; he had once been an automobile mechanic outside but found his job in prison to be more secure than competition in the *free* world of Texas or Arkansas.

When cars (the warden's, the captain's, any others) came up, they were pumped full of gas. When they were not being used, they were washed. The trucks that carried the farmers (Negro and Mexican-American inmates, who did the hardest work on the place) were gassed each morning, but the maintenance of the truck was left to the inmate who drove it.

I conceived a mad desire to drive a truck, which I had never done in my life, for a truck meant the comparative freedom of the farm. Truck drivers even went out on the highway into Texarkana to pick up manure for the fields or other merchandise consigned to the prison at the railroad station.

Since there was relatively little work at the garage (and there were generally five men for any one job in the joint), most of the inmates merely sat around and gassed (with each other) or listened to the small radio in the garage itself.

You could hear a little more on that radio than you heard over the loudspeaker installed in the cellblock, which was turned on or off from the control room at the entrance to the institution—and only played what the officer on duty wanted to hear.

This generally consisted of a steady diet of hillbilly music (instrumental and vocal), most of it supplied by a local singer who started to warble at 7:30 A.M. from the Texarkana station. Any one of these songs, if I hear them today, gives me a peculiar pain: not in the neck, not in the gut, but, of all places, in the right thigh.

Moving about in the population of the prison, you met inmates who were named Cupcake (short and fat), Bebop (Negro), Turkey (long, red neck), Snake (had one tattooed on his arm, just as another inmate had a bluebottle fly tattooed on his *glans penis* and pretended daily to brush it off for the entertainment of the other men in the shower room), Comrade (the Narrator), Mother (an old Southern expression that need not be translated here), Heavy, Slugger, Eleven, Porky, Dimples, Garbage Can (who weighed three hundred pounds and got himself committed regularly so that he could eat free), Muscles, One-Eye, Short-Timer (he had eleven years to pull), Peanut, Speedy (an emaciated addict who looked like a bird and walked on tiptoe), Lover Boy, Hadacol (local cold remedy), Kansas City, Double-O (eyeglasses), Tokio, and Buckskin.

There was more poetry in these names than in the verse I tried to write in my spare time, but the first thing that impressed me about their owners, aside from the fact that most of them were very young, was the friendliness with which they greeted my "fall partner" and me.

Biberman had been told by his parole officer (a man with dirty yellow teeth who was cordially despised by the inmates) that it would be inadvisable for us to express any of the revolutionary theories we presumably held, as most of the prisoners were very patriotic citizens and might resent it.

Patriotic they may have been, though I never saw any evidence of it. (Their favorite prison-made jingle that summer was: "I've had gonorrhea, pyorrhea, diarrhea, but I don't want no part of that *Ko*-rea.")

Class conscious (in a backhanded manner) they certainly were, for they were all convinced (and not without reason) that the *free* world was against them, the cops were against them, the courts were against them—and anyone the government was against, they were *for*. This attitude even carried over into the Saturday and Sunday baseball games, when the prison nine challenged an outside team imported for the occasion (sometimes they wore sweat shirts reading AL'S BAR-B-Q and sometimes BILLY'S BOWLING ALLEY)—the cons invariably rooted for the outside team.

Therefore, our company was always sought, and our opinions on any number of subjects on which we were not even competent to speak were solicited.

It began inauspiciously enough (for me) during quarantine, when a big Negro who was dishing out the black-eyed peas from behind the aluminum counter spooned some into my tray and said quietly, "When're you comin' out?"

"In a couple weeks, I guess."

"How's old Paul?"

This puzzled me for a moment before I passed on to the next inmate, who was serving collard greens (and the next, who had stuffed bell peppers), but I suddenly dug his question and said, "Fine."

Later, when I came out of quarantine, having forgotten all

about the incident, he approached me in the yard and said, "When did you last see Paul?"

I told him he had sung in Los Angeles that year and had appeared at a meeting in our behalf in New York the week before we went to prison (Vincent Sheean had been the chairman), and I asked him where he had met Paul.

"In Tucson, where I come from."

"What're you in for, brother?"

"Pushing dope."

There was something so friendly and open about the man that I did not hesitate to ask the next question: "How come a man with your ideas would do a thing like that?"

He smiled at me. "There ain't many things a Negro can do in Tucson," he said. "And when my kids got hungry, I accepted an offer. Easy money. I wouldn't ever do it again." (Shortly before I left the joint, I received a similar offer when a fellow con found out that I had a private pilot's license; he said that his friends would even supply the airplane if I would like to make one flight a week over the border, and I could take in maybe a thousand bucks a month. "Easy money.")

It was astonishing to so naïve a man as I was to discover how much the other inmates knew about our case and our attitude toward the world. One Negro field hand stopped me (a few weeks later, after one of the truck drivers had been released and I was given a flatbed truck to drive) and asked for a light. He was hooking up aluminum irrigation pipes in the field, and he put one foot on the running board of the truck, held my hand steady as I offered him the match, and said, around the hand-rolled cigarette, "How you like being in the South?"

The question reminded me of an incident in quarantine (the only place Negro and white were not segregated), when I had automatically stepped aside after the noon whistle blew to let a Negro inmate who was a minister stand in front of me on the chow line.

He took my arm and said, "You first."

"But you were here first."

He smiled and said, "You're in the South, brother."

So I answered the field hand's question and said, "From what I've seen so far, not much."

Then he looked at me and said, "Lots o' these peckerwoods 're gonna have to learn the hard way."

"You know, it's not *my* fault I was born with the wrong color skin."

He smiled this time and said, "You got nothing to worry about, brother. We know about you."

When I drove the truck down to the farm office that was presided over by a screw who had been a farmer himself, he told me that he much preferred running the prison farm, because he didn't like being told by the goddamned Reds who ran the country how much he could grow and how much he couldn't. He had sold his farm, he said, and (standard gag with all prison screws), "Now I got more time to pull than you."

So I was not a political prisoner, because Mr. Huber had said there were no political prisoners in the U.S.A., but neither was I a criminal—as many of my fellow inmates pointed out.

They were criminals: they had stolen cars, transported women across state lines for immoral purposes, possessed or sold narcotics, bootlegged liquor, passed phony money, evaded income tax, forged government checks, held up the U.S. mail, or sneaked in from Mexico under cover of night to look for work.

Biberman and I baffled them. One of them said to me, "I don't get you, brother. You're not a criminal like me. You're here for some ideas you got, right?"

"I think so."

"Okay, I want to ask you a question. Only, first I want you to know what kind of guy *I* am. By me, most people stink on ice. Oh, I've met a few I liked, but most of them . . . I'm a junkie and a pimp, see? I got five girls hustling for me right now, so when I get out I'll have plenty in the bank and a Fleetwood Caddy and I can lay around the best hotel in Denver and have me a ball, see? Only, here's the point: I'm for *me*. Nobody else."

"So what's the question?"

"You got a wife and a little girl, right?"

I nodded.

"It's easier for you in here pulling time than for them outside. They're living on charity, right?"

"They're living on money raised by a committee," I said. "By the time our case was lost, I was broke."

"Yeah, okay, so what right you got to make your old lady suffer for a thing like this? That's what I want to know."

"My wife agrees with what I did."

"So what about the kid? She don't know nothing but her daddy's took away, right? So what right you got to do this to the kid? That's what I want to know."

I could not answer him in any terms that he could understand (and he was a very intelligent man, as well as a very handsome one), and after a while, when he saw I could not answer, he said, "I don't get you. Birds like you, I mean. From what I hear, guys like you are always putting out. I'm taking in. Why, if you came to me in Denver after we're sprung, with your tongue hanging out, I wouldn't give you the sweat off my balls."

He paused. "Depending on how I felt, see? I might give you a grand at that."

There was no day I did not wonder how to answer that man's question, just as there was no day I did not think about my small blond daughter, who was six years old when I was "took away," the age when she would ask me, three times a day, to be Prince Charming to her Cinderella.

The week I left, she was playing "cowboy" in the living room of the duplex apartment we had rented from Edward Dmytryk, and her little girlfriend from next door was the Indian. They were taking turns hiding behind a screen: one would hide and one would stand staring at the one behind the screen.

After a time, I looked up from the speech I was writing, and since I have been hard of hearing since 1938, when I heard too much artillery on Hill 666 in the Sierra Pandóls, I had to tune in on them.

They were playing "jail."

Late that summer, my wife wrote me that they had taken home the enlarged photograph of me that had been displayed (together with pictures of the other nine) at a fund-raising dinner in Hollywood the night we went to prison.

And every day Eva spent a good half hour parading around the living room, holding my portrait aloft in both hands, and marching to the music of the phonograph: a recording of the American Revolutionary War song "The Patriotic Diggers."

DISSOLVE TO

HOLLYWOOD. 1943–1945.

"There's a war on, you know."

There was a great deal of patriotism in Hollywood during the war, much of it even genuine. The stars were busy on bond-selling tours and entertaining troops through the USO; "back home" there was the Hollywood Canteen (chairman, Bette Davis), which was, of course, made into a feature film by Warner Brothers. (And in one or two scenes, if you looked fast, you could discover that there were even handsome, light-colored Negro soldiers in the war, for they could be seen dancing in the background with extremely beautiful, light-colored girls.)

No week passed without its drive: for British War Relief, Russian War Relief, the Red Cross, the Salvation Army, and the Blood Bank (which was almost a permanent institution on the lot). Contributing was absolutely painless: when you arrived in the morning, you found a blank subscription form on your desk, and you were expected to fill it out, indicating your contribution and your authorization to the studio to deduct it from your salary. Bond drives always received enormous support, for war bonds were an excellent investment, and there was no one who did not pick up a $25 or $50 bond at least once a week at the cashier's office on the main floor of the administration building.

There was a huge rally for the Red Cross that was held on one of our largest sound stages, and while attendance was not exactly compulsory, your absence would have been noted by captains in charge of each department of the studio. This rally was addressed, haltingly, by Jack L. Warner himself and, in the ex-

[63]

pected lachrymose manner, by his older brother Harry. There were stars who made speeches, and Major Richard Bong, the ace of the Pacific Theater of Operations, made a brief appearance (he was killed shortly after, testing a jet fighter over the San Fernando Valley), and a great deal of money was raised.

There was also a private rally in the boardroom of the administration building for Jack Warner's favorite charity, the United Jewish Appeal. Every nominally Jewish writer, actor, director, and producer was practically ordered to be present (I did not see any back-lot Jews). When we were all assembled, the Vice-President-in-Charge-of-Production marched in and—to our astonishment—brandished a rubber truncheon, which had probably been a prop for one of the anti-Nazis pictures we were making.

He stood behind his table and smashed the length of rubber hose on the wood, and then he smiled and said, "I've been looking at the results of the Jewish Appeal drive, and believe you me, it ain't good."

Here he paused for effect and said, "Everybody's gonna double his contribution here and now—or *else!*" The rubber truncheon crashed on the table again as everyone present, including John Garfield, Jerry Wald, Vince (the director), Albert Maltz, and I reached for our checkbooks.

And while it might have been true that there was a good deal of conniving to obtain more red and blue (and gas) stamps than your status in the war effort warranted (my producer's steak for fifty people, I learned, had come from a friend who had a ranch and grew cattle, and it—and several other halves and quarters—hung in his huge butcher-shop freezer), it is also true that the studios did their best to cooperate with every branch of the war effort, and they made films (such as the anti-Nazi pictures) calculated to support the ideals of the war in one way or another—without ever telling you what fascism was all about.

In 1947, Jack Warner submitted to the Un-American Committee a list of such films, "forty-three of maybe one hundred or more dating back to 1917," to demonstrate his consistent patriotism and opposition to totalitarian methods. He also appended another list ("39 subjects here, all pro-American short subjects") he had made between 1936 and 1946.

But it is also a fact that many studios—either through their story departments (which friendly Committee witnesses like James K. McGuinness said were infiltrated by Communists) or through various producers who must have been extremely "liberal"—made a practice of hiring writers they had reason to believe were political progressives (and, who knows, maybe even Communists?), because, as Jerry Wald once told me, these boys knew what society in general and fascism and the war in particular were all about and could create characters and situations that bore some resemblance to reality.

Reality—in a limited sense—was very much in evidence those days in Hollywood. The Russians were our glorious allies and the Nazis and the Japanese were our enemies. And while it is true that soldiers I picked up on my way to and from work were already saying, "After this is over, we're going to have to lick the Russians" (an idea their officers were promoting even during the conflict), everyone from Jack Warner (at the bottom) to General Douglas MacArthur (at the top) was loud in praise of the glorious Red Army that was chewing the guts out of the Nazis on the eastern front.

So what was "subversion" in 1947, when the Germans and the Japanese—and even Franco—had become part of the *Free* World and the Russians had become our "implacable enemies," had been patriotic and popular and an indispensable part of the war effort in 1943–1945.

Here is a sterling example of the sort of "subversion" that was practiced on Warner Brothers films (and it is one that Jack L. Warner never did detect):

When I arrived at the studio, they were making John Howard Lawson's wonderful film *Action in the North Atlantic,* in which Humphrey Bogart, Raymond Massey, and John Garfield were starred. This is one of the few films ever made in the United States that not only acknowledged the existence of a trade-union movement (the National Maritime Union, in this instance), but even showed some scenes inside the union hall, said some honest things about trade unionism, and demonstrated, in terms of human character, what being a member of a union could mean to a man.

The ship on which the action took place had been constructed on a sound stage, and the attack on that ship by Nazi planes, as it plowed its way to Murmansk, was one of the finest pieces of technical and special-effects work ever put on any screen, with machine-gun bullets ripping across the deck as Garfield, Dane Clark, Alan Hale, and other sailors ran to man their guns and stunt men dressed as seamen leaped into a sea of real burning gasoline and swam for their lives.

And one day, Jerry Wald, who was producing *Action,* called a halt to another script I was working on for him, handed me and my partner Al a shooting script for *Action,* and pointed out some places where additional dialogue was needed to bridge two sequences.

What was wanted, said Wald, was some humor that also had a point ("topical but not typical"), and we set to work to bridge the gaps.

We had Alan Hale and Dane Clark (who was then known as Bernard Zanville) on deck at one point, and then they could hear the sound of an airplane engine coming over. They looked up at the sky.

CLARK

It's ours!

HALE

Famous last words.

CLARK
(pointing)
It's one of ours all right!

CUT TO

CLOSE SHOT. SOVIET PLANE
—its red star painted plainly on the fuselage. The helmeted and goggled PILOT DIPS his WINGS and SALUTES the ship below as CLARK'S VOICE COMES OVER.

CLARK'S VOICE
(shouting)
Soviet plane off the starboard bow!

You will have to agree that that piece of business was subversive as all hell, but apparently the audiences did not think so, because it got one of the biggest hands and round of cheers in the entire film.

There was another, even more subtle, piece of propaganda inserted later (which diabolically mixed subversion with sex). In the film, the ship ties up in the harbor of Murmansk, and Clark and Hale hang over the rail and watch the longshoremen waiting to unload the lend-lease supplies she carries. The camera pans the shore, and we immediately notice that there are also female longshoremen on the dock, husky dames but pretty as they come. Camera pans back to Clark and Hale on deck as they look at each other with incredulity, look back at the women on the dock, and Clark whistles. A gorgeous 150-pound longshoreman smiles and waves at the men aboard the ship.

CAMERA COMES TO
CLOSE TWO SHOT. CLARK and HALE
—as they turn to each other.
HALE
(with awe)
This's the first time in my life I ever wanted to kiss a longshoreman.

If Harry Bridges, the West Coast longshore leader, was highly regarded in Hollywood in those days (at least by Jerry Wald), the Russians were also *persona grata*, and every November 7 they held a magnificent party celebrating the October Revolution at their plush consulate on Los Feliz Boulevard.

There, under huge portraits of Marx, Engels, Lenin, and Stalin, drinking vodka with lemon juice and gorging caviar, smoked sturgeon, black bread, and other, more American comestibles, you would see most of the VIP's in Hollywood, including

Charlie Chaplin and Olivia de Haviland, Theodore Dreiser (before he had even announced his membership in the Communist Party), Thomas Mann, and Lion Feuchtwanger, as well as many of the biggest (capitalist) Hollywood producers, for freeloading makes strange bedfellows, too.

A representative of the Soviet film industry was also resident in Hollywood, a man who later became well known in the United States as the director of *The Cranes Are Flying*. His name was Mikhail Kalatazov, and he had an interpreter named Zina, a young woman my wife and I had known well in New York— she and her American husband had lived on the floor below us on Tenth Street.

Zina was officially employed by Sam Goldwyn as a technical assistant during the filming of Lillian Hellman's *North Star,* and she called me at the studio one day and told me that Kalatazov wanted to meet Bette Davis.

"In the Soviet Union," Zina said, "she's considered the finest American film actress, and Kalatazov wants to show her a picture and have her to dinner at his house. Do you think you can arrange it?"

So, having previously introduced myself to Miss Davis in the Green Room (and given her a couple of my own books, as well as the Dean of Canterbury's *The Secret of Soviet Power*), I called on her in her dressing room.

To my disappointment, she was reading the Dean (not me), and she slapped the book in her hand and said, "These people have the right idea!" She also accepted the invitation with pleasure, and we made a rendezvous for late the afternoon of the screening. Norman Corwin joined us, together with my wife, who was pregnant, and director Zoltan Korda. In a projection room in one of the studios, Kalatazov showed us a film called *The Rainbow* that reduced us, from moment to moment, to tears or rage.

Then we proceeded in caravan to Kalatazov's rented house, where his handsome actress-wife had cooked and then served one of those Russian dinners that go on for several hours, not only because of the number of courses that are served, but because each course is interrupted several times by toasts.

Kalatazov and his wife spoke no English whatsoever. So each toast proposed by the Soviet director—and some of them lasted all of three minutes—had to be translated into English, when the person to whom it was addressed was expected to reply; the reply was then translated, and Kalatazov replied to the reply.

The host therefore toasted his wife, Bette Davis, Norman Corwin, Zina, Korda, myself, and my wife, dwelling in her case at great length upon the child she was carrying, who would, whether it was a he or a she, carry forward the great, democratic, and even revolutionary traditions of the American people, with which Kalatazov seemed more familiar than any of his American guests.

He did not use a glass but held up an enormous drinking horn that came from Georgia (USSR), and his capacity for vodka was astounding, as well as his capacity for food. He had a booming voice that must have been heard a good four blocks away, and he would brook no interruption when he was speaking.

During this lengthy ritual, Miss Davis obviously became quite restless, especially when the attention of the host or the guests was not on her. Norman Corwin was also quite distressed, because he was suffering from ulcers, he said, and could neither drink the vodka nor the light Georgian wines nor eat the highly seasoned food.

Long before it was actually time to leave—or before the dinner itself was over—Miss Davis made several tentative moves to go. Each time she did, Kalatazov would bend a disapproving eye on her and she would sit down.

But she persisted, insisting each time anyone tried to stop her that she had to get up early, as she was making a film and had to be on the set and made up by eight o'clock. Finally she asked Corwin to get her fur coat, which he did.

She then rose with majesty and announced that she was very sorry to have to leave so early. That was the point at which

Kalatazov, not relinquishing his drinking horn for a moment, moved around the table and, placing both hands on her shoulders, roared a word or two that needed no interpretation. He meant, "Sit *down!*"

He pressed firmly on her shoulders, slopping some of the vodka out of the drinking horn, and shouted something that Zina later told me meant, "I'm the host here, and the dinner isn't over—and nobody goes till the dinner is over and the host and hostess say it's okay."

Davis, however, is not the sort of woman who can be easily intimidated by any mere male (which Kalatazov may not have known at the time, but which he learned then and there), so she merely rose again, said in a voice she had rehearsed for several decades, "I've had a perfectly *won*derful time," took Corwin's arm, and swept majestically out of the room. Kalatazov scratched his head, and the dinner continued.

There were other Russians in Los Angeles who did not appear at the homes of visiting Soviet directors nor at the annual bashes at the consulate celebrating the October Revolution or Red Army Day. They were longtime residents, even though we had never met any until we accepted an engraved invitation from someone improbably named Boris Moros.

Moros was said to have composed the celebrated "Parade of the Wooden Soldiers," which became famous in the *Chauve-Souris* revue, and he was also alleged to be a producer.

My wife and I therefore turned up, dutifully, at his swank home, ostensibly to honor a visiting Soviet sea captain who was in the port of Long Beach with his ship.

The moment we arrived, it became apparent that the invitation must have been a mistake, for we saw none of the people we had met in Hollywood up to that time and none of the writers, producers, or directors who had appeared at the Soviet parties—though we did see some famous faces.

One was the elegant profile of Leopold Stokowski, which he managed to display very effectively all evening, and one was the pudgy face of Edward G. Robinson (complete with sawed-off cigar). He was carrying a Russian phrase book, which he consulted continuously, and he announced to anyone who was not interested that he was studying the language.

But the majority of the people at that party had stepped directly out of an authentically costumed production of Chekhov's *The Cherry Orchard* (or *The Three Sisters* or *The Sea Gull*): there were gentlemen in their sixties who wore spade beards, red silk sashes across their potbellies, and Czarist decorations; there were ladies in their seventies in shiny black bombazine with high whaleboned collars and chatelaine watches dangling vertically from the peaks of enormous bosoms, and they had blue hair.

These people constantly bowed and smiled at each other—and at us—and they all spoke Russian, so we sat silently on a damasked couch at the side of the room and applied ourselves to the vodka, the canapés, red and black caviar, black bread, and smoked sturgeon until the Soviet sea captain made his appearance, which was disconcerting.

For this representative of the proletariat was decked out in a gorgeous navy-blue uniform with gold braid and epaulets, and he carried at his belt a gold ceremonial dagger on whose hilt he rested one hand as he spoke.

He spoke eloquently—and, to our ears, beautifully—for a good fifteen minutes without interpretation; we watched the Chekhov characters, and there was not a dry eye in the room. Copious tears ran down the Czarist cheeks into the spade beards, and the ladies in bombazine brought forth tiny lace handkerchiefs from their tight sleeves and dabbed at their eyes.

It was possible to make an educated guess that he was talking about the enormous casualties on the Soviet front and the devastation wrought by the Nazi armies from Moscow to the Caucasus. And the guess must have been correct, for when he concluded, the bearded gentlemen and the bombazined ladies produced checkbooks and began writing out relatively enormous checks (I peeked) for Russian War Relief, which prompted us to speculate about the astronomic sums of money they must have carried with them (or had stashed away in Swiss banks) when they escaped from the Soviets twenty-seven years before.

From time to time during the intervening years, I used to

wonder how we happened to be invited to that party: could our host have confused my name (it had happened before and has happened since) with that of Demaree Bess of the *Saturday Evening Post*?

But it was not until I was six years out of prison (in 1957) that I finally understood what had happened. For that year, Boris Moros announced—with an enormous fanfare of publicity —that he had been a double agent for years preceding, a trusted and honored spy for the Soviet Union and (simultaneously) an informer for the Federal Bureau of Intimidation.

Then I realized why we were invited to that party: he had been *spying* on us! And the FBI men outside were sedulously copying down the license numbers of the cars parked in his driveway and along the street and making new dossiers on the White Russians inside the house!

But there is something about that explanation that still does not satisfy my novelistic imagination: for if Boros Moros was— as he insisted—a spy for the Soviet Union (*and* the FBI), why didn't he speak to us that night? And why didn't he ever invite us back? Or wasn't he interested in the inner workings of Warner Brothers Burbank studio, where I worked, or the Civil Air Patrol squadron of which I was the trusted G2, charged with the task of ferreting out subversive activities? *

And if Moros was a spy for the FBI and presumably reported that I was an innocent, how come I went to prison in 1950? Or did he tell his Soviet contacts (after examining our very small contribution) that we were freeloaders? And did he tell the FBI that I was a dangerous agent who refused to speak a word of Russian? The very thought of it appalls me to this day.

DISSOLVE TO

THE WRITERS' BUILDING. WARNER BROTHERS STUDIO. Burbank, California. June–November, 1943.

* Incidentally, there *were* two genuine subversives in that CAP squadron. One was an airline executive, and the other was an automobile dealer, and both were outspoken reactionaries. But since the airline man was our commander and the auto man was his executive officer, there wasn't a soul to whom I could report them.

"Go home and change your attitude."

In July of 1943, I undertook an assignment that proved to be my undoing in Hollywood—in more ways than one.

After I had finished work on *Northern Pursuit* and had spent five weeks doing a treatment of Sutton Vane's *Outward Bound* for the late Mark Hellinger (who will never be forgotten because one Friday in his office, he asked what I would like to drink, and when I said, "Something you haven't got—Courvoisier," he not only produced it but even gave me a bottle to take home "for the weekend"—and later drank himself to death on it), I was shuttled back to Jerry Wald to work on a story called *The Very Thought of You.*

It had found its origin in a short story by Ben Hecht that appealed to the fertile brain of Jerry Wald, who then took what he wanted from it and apparently told it to a young writer named Lionel Wiggam, who wrote a screenplay with which Wald was not satisfied. Hence my assignment to the project.

The studio owned the song, Wald told me, which apparently—by Hollywood logic—was sufficient reason to use it for the title (God knows, it had nothing to do with the story). And the story raised a very controversial issue indeed: Should Girls Marry Soldiers?

Jerry said, "What I want you to do with this is to put some social significance in it. The way it is handled now, it is extremely light and frivolous and superficial, but this is, after all, a rather important question, soldiers meetings girls every day, going to war; a good many of them are not going to come back. What is our attitude about this? Do we encourage these romances between soldiers on the way to the front and girls, marriages, babies, possibly, or do we not encourage it?"

Our answer to this burning question, after many story conferences, was a forthright "yes" (corollary: *if* they love them).

This film was to star a young girl named Eleanor Parker, whom I had met at the home of Sophie Rosenstein (whose husband, Arthur Gage, was now my business manager). She had appeared in a bit role in one earlier film as the daughter of Ambassador Walter Huston Davies (Moscow), and as Sophie had predicted, she later became a big star. It also starred Dennis Morgan and Bernard Zanville (now metamorphosed into Dane Clark), and there were several supporting players, including Faye Emerson and Henry Travers (with whom I had appeared as an Oriental slave, painted brown from head to foot, in Eugene O'Neill's *Marco Millions* years and years before "on Broadway"). It was to be the second directorial job of a screenwriter named Delmer Daves, who has since gone on to write, direct, and even produce bigger and plushier Technicolor pictures that mean even less.

I was under the fond illusion that I was going to get a solo credit for my work. For it was my intention to write Lionel Wiggam out of the script entirely, and Daves did not bother me while I was working. Thus, at the only conference I had with him, I was compelled to inject a typically subversive idea:

Since our heroine (Eleanor Parker) was helping the war effort while her man was away, by working in a parachute factory in Pasadena (with Faye Emerson), it occurred to me that we might get one or two moving sequences if one of their fellow workers was a Negro girl, married to one of the pilots in the famous 99th (Jim Crow) Fighter Squadron, which had already made a name for itself in combat in Italy. I milked this idea a little and put the three girls in a car pool, and the car—a beaten-up jalopy—belonged to the Negro girl, whose name was Hope.

I submitted this idea to Daves, who enthusiastically approved it, saying, "That's great! I want to show that *all* kinds of people are working to win the war."

But I did not know the Hollywood racket well enough at that point to realize that Daves was writing "behind" *me,* for nobody had told me that he was a sweet man but watch out for him because he might put a knife in your back.

That, apparently, was what he was doing. He was taking my pages as I turned them in and rewriting them, so that when the film was finally made, it bore the credits "Screenplay by Alvah Bessie and Delmer Daves."

However, that was not all he was doing, for he was injecting new scenes and off-color gags, such as the one where Parker and Morgan enter the motel in which Emerson is living and

Morgan says, "I like it; it's what we used to call functional" (he was a student of architecture before he went in the Army), and Emerson replies with a smirk, "It still is. For what I need it, it functions fine."

Or that other gag, where Emerson and *her* boyfriend (Clark) enter the motel, after Parker and Morgan have spent an innocent evening there necking, and Emerson says, "They just broke one of my records," and Clark says, "How can you tell?" and Emerson bends down under the couch and picks up a broken phonograph record.

But when we saw the sneak preview (it's the only time they invite you to eat in the Executive Dining Room with Jack L. Warner and other VIP's, and then they whisk you to a little theater in Cucamonga in a studio limousine and there is nobody there except a theater full of people who know there is going to be a sneak preview), I really became enraged.

The Negro girl, Hope, appeared in the following scene, and this was the only appearance she made: Parker and Emerson are packing a parachute and talking about the time of Morgan's departure for the front, when Parker says, "He said it depended on the troop train. . . . I *hoped* . . ."

HOPE
(popping up from under the parachute table)
Callin' me, honey?

She was *so* light-complexioned that you would have had to read the screenplay to know that she was colored.

The writing and rewriting of this little fable occupied me from July 20 to October 1, but it did not get produced that year. And when it was "completed," Wald felt that he had to exercise the studio's right under the contract to lay me off without salary for a while—he said he had no assignment for me. (You could be laid off for twelve weeks of the fifty-two the contract ran.)

This I resisted with all my powers of persuasion, for several reasons, all of them having to do with my need for money. For

[75]

the first time in years, it had been possible for my wife and me to pay our long-standing debts; to get our teeth fixed; to buy some badly needed clothing; and (for me) to allocate a decent weekly sum for the support of my two sons by my prior marriage.

Their mother was ill in New York, and a sympathetic (and unimaginative) uncle, who was also wealthy, consulted me by long distance telephone. The upshot of our conversations involved placing the boys in a boarding school for the time being, but he did not tell me (I learned it later, from the bills) that he had chosen one of the most expensive of its kind in the state of Connecticut (and one of the worst, from what the boys had to say about it later).

So, despite my employment of a business manager, in the person of Arthur Gage, my money went out as fast as it came in, and we had such acrimonious debates about the allocation of my earnings that I had to let Arthur go, for he was trying to tell me that I could not afford to spend as much money on the boys as it was necessary to spend.

When I presented this situation to Wald, he was entirely sympathetic and said, "Okay, I'll find something for you." He maintained in his office a huge battery of filing cabinets into which he stuffed literally hundreds of ideas for film stories—ideas he had culled from newspapers, magazines, books, or merely idle conversation. These were the raw materials of films that would be topical (but not typical), and now he said, "I've always wanted to make a film that would *really* tell the truth about the newspaper racket. You used to be a newspaperman yourself."

"Okay," I said with a sigh, "I'll go on layoff."

"What do you mean?"

"We *can't* tell the truth about the newspaper business and you know it."

"Don't be ridiculous," he said. "We can tell the truth about anything. *Listen* to this idea."

Then he told me a story about a young man who went to journalism school and emerged fired with enthusiasm for his career and determined to write the truth "without fear or favor." (That became the title of the story.)

"He gets a job on a paper," Wald said, "and he rapidly discovers that he *can't* write the truth."

"You mean the advertisers control the paper?"

"We'll come to that. The point is, he covers everything for the sheet. He discovers that the races are rigged, the boxing matches are fixed, politics is—"

"And when the boss's son rapes a fifteen-year-old girl it never gets in the paper—"

"Don't interrupt me. Now *get* this: he becomes cynical as hell. Like Westbrook Pegler. He becomes corrupt; he starts to drink, fights with his wife (he's married). Now, you'll *love* this—he's done everything on the paper but be a foreign correspondent.

"There's this little war going on—in Spain—nobody knows what it's about. He asks his managing editor if they will send him, and the editor says sure, so he goes to Spain."

Jerry was becoming wound up, and he almost carried me with him as he said, "In Spain, he discovers *the menace of fascism!* He realizes that if this war isn't won, there's gonna be a world war in which America will be involved. There has to be a beautiful Spanish girl too. So he sits down at his typewriter and rips off some really hot copy and cables it home. And when he comes back, he discovers to his astonishment—"

"That it hasn't been printed."

"Right."

"The Catholic Church—"

"No, no," said Wald, "we can't touch that but—" He paused in thought for all of four seconds and said, "Maybe the owner of the paper has investments in Spain—"

"I'll buy that," I said (I was rapidly picking up the lingo).

"So he goes out to try to peddle his stories to other papers. No luck—"

"You're telling me the story of my life."

Wald was like a kid with a new toy. His broad face beamed; his triple chins trembled. "I *knew* you'd love it."

"Look," I said, "I'll take the layoff."

"*Why?*"

"Because we can't make it."

"Don't be silly," Jerry said. "They'll *love* it. The public, I mean."

"And the papers?"

"I used to be a newspaperman myself," said Wald. "I know what they'll say. *The New York Times*'ll say, 'That's not us, it's the others'; and the others'll say, 'That's not *us*, it's—' "

"Okay," I said, "I'll do it."

"Have a ball," he said, and I did. For a month and a half, I wrote this "original" story, and it was the best work I ever did in Hollywood. I decided I would put it down exactly the way it would have happened and pull no punches. I was practically inspired and was able, at times, to do whole sequences in strictly visual terms, because I was beginning to understand the motion-picture medium and sense its vast potential.

But something else was beginning to happen too. By the time the story was ready for Wald to read (it was ninety pages long), I was becoming aware that the year was almost over and that I had received only one screen credit. To my naïve mind, this seemed a very poor return to the studio for the investment of some $14,700 in (gross) salary. So I began to feel that there was a very good chance that, come January, the studio would decide not to exercise its second option, and instead of getting a $25 a week raise—to $325—I would be dropped and sent back to New York to resume work on *New Masses* at $30. (Thus money does make cowards of us all.)

What happened was simplicity itself: I began to develop peculiar gastrointestinal symptoms—I had no appetite, and a single bowl of soup in the Green Room filled me to the brim. I could not sleep at night, and I suffered constantly from gas. I had violent pains in the belly when I drove to the studio every morning, and they did not abate until I left for home at five o'clock.

On November 23, I was laid off, and the symptoms were so unbearable that I went to a doctor, who listened to my story, laid me on his examining table, and felt my belly.

He took my hand and placed it on my abdomen and said, "*Feel* that." I felt it. It was hard as a rock—well, it felt like the length of rubber hose Jack Warner had used as a gavel at the Jewish Appeal meeting in his boardroom.

"What's *that*!" I said in amazement.

"That," said the doctor, "is a spastic colon. Put on your pants."

Then he sat down and lectured me (and told me, incidentally, that he was preparing to give up general practice in favor of psychiatry). He said, "You've got to go home and change your attitude."

"How?"

"You've got to decide that you don't give a good goddamn whether you work for Hollywood or go back to New York and work for *New Masses*."

This was a difficult decision to make, but during the three weeks I was laid off, I managed it. I decided that I was definitely *going* back to New York and to hell with Hollywood. I would coast through the last month of the contract and collect our return tickets. So when I went back to the studio on December 14 to resume work on the original story, my attitude was changed. It was changed to such an extent that Wald looked at me with amazement.

He had various ideas about the story, he said. It was, he maintained, "*too* anti-Fascist," and he said that "if Jack Warner reads this, he'd fire both of us."

His ideas therefore involved initiating a process for which he was famous: first, you get a good, aggressive, honest, no-holds-barred story about a controversial issue (from a "Red," if you can find one), and then you water it down.

He wound himself up explaining to me how we could make this story after all and have an Academy Award picture, and I listened. Each time he said, "How do you like that idea?" I would reply nonchalantly, "I'll think about it."

He stared at me and said, "What's happened to you? When you first came here, you were hot as a firecracker. You were enthusiastic. You'd argue story points with me the way I like to have writers argue. Now all you say is, 'I'll think about it.'"

I did not answer his question (because I *had* changed my attitude), but I went back to work for two weeks on *Fear,* and then it was shelved. Wald called me in and said, "I was talking to some guys at my house last night, and they told me what a wonderful job the paratroops are doing in Burma."

My job was to go back to my office and work up an original story for Errol Flynn. So you call up the research department and ask them to send over everything they have on the war in Burma.

And it does not take more than an hour's reading to discover that the war in Burma is strictly a British operation, so you call up your producer and say, "Look, Jerry, there *are* no American troops in Burma," and he says, "So what? It's only a moving picture."

You protest that an American invasion of Burma will get you laughed off the screen, and he says, "So, look, put in some British liaison officers and stop worrying."

So I put in some British liaison officers (and I also put in a Jewish lieutenant named Jacobs), and this story was written in relatively record time—nineteen days—and it was a good action story, if you don't mind the fact that Burma was a British show and was not commanded by Errol Flynn. (A lot of people *did* mind, including an entire theater full of people in London, who threw things at the screen and tore up the seats until the film was withdrawn from distribution.)

There was a conference in Jack Warner's private office at this time, and it was the first and only time I was ever in the immediate Presence of the Vice-President-in-Charge-of-Production, in a relationship, that is, that permitted me to talk to him and forced him to listen.

The Very Thought of You was approaching production, and the conference involved its director, Delmer Daves, and its producer, Jerry Wald. The three of us sat in Warner's office while the V-P-in-C-of-P sat behind his desk and read the entire script to us out loud—as though we had never seen it before. He would pause at moments to suggest a very bad gag of his own, at which point either Daves or Wald (or both) would cry, "Oh, no, Jack, *no!*" and Jack would smile apologetically and say, "I was only trying to lighten it up a little."

Primed by me, Wald then told Warner that while he and Daves wanted me to do "a little polish job" on *The Very Thought*, he would also like to hold *Objective Burma* (the "original" story) for me to write the screenplay.

"No," said Warner. "Bessie can't write all the pictures in this studio. He's done enough with these two wonderful jobs. Put two other writers on it." Then he added, "I like the idea of having a Jewish officer—what's his name, Jacobs?—in Burma." He pointed one finger at Jerry and said, "See that you get a good clean-cut American type for Jacobs."

So Ranald MacDougall and Lester Cole wrote the screenplay, and Lieutenant Jacobs was played by William Prince, a good-looking, clean-cut American-type *goy*, whose dog tag—when his platoon was found, by Errol Flynn, dead after torture by the Japanese—was clean of *any* religious designation, such as the *C*'s or *P*'s that were stamped on the other dog tags in Flynn's hand in the inset.

And that is all that happened at this meeting: some bad jokes from Jack Warner (and some high praise for the job I had done on *The Very Thought*), and if I had not been so naïve a man, I would probably not have been so surprised by what The Vice-President-in-Charge-of-Production had to say about that screenplay four years later.

DISSOLVE TO

EXTERIOR. FEDERAL CORRECTIONAL INSTITUTION. Texarkana, Texas. Late summer, 1950.

The NARRATOR SITS in the driver's seat of a battered flatbed truck parked under a tree. He has a copy of Mark Twain's *Life on the Mississippi* under the seat cushion, a notebook in his hand, a pencil. He is astonished that it is possible for him to turn out two or three so-called poems a day—something he could not do even when he was a sophomore in college twenty-eight years before and fancied himself a poet and even went around for a while wearing a flowing Windsor tie (but not on campus).

> August is the hottest month,
> breeding fever in convicted flesh;

the silver column mounts inside the tube . . .
ninety-six, a hundred, one-o-five—
still climbing. . . .
You sit *inside,*
stripped down to the skin
and sweat flows from the very lobes of ears,
the tip of nose,
splashing on the concrete floor. . . .

Outside the fields are silent under sun;
the sky is brass, the very leaves of trees
(their lungs, they say)
hang silent on their twigs,
gasp and await the moving air that must—
in time—appear.

The NARRATOR LOOKS UP from his work as the fat screw named BAKER appears, WADDLING across the field. In the background, he can see the farmers working, the Negro and Mexican inmates who are stooped in the baking sun, spreading chemical fertilizer (which the Narrator has brought in hundred-pound bags from the farm).

He considers how lucky he is, being white and of the advanced age of forty-six, not to have to do this kind of labor. He can sit and read or write or even go to sleep while others work, until it's time to carry them back to the institution at four o'clock, when the flag goes up on the pole at the farm office and the whistle blows at the institution itself.

Now BAKER, dressed in gray denim, wearing a pith helmet and MOPPING his FACE with a red bandana, comes and SITS on the runnning board of the truck. He wears round steel-rimmed spectacles, and his face is more than ordinarily red.

BAKER

You got it easy. What you thinking about?

NARRATOR

Running away with the truck.

BAKER

(laughing)

You won't get very far. Maybe forty miles before every sheriff in Texas, Arkansas, and Louisiana will be on your tail.

(notices notebook)

What you writing?

NARRATOR

Notes.

Now BAKER REACHES FOR the notebook, looks through it.

BAKER

(incredulous)

Poetry?

NARRATOR

If you want to call it that.

BAKER

Why'n't you write a book while you're here?

NARRATOR

Can't concentrate. Too much noise in the block at night.

BAKER TOSSES the notebook back onto the seat of the truck.

BAKER

It's hot.

The NARRATOR says nothing, but he is thinking: Why should the weather be important/ when you are in jail?/ Because, despite our friend who said/ that everybody talked about the weather/ but no one ever did a thing about it/ . . .

BAKER

You don't talk much, do you?

NARRATOR

Nothing to say.

He thinks: . . . *outside* you can;/ *inside* you sweat it out./ He wonders whether he will remember the lines until this character goes away again.

BAKER

You ever write poetry before?

NARRATOR

When I was a kid; it works off steam.

[83]

BAKER

You think you're doing hard time, you should see your **pal** Beeberman.

NARRATOR

What's *he* doing?

BAKER

In the warehouse; he loads and unloads trucks; stacks the stuff on the shelves.

NARRATOR

He's the outdoor type. Plays tennis.

BAKER

He's older than *you* are.

(scratches his head)

You birds interest me, you know?

NARRATOR

Why?

BAKER

You're supposed to be Commonists, they tell me in the control room. Of course, I don't hold with that kind of stuff. This is a pretty good country; I don't see no way to improve it— and I been abroad—but the way I think, a man's got a right to think anything he wants. They got lots of Commonists in Europe; what I've seen of 'em, they're a pretty cruddy lot.

NARRATOR

You like this job?

BAKER

Huh? Yeh, sure. I'm not like the other custodial officers. I read. I study. You know, penology, psychology, criminology, Freud. When I got vacation, I visit other institutions. You don't *have* to.

NARRATOR

What're they like?

BAKER

Some of them I wouldn't put a dog in. But this kinda work's better than the Army.

NARRATOR

(idly)

Where were you? In the PTO?

[84]

No. Normandy. Germany. Four years.

NARRATOR LOOKS at BAKER, wonders whether he's telling the truth. The war ended when? In '45, only five years ago; and was he as fat then as he is now?

NARRATOR

You ever been in Saarlautern?

BAKER

Sure.

NARRATOR

(suspiciously)

When was that?

BAKER

(after a pause)

March of '45.

Suddenly the NARRATOR is short of breath. He puts one hand to his chest, GASPS, TAKES a DEEP BREATH.

BAKER

You don't feel good?

NARRATOR

I'm okay.

(casual)

Ever know a man named Joe Hecht?

BAKER

I should *say*!

Now the NARRATOR is convinced that BAKER is a liar because Joe Hecht was his closest friend in Spain, after Aaron Lopoff, and he was his closest friend in New York after that war and until Joe went into the Army after Pearl Harbor.

NARRATOR

Where'd you know him?

BAKER

Saarlautern. I was the sergeant of one recon patrol and he was sergeant of another. I relieved him every night.

NARRATOR

(excited—this will clinch it)

What—

BAKER
(interrupting)

That guy was fantastic! You know, there was never a night I
relieved Joe that he didn't leave me a chocolate bar, a deck of
butts, something.

NARRATOR
(to himself)

That was Joe.

(he *must* ask)

What'd he look like?

BAKER

Ugliest son of a bitch I ever met, but there was something
beautiful about him, his eyes, or maybe the fact that he was
the kindest man I ever met in my life. Always considerate.
Always thinking of the other dogfaces first.

NARRATOR

You know he was killed.

BAKER
(aghast)

No!

NARRATOR

On March 18, 1945.

BAKER

My outfit pulled out the sixteenth. I never knew that. How'd
you know him?

NARRATOR

He was in Spain—went through the whole war without a
scratch. In Saarlautern, his squad was pinned down by Nazi
machine-gun fire. They were taking heavy casualties. Joe
went out with a couple grenades and took out that gun. But
they got him. He got a Silver Star for it—posthumously.

BAKER

No shit?

(after a pause)

He was the best joe I ever knew in my born days. I never
met a man like him.

NARRATOR

(he has to say it)

Did you know he was a Communist?

BAKER

(incredulous)

He *was*?

(a pause)

If the Commonists are like—

He STOPS SHORT, glances at the NARRATOR, GETS up, PUTS ON his
pith hemet, and WALKS AWAY.

There was no other hack like Baker in the joint. He was,
without doubt, the only one who took the job seriously, visited
other institutions in his time off, read books (penology, psychology, and Freud), and tried to understand the men he supervised.

That was one good reason why he was cordially disliked by
the other custodial officers, who considered him an eager beaver
who hoped to rise in the hierarchy from officer to lieutenant, captain, associate warden—who could tell?—maybe warden in
twenty years or more.

I made a practice of asking every one of these officers whether
he liked his job, and most of them were liars, as well as being
both uneducated and vulgar men. The cons would ask: "What
kind of a guy would want to be a screw?" and the question
answered itself: "A hoosier who can't make it on the outside."

But there was no doubt that the Federal officers were a cut
above the kind of men who staffed the state and county joints.
They had tenure—and pensions—if they kept their noses clean;
they lived in neat little houses down the road, in a sort of village,
where they had wives and children. These houses cost them next
to nothing, and they got their meals in the joint itself (better food
than that of the inmates). The warden had the use of a big Buick
with a small shield on its door reading "U.S. Bureau of Prisons,"
which apparently embarrassed him, because that summer he
bought a Cadillac for himself, which was parked in front of his
very nice large house outside the institution.

[87]

But when you said, "Do you like this job?" they all said, "Sure." One, however, a punch-drunk ex-Marine (and former boxer), who was to become my personal nemesis the last month I was in the joint, was honest.

When I asked my question, Mr. Griffin replied, "Hell, no. But it's better than working for a living."

The others were a job-lot assortment. One was a fairly decent bird who also wore steel-rimmed glasses and said that he was really a landscape gardener. He had managed, once, for a few years, to get away from Texarkana, where he and his wife were born, and practice his craft in Tennessee. "But my old lady got homesick," he said, "so we came back. And there's no work in Texarkana for a landscape gardener."

There was a hack who looked like Bill Sykes in *Oliver Twist* (or so I felt) and was reputed to own a flock of motels on the Texas-Arkansas line. He was as impersonal as the screws were all supposed to be; he couldn't have cared less what went on in the joint so long as he wasn't involved in it.

There was an elderly guard known to the inmates as Asshole because he had a mouth like one (I thought of John Steinbeck's *Grapes of Wrath*), and it was permanently puckered up while he explored it, day and night, with a toothpick.

And the man who was captain the first six months of my residence was a cousin of a rather famous male movie star (though he pronounced his name somewhat differently, as though, let's say, his cousin's name was Cooper and *he* pronounced it Coper), and he was a celebrated character in the place for that reason and that reason alone.

These men were not supposed to fraternize with the cons, and few of them did (Baker was an exception, but our talks took place only when we were far out of sight of the institution). Others, like the landscape gardener, would sometimes come into the cellblock at night before the lights went out and hang around, gassing with the inmates or kibitzing as they played dominoes or chess or checkers (no cards allowed) or argued with one another about the baseball scores or the reason for dope addiction and how to handle it.

He also permitted men to visit one another's cells—which was strictly against the regulations, except that you *were* allowed to stand in the doorway—and the men appreciated him for that, because they were permanently lonely and starved for any sort of companionship.

But the Federal joints not only do not permit fraternization between officers and inmates; they also do not permit the officers to carry any kind of weapon when they are on duty or to push the cons around—physically, that is. Mental or emotional sadism is another thing, and you could be "shot" (reported to the captain or the warden) for a variety of infractions of the rules, which would result in your losing some "good time" if the warden took a serious view of the offense.

Such offenses included a marvelous misdemeanor known as "silent contempt." When you were addressed, you were expected to answer with a "yes, sir" or "no, sir." If you were insulted, which was often enough, you were not supposed to reply in kind, and if you stared at the officer with what he felt was silent contempt, you could be shot for that.

So you quickly learned to develop a pan as dead as that presented by the screws themselves and to reveal no reaction to anything that was said to you. (The experience I had had with Jerry Wald after I developed the spastic colon and went home and changed my attitude came in handy here.)

And Biberman and I were not getting along well, which I am sure augmented our mutual loneliness. In quarantine, he had bawled me out for my attitude on the ride from Washington to Texarkana. He said, "You missed a great opportunity there."

"What opportunity?"

He slumped on his cot and mimicked me. "When the marshal or the detective turned to you and asked, 'How are you, Bessie?' you lay back in the seat and moaned, 'I'm alive.'"

My God, I thought, do I have a face like *that*! So I got hot. "Are you under the impression that anything you said to those cops had any effect on them?"

He shot to his feet and stood erect. "Of *course*!" (He had once been in the National Guard, when Rupert Hughes had been his commanding officer, which fact—after October, 1947—the old man apparently considered a personal betrayal.)

"Listen, Herbert," I said, "in my opinion, I'm in the hands of the enemy. In such a situation, my obligation is to be a gentleman, say 'yes, sir' and 'no, sir,' or keep my mouth shut. That's what I'm doing."

"*Look* at you!" said Herbert, pointing at me. "You don't stand up straight. You lean against the wall! You fall into a chair and *lie* in it! I find you physically repulsive."

We didn't speak to each other for a few weeks after that, except to nod casually when we met in the yard during exercise periods, when I would sit in the bleachers taking the sun (when it was bearable) or pitch horseshoes and he would stride around the perimeter (a good quarter mile), his cap on his head, his arms pumping like a transatlantic tourist making his daily rounds of the ship's deck. Or he would lift weights, his face and neck strained in what looked like agony to me.

There was a doctor in the next cell to Herbert who was "in" for selling heroin to an addict, and he was one of the few cultured and intelligent men in the joint. He watched Herbert walking across the Atlantic Ocean and turned to me and said, "How old is your friend?"

"Fifty."

"He'll drop dead of a heart attack."

"Not Herbert," I said. "He's the outdoor type."

Our second quarrel came a couple months after our arrival in Texarkana. The newspapers carried a story about Edward Dmytryk, who had issued a statement through his attorney, Bartley Crum, from the prison in which he and Albert Maltz were confined.

In that statement, Dmytryk said, in effect, that he had made a sad mistake, that his country was at war (which was more than Truman admitted), and "my country right or wrong."

I blew my cork and cursed Dmytryk, saying that he hoped to shorten his six-month sentence and predicting that he would become a renegade. Herbert became livid with rage.

"You don't know what you're *talking* about!" he shouted. "He may be weak—he had a visit from his wife just before he made that statement—but Eddie will *never* go over to the enemy! You don't *know* him. You show no understanding of people whatsoever when you say a thing like that!"

DISSOLVE TO

THE WRITERS' BUILDING. WARNER BROTHERS STUDIO. Burbank, California. Winter, 1943–Spring, 1944.

"You're the father of a lovely little girl."

It was during the final rewrite of *The Very Thought of You* that my only daughter, Eva, was born. That was on March 1, 1944, but two months before she made her first appearance on the scene, Errol Flynn had spotted her.

My uncomfortable wife was in the habit (under doctor's orders) of taking a walk every afternoon, and we were living on Montcalm Avenue, in a cute little pastel house that belonged to a *tapette* who was helping out the war effort in the Navy (Stateside). So every afternoon my wife dutifully walked out of the pastel (green) house and turned the corner into Mulholland Drive and promenaded her enormous belly along the right side of the road.

She was walking downhill toward the Valley one afternoon, when Flynn came roaring uphill in his convertible, unaccountably alone. He saw her and drew to a shrieking halt and flashed his brilliant teeth.

"Hello," he said.

She said hello, being a very polite lady.

"Hop in."

"No thanks, I'm going the other way."

"I can go *both* ways," said Flynn.

Helen Clare remained silent as he smiled at her, and she decided that she had better continue to walk, when he said, "Why don't you come up to my place, baby, and I'll show you a good time?"

"I don't think my husband would approve," she said politely and continued to walk downhill toward the intersection of Mulholland and Woodrow Wilson.

Flynn did not mention this episode in his much ignored but very moving autobiography, *My Wicked, Wicked Ways*, but perhaps the omission was an oversight.

My wife and I were realizing two of our life ambitions that winter and spring. She was producing her first and only child; I was studying for my pilot's license; and we moved just before Eva was born to a house in the Valley, on Coldwater Canyon, a block from John Howard Lawson and his swimming pool.

Jack's lovely house (and pool) was four thousand miles and nineteen years removed from the place we had first met, when he worked on the top floor of a ramshackle house in Patchin Place, Greenwich Village, and I lived in the cellar and worked nights as an extra in his play *Processional*.

We extras shuttled every night by cab from the theater that housed Sidney Howard's *They Knew What They Wanted*, where we were Italian-American vineyard workers, to the old Garrick Theater, where we were coal miners and (in a later scene) members of the Ku Klux Klan. (The Guild saved a lot of money that way.)

It was in this latter role that I made my most enduring impression on the Theatre Guild's director, Philip Moeller, who suggested during rehearsal that the Klansmen should come on stage and "do something funny."

Since I was accidentally first on stage and since I was only twenty-one, it was still possible for me to take a short run in the wings and make a very elevated flying leap onto the stage, freeze, and then stalk with exaggerated tiptoeing movements to my proper place. The other Klansmen followed suit.

Moeller, watching from the audience, said, "That's *great*! Keep it! How did you *do* it?" With the sort of arrogance I have never been able to muster since, I replied (in the presence of the entire company), "Genius."

That almost finished my career at the Theatre Guild, for Moeller could never take me seriously after that, and my life onstage almost ended again in 1927 when Walter Hampden told me that I was not tall enough to play classical drama.

This infuriated me, and I decided then and there to end my theatrical career in a blaze of notoriety, and I waited for three months to get a chance to do it. It would have been so simple. I was understudying the part of the Vicomte de Valvert in *Cyrano de Bergerac,* whom Cyrano (Hampden) kills in a duel while reciting a ballade (*à la fin de l'envoi, je touche!*), and the dueling was distinctly third-rate in my eyes, for I had been a member of the Columbia fencing squad. So I decided that when M. le Vicomte got sick some night and *I* played the role, I would simply *refuse* to be killed and would keep Cyrano dueling all over the stage for at least three minutes, then, cooly, I would run him through with my own *épée.*

They would have had to ring the curtain down, and the exploit would have made the front page of every paper in New York. *Mais, hélas,* it never happened, for the simple reason that the actor who played de Valvert never missed a performance during the entire run of the play.

Jack Lawson's success with *Processional* and then with *Success Story* and *Gentlewoman* (for the Group Theater) had brought him to Hollywood in the 1930's, where he became not only one of the busiest (and best) and most successful screenwriters in town, but also one of the organizers and the first president of the Screen Writers' Guild, thereby becoming the permanent bête noire of every reactionary in Hollywood.

Jack's attitude when I arrived in January, 1943, was optimism personified and certainly the opposite of that expressed by Dan Fuchs. He told me at lunch that first week that I would have an opportunity to do my best work and that, despite the monopolistic character of The Industry and the total control that the producers exercised over the content of film, any decent writer could develop honest characters and situations in the work he had to do and could contribute to the stature of a medium whose potential could be seen by anyone who looked at the screen. (I think he has changed his mind since then.)

I had begun to question that concept during the writing of

Northern Pursuit, Objective Burma, and *The Very Thought of You,* but what followed these assignments convinced me that such ideal conditions might obtain for a man like Jack, who had a reputation in The Industry and therefore a bargaining position, but not for me. Jerry Wald promptly assigned Jo Pagano and me to write an original story to be called *Invasion,* about the Anzio invasion that had taken place a little over a month before, and we worked enthusiastically for a month—and it was shelved.

Then I was on layoff for five weeks, during which I spent a lot of time observing my newborn daughter, Eva, who had arrived on March 1, and attending classes at night at the Civil Air Patrol (Los Angeles Squadron 3), learning what I could about navigation and meteorology, aircraft and engines and doing close-order drill on Sunday mornings in Warner Brothers old studio on Sunset Boulevard. And I also spent a lot of money at Lone Pine in the Owens River Valley, taking dual instruction in a series of Piper Cubs and Luscombs—at eight dollars an hour.

I was a solo pilot again (as I had been in 1937, before I went to Spain) and, as such, rated a sergeant's stripes in the CAP and an Observer's Wing. And the CAP was a ball for the job-lot assortment of 4-F's and older men and women who enlisted in it and spent their time in the air in "navigational training missions" or scouring the canyons and passes of the Sierra Madre Mountains for the Army, Navy, and Marine planes that invariably got lost in the fog when they were on instruments and ran into clouds with solid linings.

The squadron commander and his executive officer each owned a private aircraft and got free gas to fly around the countryside. The rest of us rented planes at Lone Pine and were quartered, when we stayed the weekend, in the Japanese "relocation" camp at Manzanar, across the road from an auxiliary airport for the airlines.

My closest friend at the time was a CAP lieutenant named Paul Pierce, who had his private license and worked as a chorus man at the studio in such things as *Shine On, Harvest Moon,* which was written by that sweet man, Dick, who kept his war bonds in his jacket pocket.

Paul really wanted to be an actor, and I even took him to Sophie Rosenstein one day for an audition, which he admitted later had been dreadful (so did she), so he abandoned that ambition; and when his contract (at $100 a week) ran out, he took what money he had and bought more instruction and eventually got his commercial license with an instructor's rating. Then I took instruction from him as well as from a fat little man named Phipps, who looked like a country grocer but was the best flight instructor I had ever known.

Pierce took me on one navigational training flight to Quartzite, Arizona, and promptly got airsick in San Gorgonio Pass and turned the ship over to his incompetent copilot, whose only job was to keep it on an even keel while Paul heaved out his window and all over the side of the plane.

From Quartzite we flew to Baker, California (after Paul had recovered and we had scrubbed the fuselage with a wire brush), and from Baker we flew back through Cajon Pass into the coastal valley and a haze so thick that you could see straight down but not ten feet ahead.

We were trying to find the small airport in the foothills of the Sierra Madre that had been assigned to CAP as a base from which to fly (on prescribed course) out of the coastal area, and we could not find it. But we did find a farmhouse on the ground, and Paul made steep, descending spirals till we were right over it, and three men, hearing our Continental engine, came running out and looked right up at us.

Idling the engine, Paul yelled out of the window—something I am sure no pilot had done since the 1920's: "Which way to *Pomona?*"

The three men pointed in three directions, and Paul intelligently decided that the one in the middle was probably right; within fifteen minutes (and in a sea of perspiration), we passed over the airport at Monrovia and came into the landing strip near the tiny reservoir and sat down with a collective sigh.

But finding your way through haze and smog was a lot easier (I came to realize) than finding your way through the mind of a producer named Lou, to whom I was assigned (again with Jo

Pagano) on my return from layoff. Or rather, we had to find our way not only through Lou's mind but also through the mechanics of making a film from a novel by Vicki Baum called *Hotel Berlin,* which was a quick rewrite of her earlier best seller *Grand Hotel,* brought down to date—to Hitler time, that is.

We had a technical adviser on the film whose name we knew immediately: Leonhard Frank, who was remembered for his post-World War I novel *Karl and Anna,* which he had dramatized and which had played all over Europe and had made him a rich man—till Hitler came to power. Frank, who was in his early sixties, was a small man with white hair and startling blue eyes. His history was as spectacular as his appearance was ordinary. He was a fervent anti-Nazi (and perhaps a Red) who used to spend his time arguing with me about the current line of the Communist Party under Browder.

"What is this shit?" he said indignantly. "Progressive capitalism! Whoever heard of such a thing? Capitalism is going to lie down and *die*? The workers will take over without a *struggle*?"

He pulled on his long white hair with both hands and shouted, *"Verrücktheit!"* and all our conversations were conducted in his (and my) bad French and my worse German, of which I had had one year in college, twenty years earlier.

Frank fled Germany with a price on his head and took refuge in France, where he was promptly interned by the Vichy regime. When the Nazis occupied the north, he escaped to Southern France dressed as a woman, walking by night and hiding during the day (he was almost sixty then). And when all of France was occupied, he managed to get to the United States through the efforts of an organization called the League of American Writers, of whose executive board I was a member. Part of the League's function involved helping anti-Fascist refugees get out of Europe, among them such distinguished artists as Franz Weiskopf, the French novelist Vladimir Pozner (who also turned up at Warners and worked dubbing films into French before they trusted him to write a screenplay), and the Germans Ernst Toller, Stefan Zweig, and Lion Feuchtwanger.

To obtain the cooperation of the United States government, it was helpful if the League could assure the Immigration Service that the refugee it was sponsoring would not become a public charge and would have a job and a salary upon arrival. By pulling certain strings and making certain telephone calls, it was therefore possible to obtain a job for Leonhard at Warner Brothers, nominally as a technical adviser, and his personal sponsor was Max Reinhardt's son Wolfgang, who was one of the most pleasant human beings (and cultured producers) on the lot—and therefore one of the least successful.

Lou, our producer, was a vulgar and stupid man, but he had lined up a distinguished cast, including Helmut Dantine of *Northern Pursuit* (who was now an *anti*-Nazi), Raymond Massey (a Nazi general), Peter Lorre (an anti-Nazi professor), and Faye Emerson, whom I had thought was a wonderful actress when she appeared in *The Very Thought of You,* but then I saw her play a scene opposite Helene Thimig, the widow of Max Reinhardt, in *Hotel Berlin,* and the difference between a performer and an artist became painfully apparent.

Leonhard Frank—since he was a German and an anti-Nazi and presumably knew something about what was happening under Hitler—was assigned as technical adviser at the munificent salary of $100 a week. This fact was enormously embarrassing, both to my collaborator (who earned five times as much) and to myself (who was then earning four), but it did not seem to bother Leonhard at all. He was, in fact, delighted that the studio had been kind enough to provide him with a bilingual secretary so that he could make contact with his other colleagues.

But when the two writers read the so-called novel, they were appalled, for the central situation called for an anti-Nazi underground leader (Dantine) to be trapped in the Hotel Berlin (the Adlon, of course) and to take refuge in the bedroom of a woman (Andrea King) who was the mistress of a general of the Nazi General Staff (Massey). What was worse, they were to fall in love with each other.

Frank, of course, was of one mind with the two writers about this situation, and the three of us went to Lou, our producer, forgetting to bring along Leonhard's bilingual secretary.

We told Lou this situation would have to be changed; it simply would not work. In fact, it would be laughed off the screen.

MED. SHOT. INTERIOR. LOU'S OFFICE.
LOU SITS behind his desk. PAGANO and BESSIE SIT in facing chairs. LEONHARD FRANK PACES UP AND DOWN; he wears a white silk scarf around his neck.

LOU

Why won't it work?

BESSIE

Because a leader of the anti-Nazi underground—

PAGANO
(interrupting)
—if such exists—

BESSIE

—if such exisits in Berlin today—could not *possibly* fall in love with the mistress of a Nazi general.

LOU
(judicially)
In love, anything is possible. What's the matter with you guys? Don't you believe in *love*?

I looked at Leonhard and was amazed that he seemed to be understanding every single word that was said; he *must* have or his face would not have become so red.

We assured Lou that we believed in love but that in this particular situation, it was impossible.

BESSIE
(ticking off points on his fingers)
One, underground leaders in Nazi Germany are men of a special breed. Two, they are highly political fellows and—you should pardon the expression—probably Communists and—

[98]

Three, it is *impossible* for a Communist leader to fall in love with a Nazi woman!

Lou shook his head, and the argument continued, with Jo and I appealing to authority in the person of Leonhard Frank, who suddenly started speaking his peculiar brand of French, interspersed with German. I "translated" for him. This went on for a few moments, until . . .

LOU

(interrupting, pointing at FRANK)

Why should I listen to *him?* Who the hell is *he?* A $100 a week technical adviser!?

(pause)

Besides, he can't speak English!

We tried to tell our producer that Leonhard was one of the world's best-known and most respected novelists and dramatists, that he was a German, an anti-Nazi, a man who had lived through the whole thing we were writing about, and—as a last resort—that he had been one of the most successful and *richest* writers in Europe.

LOU

(very angry)

Never *heard* of him!

(to the writers)

Now listen, Vicki Baum's one of the greatest writers in the world. Her books sell millions of copies. We bought this book, and we're going to make it exactly the way she wrote it!

If you think we gave up at this point, you do not understand the role of an honest writer in a corrupt world—nor the influence that Jack Lawson's assurances still had on me. Always, in Hollywood, the honest writer attempts to improve on the frequently shoddy material given to him to adapt for the films; he frequently succeeds—and this is sometimes called "subversion."

So the two writers and their technical adviser sat in their office and discussed the problem for almost a week, and they came up with an idea and went back to their producer.

INTERIOR. LOU'S OFFICE

—as LEONHARD FRANK PACES UP AND DOWN and LOU stares at him from behind his desk, but listens to the writers anyhow.

> PAGANO
>
> Lou, we have an idea. And we'd like to tell it to you. But please—*please* don't interrupt until we're finished. Then, if you don't like it, we'll try to find another.

PAGANO suddenly chickens out, looks helplessly at his collaborator. LOU LEANS BACK in his chair, an expression of patient resignation on his out-of-focus face, and BESSIE LEAPS IN.

> BESSIE
> (eagerly)
>
> The anti-Nazi underground leader *doesn't* fall in love with the mistress of the Nazi general.
>
> (LOU makes a gesture; BESSIE starts to shout)
>
> *But,* he *pretends* to fall in love with her—in fact, he *seduces* her in order to get the secrets of the Nazi High Command!

> LOU
> (beaming, sitting forward in chair)
>
> I'll *buy* that!
> (slaps desk)
>
> *That* I like!
> (spreads hands apologetically)
>
> All I wanted, boys, was the bedroom scene.

> DISSOLVE TO
>
> THE GREEN ROOM. WARNER BROTHERS STUDIO. Burbank, California.
> CAMERA MOVES IN TO

—a variety of short scenes in which the NARRATOR is SEEN trying to feel his way through the Hollywood jungle, more or less by instinct, since he has not been able to develop any real guile, nor has he learned to play his cards right, nor will he ever.

1. CLOSE SHOT. NARRATOR.

He is eating alone but contemplating the perfect features of Miss HEDY LAMARR, who is EATING lunch at another table with her husband, the actor JOHN LODER. She is in costume, and in addition to her flawless face, she has magnificent swelling breasts under the period costume. The NARRATOR is cogitating over a typical *New Yorker* story he has in mind—and which has been inspired by the sight of Miss LAMARR, whom he had seen the day before, in street clothes. The story begins in his mind:

"What lovely breasts you have today, darling," said Timothy Swabish to his bride Ellen as they lifted Martinis to each other. "You didn't have them last night."

The NARRATOR wonders how to continue the story from that point but gives up.

DISSOLVE TO

2. CLOSE TWO SHOT. AT TABLE IN GREEN ROOM. BETTE DAVIS and NARRATOR.

They are having lunch together, and this situation rises out of the NARRATOR's shameless attempt to curry favor with the reigning queen of Hollywood.

Early in 1943, he had given her copies of his books; and nine years before he met her, he had "decided" (1) to meet her; (2) to write a film for her; and (3) to marry her before he died.

He will never, of course, achieve the second or third objectives; in fact, the third, when expressed obliquely at The Writers' Table in the form of a remark to the effect that the lady was enormously appealing in a physical way—among others—brought glances of scorn and contempt from his fellow writers, including the muttered remark, "She's a dog."

DAVIS IS now SPEAKING of the heroine of the NARRATOR's novel *Bread and a Stone*.

DAVIS
(emphatically)

I want to play that woman.

[101]

NARRATOR

I want you to.

DAVIS

There's only one thing wrong. You've got to find some way to save the man's life. He simply *cannot* be executed.

NARRATOR

But it's the logic of his life and—

DAVIS

(impatiently)

I *know* that. But it makes for a downbeat ending. It will send people out of the theater feeling sad.

NARRATOR

(vapidly)

It's a sad story.

DAVIS

You think about it, Alvah. You find a way to save his life, and I'll get Jack Warner to buy it.

NARRATOR

(feeling doomed)

I'll think about it.

(brightly—he knows the answer)

Tell me why the woman interests you so much.

DAVIS

She's real. She's solid. She's in one piece. She's a strong woman. I like to play strong women.

NARRATOR

Then tell me—how is it that you're so wonderful at playing neurotic women?

DAVIS

(deadpan)

Probably because I'm the only *non*neurotic woman in the United States.

DISSOLVE TO

3. ANOTHER TABLE. GARY COOPER.

COOPER and Ingrid Bergman (absent today) are making *Saratoga Trunk* (with Katina Paxinou). Rumor has it that COOPER and Bergman are what Walter Winchell calls "an item," but if they are, they are itemizing off scene, because they rarely eat lunch together. Today, as usual, COOPER is sitting alone as the NARRATOR APPROACHES him.

NARRATOR

Mr. Cooper, I'm a writer here.
Alvah Bessie.

COOPER

Yeh, hello.

NARRATOR

Do you know when *For Whom the Bell Tolls* will be released?

COOPER

Purty soon, I reckon.

NARRATOR

I'm anxious to see it because—
(significant pause)
—I'm one of those guys you played in the picture.
He SITS down without being invited.

COOPER
(chewing)

That so?

NARRATOR

I wasn't one of the guerrillas; we only had four American guerrillas. I was in the International Brigades.

COOPER
(chewing)
Terrible thing, civil war. Brothers fighting each other.

NARRATOR
It wasn't really a civil war, Mr. Cooper.

COOPER
(mouth open)

It wasn't?

NARRATOR
It was a war of invasion on the part of Germany and Italy —against the legal government of Spain.

COOPER

That so?

(swallows)
That's what's so great about this country.

NARRATOR

Huh?

COOPER

What I mean—a guy like you can go and fight in a war that's
none of your business.

DISSOLVE TO

4. ANOTHER TABLE.

—as the NARRATOR, who has now seen *For Whom the Bell Tolls*
at its *première* at the Carthay Circle Theater, APPROACHES KATINA
PAXINOU, who played Pilar in the film, a character modeled after
the great Dolores Ibarrúri (La Pasionaría) despite Hemingway's
obvious dislike for the Spanish woman leader. Paxinou's performance is the only one he can remember—one week after the film
was released. He does remember, however, that all the characters
except Bergman and Cooper had *green* faces and that the *première* audience, during the intermission, was hotly debating
which were the good guys and which were the bad guys and
asking plaintively, "Who're you supposed to root for?" and,
"What's the damn war all about, anyhow?" *

NARRATOR

(bending over table)
Miss Paxinou, I want to thank you for your performance in

---

* The ambiguity of the film version of *Bell* was pointed up by the contention of its director, Sam Wood (no less), who insisted that it took no
sides in what he chose to call a battle between communism and fascism;
by a spokesman for Paramount (which produced it), who said the film
"really isn't about anything"; and by a question and a reply at the Writers'
Congress held at UCLA in 1943, in a seminar on "The Nature of the
Enemy," when screenwriter Dudley Nichols was asked by a member of
the audience:

Q.: Mr. Nichols, who prevented you from naming the Fascists in *For Whom
the Bell Tolls*?
CHAIRMAN: You need not answer that, Mr. Nichols.
NICHOLS (grins): I can answer that in two words—the Fascists.

For Whom the Bell Tolls. You were the only person in the film who convinced me he was Spanish.

> PAXINOU
> (smiling)

Thank *you.*

> NARRATOR

You must have spent a lot of time in Spain.

> PAXINOU

I have never been in Spain in my life.

> NARRATOR
> (he doesn't)

I see.

> PAXINOU

That war meant a great deal to me. Especially a particular Spanish woman. I heard her speak one night at a big meeting in Paris, at the Vél' d'Hiver . . .

> DISSOLVE TO

THE WRITERS' BUILDING. WARNER BROTHERS STUDIO. Burbank, California. 1944–1945.
The Narrator is something of a success, depending on how you look at it. Starting at $300 a week, he managed to survive an entire year and started 1944 at $325, ending it at $350. At the end of 1944, his agent went to the story editor (Jim Geller having moved on to other and perhaps greener pastures), a gentle, intelligent, and unaggressive fellow named Finlay McDermid.

He told McDermid that the Narrator was "unhappy," which was a euphemism that could be translated into "he wants more money and thinks he deserves it," and in view of the fact that he had "won" screen credits on *Northern Pursuit* and *The Very Thought of You, Objective Burma* and *Hotel Berlin,* the contract was rewritten and called for a $75 a week raise beginning January 1, 1945.

He has therefore become a third- or fourth-class writer, for writers who earned $4,000 a week did not speak to those who only got $3,000, and those who earned $1,000 did not speak to those who only got $425—except in a casual, passing-the-time-of-day manner—and these class distinctions also obtained among those who were considered progressive or even "Red."

Such distinctions are merely a reflection—in what Marxists call "the superstructure" of (Hollywood's) society—of what goes on at the economic base. What goes on, in turn, is best expressed in that classic gag concerning the institution known as the story conference, wherein script problems are solved through the intervention of the producer, who frequently fancies himself a creative artist and has the power to impose his fantasies on those who really are. Like that famous paragraph in the writer's term contract which stipulates that the studio is the author of his work, this gag details precisely the relationship between the writer and the medium:

Following a violent argument between producer and writer over a story situation that the writer does not like but the producer does, the producer rises, takes the writer's arm, and leads him to the window of his office. Pointing to the studio parking lot, he asks the writer, "Which is your car?"

The writer indicates a secondhand Chevrolet.

"See that car?" says the producer, pointing to a Cadillac. "That's *mine*. The situation stays *in*!"

But when the new contract went into effect, the Narrator was "off" *Hotel Berlin*, the writing of which had taken from May to November, 1944, and two days after the job was finished, he was reassigned to producer Wolfgang Reinhardt, which delighted him, and to the remaking of a film that he personally thought of as *The Amazing Dr. Clitoris*.

This was, of course, *The Amazing Dr. Clitterhouse*, which had been released ten years earlier, starring Edward G. Robinson. Upon receipt of this assignment, the Narrator began to think of himself as a permanent fixture who could sell ideas to the stupidest producers; he also thought of himself as fighting a holding action (as in Spain), fighting to prevent his producers from making pictures that were stupid, antihuman, or outright reactionary.

But there were ideas that he could not sell, and Leonhard Frank (now promoted to the rank of writer himself—at $200 a week) was involved in one of these fiascos with the Narrator.

They were fairly close friends by then. Leonhard turned up regularly at the Narrator's ranch-style house on Laurelgrove Avenue in the Valley (rented from the actor Alan Baxter, whom he had never met, except on the transcontinental telephone). Frank would drive up in an ancient Packard convertible, which he had picked up for fifty dollars, wearing a white silk scarf around his neck like a World War I pursuit pilot.

He liked to cook for the Narrator and his wife, his specialty being *Weisswurstl*, and he gave the Narrator's daughter Eva the first dress she ever wore: a dark blue affair with large white polka dots, which her mother still cherishes.

Hollywood engages in the practice of the remake for a very simple reason: a film has been a huge financial success; to repeat the success (they hope), they often will remake it—give it a different title, rename the characters, change the locale, but the story will be essentially the same. Then the new audiences sit in the theater and wonder, "Where have I seen *this* one before?"

In this instance, we had Dr. Clitterhouse, who is a sort of psychiatrist who has been called to court many times to testify as an expert witness in criminal trials. He therefore becomes interested in criminals and decides that most of them are very stupid men and that he can commit a much better crime himself. So he organizes a gang of thugs, serves as their mastermind, and pulls off a number of fantastically successful jewel and bank robberies. He plans them; the gang carries them out. Eventually, of course, he makes a mistake and is caught; his lawyer pleads insanity, and he is sent to a mental institution for a short time (like many another rich criminal) instead of to prison for a long stretch.

Wolfgang Reinhardt, Leonhard Frank, and I sat in the projection room, and they ran the original film for us and gave us copies of the screenplay—and we were in despair. For the film—after ten years—was so exciting and so well executed that we could see no way, offhand, to either change it or improve it.

Wolfgang had told us that he had available as actors Peter

Lorre (again); Sydney Greenstreet, the very fat and very fine actor of British background; a beautiful young girl (whom Wolfgang—unlike many other Hollywood producers speaking of their female stars—*never* referred to as "the cunt"); and many others. So Leonhard and I sat down to think.

After stewing over it for a few weeks and arguing about the current line of the Communist Party and the way the war was going in Europe (the long-delayed Second Front had finally been opened on June 6, 1944—two days after my birthday), we finally reached a momentous decision: we would move the locale of the story from the U.S.A. in the twentieth century to London in the nineteenth. We thought it might be interesting (and pathetic) to have Greenstreet (who would play Clitterhouse) seriously in love with the young girl, who would treat him like a dog but make him regular promises of her "love" in exchange for furs, jewels, and expensive clothes.

We added some new characters and cast Peter Lorre in the role of a feebleminded gangster called Willie the Weeper, who was constantly trying to snitch Greenstreet's whiskey, so that Greenstreet could whack him on the back of the hand with a ruler and roar, "Whiskey's not for children!"—and Willie would weep.

We worked five or six weeks on this treatment of the story—a long narrative showing how it would be handled in film—and Wolfgang was delighted with it. While we were engaged on this minor masterpiece, the American troops were taking a shellacking in the Battle of the Bulge, but no one in Hollywood seemed to notice the fact.

Wolfgang was convinced that we had an imaginative, clever, moving, and entertaining film that not only would increase his stature at the studio but would so successfully disguise the original story that audiences would have a hard time remembering where they had seen it all before.

Such treatments usually went to the story department and occasionally to Jack L. Warner, Vice-President-in-Charge-of-Production, but Warner was (as usual) on vacation somewhere, playing roulette at Cannes or who knows? So it went to his administrative assistant, a man named Steve, and Steve called a story conference in the administration building.

CAMERA MOVES IN TO

MED. SHOT. STEVE'S OFFICE.

Present are Producer REINHARDT and his writers FRANK and BESSIE. STEVE THROWS the manuscript on his desk.

STEVE
(pointing to manuscript)

What's *this*?

REINHARDT

That's *The Amazing Dr. Clitterhouse,* that we're remaking.

STEVE
(scratching head)

I don't understand. Sydney Greenstreet is Clitterhouse?

REINHARDT

Yes.

STEVE
(outraged)

Greenstreet *in love* with a young *girl*?
That's *disgusting!*

BESSIE
(mildly, remembering his spastic colon of 1943)

We thought it would be interesting—since Greenstreet's a very fine actor, and not merely a heavy—to have him play this straight. He could get a lot of pathos out of the situation.

STEVE
(shouting)

People will laugh it off the screen!
That comes *out!* And who's this character called Willie the Weeper? Is this a *child*?

FRANK
(in German, which Steve understood)

No, that's Peter Lorre. He's feebleminded.

[109]

STEVE
(scratching head)
He *must* be a child.
(points at script)
It says right here, "Whiskey's not for *children!*"
STEVE STANDS UP, STARTS PACING his office like Napoleon (or
Darryl Zanuck).

STEVE
(whirling on others, pointing)
Now look! We're going to remake *The Amazing Dr. Clitterhouse.* It was a very successful picture. It made a lot of
money. I don't mind your putting it in London in the nineteenth century, that's good—good atmosphere, spooky, fog,
mysterioso—but *I want this to be exactly the same picture
we made before!*
(pause for breath)
Take out the girl!—that's *revolting!* Take out the feebleminded gangster. *I want exactly the same picture—word for
word!*

So, Leonhard and I went back to our office and spent another
three weeks making a new treatment that would be exactly the
same as the original screenplay, except for those necessary
changes to adapt it to the nineteenth century London locale.

                                                    BACK TO SCENE
INTERIOR STEVE'S OFFICE
—he THROWS the new script on his desk, TURNS to face REINHARDT,
FRANK, and BESSIE.

STEVE
What's *this?* This is exactly the same as the original screenplay!

REINHARDT
(sighing)
That's what you said you wanted, Steve.

[*110*]

FRANK and BESSIE
(together)

That's what you said.

STEVE
(screaming)

I said no such thing! What do you think I am—*crazy*? If I
wanted to have the same picture we made with Eddie Robinson, I wouldn't have it remade *at all*! I'd just release the
original film!

REINHARDT
(pathetic)

But, Steve, we were *all* here when—

STEVE
(suddenly)

Listen, is this Clitterhouse *insane*?

REINHARDT

Of course.

STEVE
(bellowing)

I don't want to make a picture about a crazy man! Forget it!

FADE OUT *

FADE IN

FEDERAL CORRECTIONAL INSTITUTION. Texarkana, Texas. Fall of
1950.
The Narrator has petitioned for parole and has been denied,
and though he still carries his trusty's pass, he has been pulled
inside the fence and now works as a clerk in the warehouse, typing inventories, receiving reports and bills of lading (in quin-

---

* We forgot it. It was then given to two other writers, who went back to
our original treatment, Willie the Weeper and all. Then it was shelved for
good. After the war, Frank returned to his hometown, Munich. The German
Democratic Republic gave him its National Prize (100,000 Deutsche marks
and a medal), and the German Federal Republic countered with its own
award. He proudly displayed both, saying, "This is my personal reunifica-
tion of Germany." He died on August 18, 1961, at the age of seventy-nine.

[*121*]

tuplicate) in the office, while Herbert Biberman (soon to be released after serving five of his six months' sentence) loads and unloads trucks and stacks supplies of all kinds on the metal shelves in the warehouse itself.

Steve may not have wanted to make a film about a crazy man, but if he had, he would have found lots of fine material in Texarkana—and not all of it confined to the inmate population. It is a tragic fact that large numbers of prisoners, who almost invariably come from the poorest levels of our population, are also high-powered neurotics when they are not actually psychotic; and just as they receive no occupational rehabilitation worthy of the name, neither do they receive any psychiatric treatment.

The young man in the next cell was a beautiful example of good human material that could have been saved or rehabilitated, had anyone been interested. His name was Del, and he worked in the parole office under my mentor, Mr. Huber. Tall, handsome, with dimples in his cheeks, he was the epitome of masculine charm, which accounted in large part for his presence in the Texarkana institution. Del was a confidence man.

His story, which I tried hard to believe, went like this. During the war he had been a tail-gunner in the Naval Air Service, stationed in the Pacific Theater of Operations. On his return, he married a girl from the state of Washington (he showed me an eight-by-ten glossy photograph) who looked so much like Frederic March's daughter in *The Best Years of Our Lives* that, for all I know, it might have been a photograph of Teresa Wright herself. They had a baby son and were living in Ohio, where Del had a good job as a salesman (following an earlier post as aircraft and engine inspector for the Civil Aeronautics Authority).

Then (and the plot began to thicken) his wife's father in Seattle fell ill. "My wife's devoted to her old man; she's practically nuts about him; she insisted on going to him—to be with him and nurse him back to health." Del said he did not have the money for the fare, but instead of borrowing it (which he could have done; he had a good job, as he said, as well as connections with the Veterans of Foreign Wars), he simply wrote a check for a couple hundred dollars, cashed it in a department store, and gave it to his wife, who left for Seattle, taking the baby with her.

Then, said Del, when he realized what he had done, he just "took off." He not only took off, but lived high on the hog for the next couple years, traveling on the airlines, laying all the hostesses (he said), cashing checks all over the landscape by the simple expedient of being good-looking and well dressed, talking to strangers in bars and hotel lobbies, and displaying his expired CAA inspector's identification card.

When they finally caught up with him in New Orleans, he was arrested—*not* for being a confidence man (he got a big charge out of this), but for "impersonating myself," which means he was impersonating an employee of a Federal agency. He got four years, and the department store in Ohio and a hotel in Washington, D.C., where he had run up a big tab and then skipped, both put detainers on him. Which meant that if and when he got out of Texarkana, he would be tried for the two grand thefts he had committed (or which had been detected) in Ohio and the District of Columbia.

Del was up for parole (he had served a year and a half at the time), and he was determined to make it. In preparation for his hearing before the parole judge, he wrote two letters, which he brought to me. "My English ain't so good," he said. "I never had more than a couple years high school."

One letter was to the department store in Ohio; the other was to the Washington hotel—and they were almost identical. In both, Del told how he had committed his particular crime and why (the pressure on his wife, his love for her and their baby, her devotion to her father, his insolvency); how he realized that he had made a foolish mistake; how he had now served a third of his prison sentence and had certainly learned his lesson.

He promised both the hotel and the department store that if they would ask the local district attorney's office to lift their detainers, he would pledge to come back to Washington (and Ohio) and work for the hotel (and the store), at any salary they offered, until he had paid off every cent he owed—with interest compounded semiannually at four percent. (He also wrote to his VFW chapter, begging their intervention in his behalf.)

Illiterate these letters certainly were—he could neither spell nor construct a simple declarative English sentence—but as I read them, I was moved to tears. I told him that I would not change so much as a comma; they were beautiful letters; they gave a perfect picture of a man who had not had an opportunity to get an education; and they were so patently honest and sincere that *anyone* would be moved.

Del was well liked by Mr. Huber (which was in his favor too), and he was doing a good job in the parole office. The screws liked him, as well, and our fellow cons admired him, although he did not fraternize with them very much. So far as I could see, I was the only man he "buddied" with, and we spent long hours in his or my cell discussing the state of the world, the movies we saw every Saturday night, women, the war, our respective crimes, my Spanish war experience and his Navy exploits, flying, sex, and narcotics addiction (he was not an addict, though twelve of the twenty men in our cellblock were), and playing chess.

I had taught him the game, and within two weeks he was pushing me hard (chess has always hurt my head, anyhow); and on one memorable evening late that fall he almost won, and I made the stupid mistake of saying (thinking I was kidding him), "What's the matter, Del, can't you win a game?"

His face went white and his lips tightened as he looked at me. "Don't you talk to me like that, you son of a bitch," he said. "You want me to tear you a new ass*hole*?" His voice rose as the question was concluded; he rose with his voice and strode out of my cell, and he didn't speak to me for two weeks, even though I wrote him a note that very night (and put it on his cot) apologizing for my insensitive and tactless gaffe.

It was close to Christmas, and although I was expecting a visit from Helen Clare and Eva, I was about as low as you can get in such a joint without slitting your throat with a razor blade, as one young fellow who had robbed a post office had done the week before (but not too enthusiastically).

My parole had been denied despite a moving document that I had written as early as September. It had been denied despite the recent decision (December 11, 1950) in *Blau* v. *United States*, in which the Supreme Court reversed a judgment for contempt for refusing to answer questions relating to membership in the Communist Party. The Court ruled that such questions violate the privilege against self-incrimination, whether or not the defendant raises the privilege in the "correct" legal terminology or not.

And Herbert Biberman had gone home. The afternoon he left we sat in the yard, and he said, "Alvah, I had hoped never to have to talk to you like this, but before I go, I—"

We were sitting on the ground near the horseshoe pits, and he went silent for a moment. Then he said, "First, I want to say that if there were any way I could serve half of the balance of your sentence, I would do it."

"Thank you," I said. "I believe you would." (I *did*.)

"I can't. But I can give you a warning. I *can* say to you, Alvah, that I'm *terrified* of what may happen to you after I'm gone."

I must have looked blank, because he paused and said, with all the force at his command (and it is considerable), "Alvah, the men here hate you!"

"They do?" I said with astonishment. "I was under the impression I was getting along pretty well."

"Alvah, they *loathe* you! Any number of them have said to me, 'What's the matter with that guy, anyhow? I say hello to him, he grunts. What's eating him that ain't eating me?'"

I was struck dumb. For Herbert speaks with such authority and conviction that it was impossible not to believe him. I believed him. I was not only struck dumb, I was terrified. I was *so* terrified—and so bewildered by having seen no indication whatsoever that the other men loathed me—that I did not go out in the yard for the next two days but sat in my cell trying to read Sholom Asch's *The Nazarene* and *The Apostle* at the same time.

Then came Sunday, when you were allowed to wander freely around the institution and visit in other cellblocks, so I called on the doctor who was there for selling heroin and who lived in the cell next to the one our departed Herbert had occupied. He sat on his bed and listened as I repeated what Herbert had said, and to my amazement he started to laugh so hard that he finally rolled off the cot onto the concrete floor, which was scarcely a dignified thing for a doctor of medicine—and a short fat man, at that—to do.

When he had recovered himself, he gasped, "Al-vah . . . the . . . men . . . hate . . . *Her-bert!*"

Although I didn't believe this, I had observed a few things that made me somewhat uncomfortable. Bad enough that Herbert had chewed me out for my "attitude" on the ride from Washington to Texarkana; bad enough (but understandable) that he did not like the way I slouched about, leaned against walls, and collapsed into chairs. Worse, to my con-wise way of looking at things in those days, was the fact that when he entered the warehouse every morning at eight, he said, "Good morning, Mr. Portly, good morning, Mr. Heel," to the two screws who ran the place, as lousy a pair of creeps as I have encountered in my lifetime. (Their names were not *really* Portly or Heel, but that's the way I thought of them, and they do suggest the originals.)

The five other inmates who came to work with Herbert also said, "Good morning, Mr. Portly, good morning, Mr. Heel," and when they all left at four o'clock, they each said, "Good afternoon, Mr. Portly, good afternoon, Mr. Heel." But I could never bring myself to say anything to either of those pinheads unless they spoke to me (when I generally grunted in reply), and the day after Herbert left for home, not one of the other cons ever again said good morning, good afternoon, or go fuck yourself.

I was also in trouble with Mr. Portly. He had given me permission to use the office typewriter for personal needs after I had finished the day's bills of lading, receiving reports, and inventories (in quintuplicate), and I had typed up most of the seventy-odd so-called poems I had written to that point. And one weekend I lent the manuscript to the good heroin-selling doctor, who could not return it to me—because it was removed from under his mattress during a Sunday shakedown.

Portly, who always wore a railroad engineer's striped denim cap and a huge railroad watch on a long gold chain ("My daddy was an engineer," he told me), was outraged that I had used the typewriter for such a purpose, in spite of the fact that he had given me permission to do so.

"Why can't you be like Mr. Beeberman?" he said. (I was astounded by the use of that word by a screw; I knew that the other cons called Herbert "mister"—a fact of which he was inordinately proud—but a *screw!*) "That man," he said, "is the best inmate I have had in over twenty years of custodial work. Always polite, always courteous, a perfect gentleman, a model inmate."

In vain I tried to convince Portly that I had written nothing subversive, nothing that could disgrace him (or myself), but he muttered, "That ain't what they say in the control room."

I went to the control room and spoke to the captain. There was a new one now, the cousin of the movie star having moved on to a higher post in El Reno, Oklahoma, after visiting me in the prison hospital when I had flu. He had stood grinning at me and said, "When a man can stand on his feet, I send for him to tell him this kind of thing, but since you're flat on your back already, I come to *you*." (Wide grin) "Your parole's been denied." (Loud laughter. Exit.)

CAMERA COMES TO
CLOSE TWO SHOT. NARRATOR. CAPTAIN. CONTROL ROOM (AT CAPTAIN'S DESK)
—as NARRATOR STANDS before the new CAPTAIN, who SITS behind the desk and looks up at him with a scowl on his face.

NARRATOR
(tightly controlled voice)
I understand that a piece of my personal property has turned up here.

CAPTAIN
Wha's that?

NARRATOR
A book of poems.

CAPTAIN

Yeh. An' what right you got to *have* a thing like that?

NARRATOR

I wrote them.

CAPTAIN

You wrote 'em. An' you won' get 'em back, *neither*. They're derogatory to the institution.

NARRATOR

(heart beating wildly)

I spent months writ—

(a pause)

I don't see how they could be derogatory to the institution. I don't *feel* derogatory.

CAPTAIN

(a growl)

I oughta know. I sat up half the night readin' 'em.

NARRATOR

(politely)

I'm sorry, sir. I'd like to have—

CAPTAIN

Get outa here!

That night I copped out: I wrote a letter to the warden (who was on vacation in his new Cadillac), explaining the situation as best I could and asking to have the manuscript returned after he had read it. I knew this would spike any attempt by the captain (should he be so inclined) to flush my poems down the nearest toilet.

The temporary loss of Del's friendship hit me hard. He was not only about the only con with whom I could hold extended and fairly intelligent conversations and the only one of whom I was personally fond, but also my personal commissary. The ten chocolate bars and the carton of cigarettes I was permitted to buy weekly were always consumed long before the commissary came around again, and Del—who bet successfully on football, basketball, and baseball games (on the radio)—was always loaded with the stuff. No chocolate bars! No cigarettes!

But Del was an excellent con man (after all, he always won his bets on the games), and he had considerable vanity. So when he decided to make up with me, just before Christmas, he showed me two letters from district attorneys in Ohio and the District of Columbia informing him that, at the suggestion of the hotel and the department store and in view of his promise to return to both places and make restitution (apparently the respective DA's did not know about each other), the detainers had been lifted.

"My God!" I said. "*I'm* supposed to be the writer, but *you're* going to write yourself right out of here!"

He grinned (showing his dimples) and said, "No shit, brother," and offered me a chocolate bar without being asked.*

When I wrote to the warden asking for the return of my manuscript, I also made another request: to grow a moustache, which I had worn since 1920, in spite of the fact that my father had always worn one and we did not like each other. The moustache had been shaved the day I arrived in quarantine ("take that thing off!"), and I wanted to have it when my daughter arrived with her mother Christmas week to visit me. She had never seen me without it, and the visit itself would be strange enough for her without encountering a father who did not resemble the one who had been "took away" from her six months before.

The request to grow a moustache came back "Granted," together with an invitation to call on the warden on Saturday after-

---

* At Del's request, I called his mother after my release in April, 1951, and reported that her son was well. Four months later, working in San Francisco, I received a call one night from New York. The voice said, "Hi, Al. Want a chocolate bar?" He told me he had won parole, had worked in Philadelphia, New York, and Miami and would come to San Francisco some day to see me. Three months later, when I was putting out the biweekly newspaper of Harry Bridges' International Longshoremen's and Warehousemen's Union, the phone in the printshop rang, and the same voice said, "Need a chocolate bar?" "Where the hell are *you?*" "In a bar down the street from your office." An hour later, we met. He was well dressed, *said* he was driving a truck for a farm-produce outfit in Sacramento, *said* he was going down to Bakersfield to "lay down the law" to his ex-wife, and asked me whether I needed any money. I said I had a pretty good job, and he said, "You were pretty decent to me in Texarkana. You ever get in any trouble, need some dough, you get in touch with me." He gave me his address, and I have never heard from him since.

noon. I had seen him many times when I worked on the truck during the happy months outside the hurricane fence, and I had never seen him smile. He drove his Bureau of Prisons Buick slowly around the seven-hundred-acre farm, parking it and watching the inmates from the window, occasionally talking to one of the screws who supervised the work, and chain-smoking cigarettes.

CAMERA COMES TO CLOSE TWO SHOT. WARDEN. NARRATOR. In the WARDEN'S OFFICE. As the NARRATOR ENTERS, the WARDEN INDICATES a chair opposite his desk and TOSSES the manuscript of poems onto the desk itself.

WARDEN

I don't see anything derogatory to the institution here.
(after a pause)
Of course, it's derogatory to the entire prison system.
(looks at NARRATOR)
You're pretty bitter about this experience, aren't you?

NARRATOR

I suppose I am.

WARDEN

You don't usually write poetry, do you? That's not in your line.

NARRATOR
(astonished)
Not since college, sir. But it's impossible to write an extended piece of work here. How did you know?

WARDEN
(deadpan)
I know quite a bit about you, Bessie.
(pauses, touches manuscript)
You don't use language like this ordinarily, do you?

NARRATOR

No, sir.

WARDEN

Then how come you write it here?

[120]

NARRATOR

I just put down what I hear around me.

WARDEN

(nods)

I'll give this back to you, and I want you to cut out all those words, then return it. You have a young daughter. I'm sure you wouldn't want her to read words like that.

NARRATOR reflects that this sounds pretty naïve of the man, but he tries to show nothing on his face. After all, it would be simple, once he got home, to restore the crossed-out words.

CAMERA COMES TO ANOTHER ANGLE. WARDEN. NARRATOR.

—as NARRATOR SHIFTS uncomfortably in his chair.

NARRATOR

No, sir, I wouldn't.

WARDEN

I'll hold this for you till you're released.

NARRATOR

Thank you.

WARDEN

(after a pause)

I don't suppose you can be blamed for being bitter, since you don't believe you've done anything wrong.

NARRATOR

I'm not really bitter, sir. I just consider this a total waste of time.

WARDEN

It needn't be. If you learn how to use your time and write something you can sell later.

NARRATOR decides that he likes this man with the dead Scottish face and the constant cigarette, and suddenly he pours out everything.

NARRATOR

Sir, I'm sorry the relationship between us is what it is, because I'd like to talk to you.

WARDEN

Talk. What do you suppose I come in here for on Saturdays? I don't have to.

NARRATOR

I've been here six months now, and I've observed a few things and listened to the men for hours. I don't like the fact that the officers don't seem to give a damn about the men, how they came to be here, or what's going to happen to them when they get out.

WARDEN

You're wrong. Under our regulations, they're not allowed to fraternize with the men, but you'd be surprised how often they come to me with problems the men have talked about to them and how concerned they are about them.

NARRATOR
(emboldened)

I've never seen any signs of it. In my opinion, they're a pretty crummy bunch of human beings.

WARDEN
(deadpan)

When you pay the kind of wages these men get, you don't get very high-class men.

NARRATOR

May I ask a question, sir?
(WARDEN nods)

How many people are in prison in the United States?

WARDEN
(looks at ceiling)

The Federal prison population averages about twenty thousand, year in, year out. Counting state and county institutions, you could say that at any time there are well over three hundred thousand people in prison in this country.

NARRATOR

Most of them are young?

WARDEN

The vast majority are between fifteen and thirty-five.

NARRATOR

What percentage of the men released from prison come back
again?

WARDEN

It differs with different types of crime, but I'd say the over-
all average is well over sixty percent.

NARRATOR

(growing hot)

I know this is a small institution and there's no prison industry here, but what about the big tops? What do you
think about the rehabilitation system there?

WARDEN

What rehabilitation system?

NARRATOR

(pseudonaïve)

I thought there was one.

WARDEN

Bessie, there's no interest in this country in rehabilitating
prisoners.

NARRATOR

(playing it cool-astonished)

There *isn't?*

WARDEN

(lights cigarette, looks over NARRATOR's shoulder)

I've been in this work for over forty years, and once upon a
time I had an idea—but nobody was interested in it.

NARRATOR

Tell it to me. I'm interested.

CAMERA COMES TO

CLOSE SHOT. WARDEN.

As he SPEAKS, without looking at NARRATOR, his face shows more
animation, his eyes almost sparkle (but not quite).

WARDEN

I had an idea that for any man who had a long sentence—
let's say a year or more—and who made a good adjustment,

[123]

there should be a sort of community to which he might be sent.

(pause)

This community wouldn't be any different than any other small town in the U.S.A. There'd be no walls, no fences, no guards in uniform. The man would have been trained, during the first six months of his sentence, in a skilled job—if he didn't have one—so that when he went to this community, let's say as an automobile mechanic, he'd be the mechanic for that town and would be paid the prevailing wage.

(looks through cigarette smoke, squints)

If the man had a wife and children, let's say, they could join him there. It would be a sort of halfway house between the institution and the *free* world.

(pause)

He'd spend as much time there as necessary, and when it came time for him to leave, I'd see to it that he got a job as a mechanic or whatever he was, in a town he chose—whether it was the place he came from or any other he wanted to go to.

(pause)

Then I'd pass a law that would make it a criminal offense—once the man was released and working in his job—I'd make it a criminal offense for anyone to even *say* the man had ever been in prison.

CAMERA COMES BACK TO

TWO SHOT. WARDEN. NARRATOR.

The NARRATOR looks as though there is something he wants to say very badly, but is afraid to say it. He SWALLOWS the words in his mouth: "You know, there *is* a place where this philosophy of criminology is actually practiced."

NARRATOR

(licks his lips)

It's a hell of a good idea. Why wasn't anyone interested?

[*124*]

WARDEN

(a faint smile on his face)

Bessie, I know you.

(pause)

You know as well as I do why there was no interest in it.*

The WARDEN RISES from his chair and looks down at the NARRATOR.

WARDEN

Since your wife and daughter can only make one trip here
from Los Angeles, I've granted them permission to visit you
three times the week they'll be in Texarkana.

NARRATOR

(he *loves* the man)

Thank you, sir.

WARDEN

One other thing. Since I'll have to read anything you write in
the next four and a half months, please don't write too much.

The NARRATOR STANDS and wants very much to shake the man's
hand and say something sloppy, but he manages to control himself.

NARRATOR

I won't. Thank you, sir.

The WARDEN NODS, LIGHTS another cigarette, as we

DISSOLVE TO

WARNER BROTHERS CONCENTRATION CAMP. Burbank, California.
1945.

That was the year I really began to realize what I was involved

* Twelve years after this conversation, the Associated Press carried a
story out of Chicago (by G. K. Hodenfield) concerning the establishment
by the U.S. Bureau of Prisons of three "halfway houses," which had been
opened in the fall of 1961. They were located in Chicago, Los Angeles, and
New York and constituted a three-year "demonstration program." Young
offenders were living in these homes, got jobs in the respective commu-
nities, and lived a social life centered around the establishment, with gradu-
ated freedom offered for nights and later for weekends. The San Francisco
Chronicle's account (July 9, 1962) reported that the centers seemed to be
working well, but only a few hundred young men were involved out of a
Federal "population" of five thousand young offenders—and forty thousand
more in state institutions.

[125]

in, in working for The Industry. It was a year of progressive disillusionment with the possibility of doing the sort of job Jack Lawson had assured me that any honest writer could do, even though I had not yet arrived at the point where I could agree with Dan Fuchs's abysmal analysis of the role of the writer in Hollywood.

For one thing, I had come to feel that writing screenplays was the easiest way anyone could devise to make easy money. Nobody seemed to know a good screenplay from a hole in the ground (the producer least of all), and you could therefore get away with murder—and many people did.

Here are two examples, both real, of how it works. When you run into a story problem, the producer will sometimes say, "Okay, let's open that can of beans." One classic can of beans involved a conference between a producer, a writer, and a star comedian.

Nobody knew what to do with the beans that had been discovered until the comedian said, "I got it! At that point, I reach down behind the desk, pick up a baseball bat, and crown the bastard!"

"Great!" said the producer. "I'll *buy* that."

"Wait a minute," said the cautious writer. "How did that baseball bat get behind the desk in the first place?"

The producer and the comedian looked at the writer with indulgence, and the comedian said, "If it wasn't there in the first place, how could I pick it up?"

Then there is the marvelous story about William Faulkner—which I never bothered to ask him about, because we used to talk of other things whenever I visited his office or we had dinner with my wife at Musso Frank's on Hollywood Boulevard.

The story had it that once, early in Faulkner's Hollywood career, he sat in his office for several weeks doing nothing (sometimes he played dominoes, sometimes he played chess). And there came a day when the producer, tired of waiting for "pages," came to his office in person (which was really a breach of Hollywood protocol) and wanted to know how he was getting on.

Faulkner, who had not written a single line, reached for an old screenplay he had found in his desk and said, "Ah'm not satisfied with it." Then he slowly tore it up, page by page, and dropped it in the wastebasket.

The producer reported back to his own boss, "That fellow Faulkner's great! Tore up a whole screenplay because it didn't satisfy him. Conscientious. I wish we had more writers like him. See that he's not disturbed."

These examples are no more fantastic than the things that happened at Warner Brothers every day. Example: the studio was planning a great epic about the war, a four-part story in which one episode would be devoted to American participation, one to the British, one to the French (Free French, that is), and one to those dirty Russians, who were our glorious allies before they became our implacable enemies.

There was a fellow at the studio who had achieved some notoriety (and success) with an "original" screenplay that (rumor had it) had been written by his wife, who (rumor had it) wrote *all* his stuff. This man had been in the silent service at one time, and when Jerry Wald was planning a submarine story, he sent him to a submarine base in Connecticut to brush up on the latest stuff.

He spent some weeks on location at studio expense and came back with a story that Wald promptly threw in the wastebasket. The idea was then handed to Albert Maltz (later one of "The Ten") and Maltz, who had never seen a submarine in his life, sat down and wrote *Destination Tokyo,* which starred John Garfield and Cary Grant and not only was a huge success but was adopted by the Navy as a training film.

Meanwhile, our silent-service expert, who was easily one of the loudest anti-Soviet writers in the place, was put to work on the great war epic—writing the Soviet episode, of course. This was promptly junked when he had finished it, and it was given to Faulkner (who was busy cooking up a novel that he told us at Musso Frank's was to be a modern parable of the Christ story), and then the whole epic went down the drain; our silent-service expert's option was dropped, and he went to another studio—at a large leap in salary.

Hotel Berlin and *Objective Burma* were the third and fourth (and last) credits I ever "won" at Warners, and despite the fact that both were written in 1944, I remained there, with regular salary increases, until January, 1946. In the interim there was work on a series of four stories about which I can remember literally nothing except their titles. There followed a layoff that lasted from April 17 through June 3, during which I intensified my daughter-watching, weekend flying, and teaching of classes in short-story writing for The School for Writers in Hollywood. This last fact was duly noted (two years and some months later) in the dossier presented by investigators for the Un-American Committee. For the teaching of short-story writing, even to the last wife of the late John Barrymore, is no doubt subversive as hell.

On my forty-first birthday, I returned to the studio to work on a treatment of *The Law and the Lady* (producer forgotten), and then, for Jerry Wald, I collaborated with Emmett Lavery and Howard Koch (who wrote the screenplay for *Mission to Moscow*) on a documentary-type thing, which Jack Warner wanted momentarily to make, called *The Ghosts of Berchtesgaden*. The purpose of the film was to point to the continuing danger of fascism and Fascist ideas everywhere in the world, especially in our own country, now that the Nazi Wehrmacht had been destroyed and the Japanese were on their way toward unconditional surrender. (The picture was never made, of course, because the screenplay pointed its finger at individuals and financial interests whose exposure might have embarrassed the financial octopus known as Warner Brothers.)

There was a whole flock of other things between June and October for Wald and Wolfgang Reinhardt, but on my return from layoff, I had noticed that my secretary was busily engaged typing a manuscript. I asked what it was, and she said, "A novel for Jerry Wald," so I picked it up and started to read it. It was a very bad piece of writing, but what fascinated me about it was the fact that the action was laid in Spain during the little war in which I had participated. There were American volunteers, and they were fighting—of all places—at University City in

Madrid, a battle that took place almost a year before the first American volunteers arrived.

So, I did something you simply do not do in Hollywood: I marched up to Wald's office and asked him what it was all about.

"Oh," he said, "it's a novel Richard Brooks is writing."

I had seen the young man, still dressed in his military uniform, and had been told that he was a junior writer. He had published a short novel called *The Brick Foxhole*, which had brought him to Wald's attention and which was later made into a film at RKO by Adrian Scott and Edward Dmytryk under the title *Crossfire*. This was probably the first Hollywood film ever to make an outright attack on anti-Semitism, an interesting thing in itself, considering the fact that the novel dealt not with anti-Semitism but with homosexuality.

"Was Brooks in Spain?" (I knew the answer to that.)

"No."

"Then he shouldn't write about what he doesn't know. He's got American volunteers fighting at University City in Madrid in 1936."

"I'll let you read it when we have a complete script. You'll find it very interesting," said the irrepressible Wald.

What happened after that was even more fantastic than the mere shift of subject matter from homosexuality to anti-Semitism, and it makes a many-faceted story:

Facet 1: A son-in-law of one of the brothers Warner, by name Milton Sperling, had moved onto the lot as an independent producer, which was a laugh, because his financing came from Warner Brothers.

Facet 2: He employed as his story editor a very attractive young lady whom I met in the Green Room and with whom I had the following, brief conversation:

NARRATOR: What sort of stuff is Sperling going to make?
YOUNG LADY: Well, we have a newspaper story at the moment.
NARRATOR: That's interesting. I once wrote a newspaper story for

Jerry Wald, but it was shelved. I'll send you around a copy and maybe you can steal some ideas from it.

YOUNG LADY: You do that.

I did. I sent for one of the messenger girls, who peddled their asses around the lot in skintight pants hoping to be "discovered" by a big producer, and sent the lady story editor the manuscript of *Without Fear or Favor*.

DISSOLVE TO

THE GREEN ROOM. A few weeks later.

NARRATOR and YOUNG LADY are having lunch together. He has sort of a yen for her, which will do him no good whatsoever, since she is the wife of a prominent writer.

CAMERA COMES TO

TWO SHOT. NARRATOR. YOUNG LADY (AT TABLE)

—as he vainly uses what his wife calls his "deep-books look" on his luncheon companion.

NARRATOR

Did you ever get that newspaper story I sent over?

YOUNG LADY

Of course.

NARRATOR

What did you think of it?

YOUNG LADY

(deadpan)

Well, of course, that's the story we *have*.

NARRATOR

Come again?

YOUNG LADY

I said, that's the story Milton bought from Warners.

I went back to my office and sat contemplating this interesting fact. Suddenly, as in a cartoon strip, a light bulb bloomed over my bald head, and a few more facets of the little intrigue seemed very apparent:

Facet 3: Wald had shelved *Without Fear or Favor* because it was "too anti-Fascist" and because Jack Warner would have fired both of us if he had read it.

Facet 4: Wald had read Brooks's short novel *The Brick Foxhole* and had imported him to the lot.

Facet 5: Without showing Brooks my original story, Wald, I suspect, had done to him something he had done to Lionel Wiggam and to me, with *The Very Thought of You*: he had *told* him a story he "had in mind" and suggested that Brooks work up an "original" around the idea.

Facet 6: Brooks had written a novel on studio time and a weekly salary.

Facet 7: Wald had probably "bought" this novel from Brooks (with studio money).

Facet 8: Finding no immediate use for it, Wald had apparently "sold" it to the new producer on the lot, Harry Warner's son-in-law, Milton Sperling.

With the light bulb over my head still burning brightly, the telephone rang:

SPERLING'S VOICE
(over phone)

How would you like to work for me?

NARRATOR

Love to.

SPERLING'S VOICE

On your newspaper story, I mean.

NARRATOR

I'm your boy.

SPERLING'S VOICE

Come over and talk to me about it after lunch and maybe I can arrange to borrow you from Warners.

We talked about it after lunch, and Sperling said that of course it couldn't be made the way it was, but he thought that he had "a way to make it," and we would discuss it later. He would call Finlay McDermid, the story editor, and see whether he could borrow me.

That was the last I ever heard of the newspaper story, but it was not the last I heard of Sperling, for I mentioned to him one day that two guys I knew who had been guerrillas in Spain and OSS men in World War II were in town.

This time a light bulb lit up over Milton's head, and he said, "I want to meet those guys. I was in the OSS myself for a while, and there's a hell of a moving picture in that outfit."

I had listened to my two pals, one of whom had been an organizer for the United Electrical and Machine Workers Union and one of whom had been an organizer for the Young Communist League between the wars, and the stories they had told me were fabulous. I teased Sperling with a couple of these tales, without going into specifics, and he was hot to meet the two guerrillas and said that he would make them a good offer for their story.

One was a man who was as wide as he was tall and as powerful as any gorilla should be. Before he went to the war in Spain, he had been an adagio dancer! The other was as thin and wiry as the first was broad and powerful, and they sat in Milton's office and told him a number of their stories while he listened with his eyes bugging out.

Sample story A: They had run into General (Wild Bill) Donovan, head of OSS, in Italy.

GUERRILLAS: Look, General, there's a man we need here—need him badly.

DONOVAN: Who's that?

GUERRILLAS: He was the last commander of the Lincoln Battalion in Spain.

DONOVAN: I know him. Talked to him just before we got into the war. Fine fellow. Where is he?

GUERRILLAS: Well, he was kicked around the States for a long time, trying to get into a combat outfit, but they sent him to a camp in the Southwest that was restricted to German and Italian nationals suspected of disloyalty.

DONOVAN: No shit.

GUERRILLAS: Then he applied for combat duty again and was sent to OCS, made top grades in his class, and was shipped back to his original outfit without a commission.

DONOVAN: Go on.

GUERRILLAS: Then he applied for transfer again and was sent to Seattle, where he rode around in a motorboat on Puget Sound, patrolling the port to watch for Japanese submarines.

DONOVAN: Where is he now?

GUERRILLAS: He finally made it to Burma, where he's training Chinese guerrillas for Vinegar Joe Stilwell.

DONOVAN: You want him here?

GUERRILLAS: We *need* him here.

Thirty-six hours later he was there.

Sample story B: They never gave him anything to do once he got to Italy, but he and the two guerrillas had a fine time and picked up a lot of interesting information about the OSS operation on the peninsula.

They noticed, for example, that we regularly dropped thousands of dollars in American currency to the Italian partisans operating behind the Nazi lines, as well as food and ammunition. And they ran into a fellow who had been a high-ranking political officer in Spain, where he was known as Luigi Gallo, and who was now the American Army's contact with the Italian guerrillas. Gallo told them that he had received word that the American Command wanted a general strike in northern Italy, to coincide with our push up the Italian boot, and it had been arranged. In every town in northern Italy on that date and at a given hour, the Italian workers went on strike, crippling the Nazi rear, and the American offensive started rolling.

But there was another piece of information they picked up, independently: as the American army rolled north, it was under orders to pick up and jail every Italian partisan it could find, because everyone knew that these fighters were all Communists anyhow. This outraged the American OSS men, and they went to Gallo and told him about their information.

He smiled and said, "We know about that."

"Well, what the hell are we going to *do* about it?"

"Well, comrades, what do you think is the most important thing right now?" said Gallo. "To save our comrades from what will, after all, only be a short jail term or drive the Nazis out of Italy?"

They agreed, of course, that the latter was the more important objective, and Gallo assured them that the moment the partisans took a town, they would hold it only long enough to hear the approach of the American forces, and then they would disappear, which most of them managed to do.*

(Incidents like this may account in part for the fact that in the 1963 elections, the Italian Communist Party polled more than twenty-five percent of the total vote.)

I had warned my friends that it was foolhardy to tell Milton these stories, because stories had a way of being purloined in Hollywood, but they had answered with the cogent argument that if they didn't tell some of the stories, how could they sell Sperling on the idea? **

CAMERA COMES TO
MED. SHOT. INTERIOR. SPERLING'S OFFICE
—as the two GUERRILLAS, SPERLING, and the NARRATOR are in conference.

SPERLING
(eagerly)

You're my boys, all right. I want to put you to work right away, and I'll get Alvah to work with you on the screenplay. How would $1,000 apiece seem to you?

The HEAVYSET GUERRILLA SITS BACK in his chair and after a pause delivers himself of the following considered statement:

* Gallo's real name is Luigi Longo, and on the death, in 1964, of Palmiro Togliatti, he became the general secretary of the Italian Communist Party.
** The three American OSS men were each awarded the Legion of Merit for their fine work in Italy, and Donovan told them that if they ever needed a job they should come to see him, but two of the guerrillas said what they were now about to say to Sperling.

HEAVYSET GUERRILLA

Well, Milton, there are only two reasons we would work on
a movie. One, a chance to make a really *good* movie that
would tell the truth about what happened during that operation. We'd even do it for free.

(pause)

The other would be to make a lot of money—if we can't make
an honest story.

SPERLING

I'm with you. What do you think of the offer?

GUERRILLAS

(together)

We don't like it.

SPERLING

How much do you need?

HEAVYSET GUERRILLA

Five grand apiece, since we get the feeling already that we
couldn't make the sort of movie we'd like to make.

SPERLING

I can't go that far, boys.

HEAVYSET GUERRILLA

Forget it.

(indicates THIN GUERRILLA)

My pal here is going back to United Electrical anyhow, and
I can always get a job as an organizer for the Party.

And that is precisely what the two guerrillas did, but Milton
later made a film called *Cloak and Dagger,* about the OSS,
though he was extremely careful not to use any of the material
my two guerrilla friends had supplied; or perhaps "careful" is not
the word, for these were highly political stories—and both were
extremely critical of the outfit that was called Oh-So-Secret—and
Milton was scarcely a political fellow himself.

Cloak and Dagger was written by Albert Maltz and Ring
Lardner, Jr., and it involved one of those marvelous contretemps
that can only happen in Hollywood. Maltz had finished *Destina-*

tion Tokyo and a screenplay of Lloyd Douglas' *The Robe* (for another studio), and word had got around town that these were both fine jobs. But Albert wanted to take six months off to write a novel and told his agent that he would not accept a film assignment till he was finished. His salary was $500 a week at the time.

The agent immediately began getting offers; one of which was from Milton Sperling for *Cloak and Dagger*. Albert said, "No soap."

But Sperling bugged his agent day and night, and finally she said, "Albert, I've got to give the man *some* kind of definite answer. You're in demand, you know. What shall I say?"

"Oh," said Albert, "ask something ridiculous. Ask for $5,000 a week."

An hour later his agent called in despair. "Albert," she said, "Sperling kept after me, and I took your advice and said you wanted $5,000, and he said, 'You've got a deal.'"

FADE OUT

FADE IN
HOLLYWOOD. January, 1946.
January was more than a beginning, for despite what was still to happen in 1947, it was actually the zenith *and* the nadir of my Hollywood career. During that month, I lost my job at Warners, and *Objective Burma*, which had been released in 1945, was nominated for an Academy Award in the "best original story" category.

My own release from Warner Brothers Concentration Camp followed upon a really momentous event that showed which way the Hollywood wind was blowing—despite the anti-Fascist war, the pretensions of The Industry to devotion to democracy, and the lip service paid to honest trade unionism in Warners' own *Action in the North Atlantic*. A strike had begun in March of 1945 under the leadership of the Conference of Studio Unions (CSU). This was a loose organization comprising members of the painters' union, the set decorators, some machinists and electricians, building service workers, plumbers, and—to the amusement of some observers—screen cartoonists, publicists, and story

[136]

analysts (readers). The CSU was organized for two purposes: to try to develop an industrial union in Hollywood to replace the old-line craft unions under AF of L leadership; and to get some democracy into these predominantly reactionary and hopelessly corrupt organizations, which were dominated by Roy Brewer's International Alliance of Theatrical Stage Employees (IATSE).

When the painters and set dressers struck, Brewer * chose to call the strike jurisdictional, and the newspapers—always on the side of the employers in that company town—denigrated it by saying that it was all a silly quarrel over who had jurisdiction over the set decorators. But there was a great deal more than that involved.

It came to a head on October 5, when the CSU put a mass picket line outside the Warner Brothers studio on Olive Avenue in Burbank, and the way the studio handled that situation did not, somehow, equate with the wording of the great advertising sign outside the place that spoke of good citizenship *and* good picture making. The IATSE supplied strikebreakers and goons, who were mobilized in the side streets and armed with clubs, baseball bats, and tire irons; the Burbank police cooperated by turning on high-pressure hoses and using tear gas; and various people, inside the studio (unidentified) took advantage of the melee to throw blocks of wood and steel bolts from the roofs of the sound stages onto the picket line below.

Many workers were injured, and many got extremely angry and not only stopped cars trying to run the picket line but rocked them violently and even overturned a couple. The major casualties were among the striking workers, many of whom went to the hospital, including a comrade of mine from Spain who had gone through that conflict without a scratch and had been employed at Warners as a story analyst.

The day the mass picket line was set up, all the writers appeared for work as usual and—seeing the demonstration—gathered diffidently across the street from the administration building, in front of the drugstore. I was at that time the chairman of

* This sterling trade-union leader later went on to his reward and became a studio executive himself—with Allied Artists.

the Screen Writers' Guild chapter in the shop, so they asked my advice. I suggested that we all go to the SWG office in Hollywood and sit down and discuss the situation.

Because I was chairman, I took no part in the discussion myself, but the screenwriters decided on a course of action: our contract did not give us the right—which is written into the contracts of most militant and progressive unions—to respect picket lines, but it did have a provision stating that we were not required to go to work if there was a situation that might endanger our lives or limbs—and who could tell what those dangerous pickets might do to us if we tried to cross their lines? So the writers voted to stay out until the mass picket lines were withdrawn, and this vote was respected by all but one writer, whose name was Thames Williamson and whose action distressed me because he had once written a fairly good novel called *The Woods Colt*.

When the strike was over and we went back to work (the cause was lost and the CSU was ultimately destroyed), a friendly producer took me aside and told me that my option would not be picked up in January.

NARRATOR: Why not?

PRODUCER: Jack Warner's convinced that you and Howard Koch were responsible for the strike.

NARRATOR: *What!*

[I am ashamed to say that I had nothing to do with the strike beyond (*a*) writing two leaflets on request of the story analysts' guild and (*b*) observing the picket line from across the street at the behest of the SWG, with Howard Koch, who had done two things that were even more heinous—he had written the screenplay for *Mission to Moscow* and had even sent a telegram to Jack Warner urging him to settle the strike.*]

PRODUCER: In the Executive Dining Room the other day, at lunch,

---

* John Howard Lawson went even further. Not employed at Warners, he *walked* on the picket line with many other film workers, and his picture appeared the next morning in all the papers—and this fact was dutifully recited before the Un-Americans in 1947.

Steve [Warner's right-hand man] told everybody that that was what Jack felt.

NARRATOR (fascinated): Tell me more.

PRODUCER: Steve said that Blaney Matthews ["plant protection" director, that is, studio cop and Gestapo man] had a dossier on you that high; that he knew every meeting you went to, who came to your house, whom you visited, and even had your telephone tapped. Steve said it was too bad you were the chairman of the Screen Writers' Guild but they could get around that by waiting till your option comes up, then dropping it. [Koch's contract was bought out by Warner.]

The friendly producer's prediction was correct; shortly before the first of January, my agent received word that the option would be dropped; so we started the bright new year without a job, and I was reluctantly forced to conclude that either I had been born under an evil star or I am what the psychiatrists call calamity-prone. For example: *Men in Battle,* my book about the Spanish war, had received excellent reviews, but it appeared the week Hitler invaded Poland, and nobody read anything but newspapers for months thereafter. The novel with the character I had wanted Bette Davis to play, *Bread and a Stone,* was published a month before Pearl Harbor: *ergo,* nobody read anything but newspapers for years thereafter. And then, as a sort of climax-anticlimax, *Objective Burma* was nominated for an Academy Award, which normally would have raised my stock at the studio and in The Industry itself, but I *had* no studio and I was temporarily out of The Industry.

However, we had a few dollars in the bank, and during the weeks before the annual self-adulatory rites were scheduled to take place, I luxuriated in a pleasant fantasy about the speech that I would make when the Oscar was awarded to me. (It was the sort of fantasy I had indulged in years before when I was furious at Walter Hampden and planned to kill him onstage during the first act of *Cyrano de Bergerac.*) After the applause had died down and I stood there in Lester Cole's borrowed tuxedo, with the Oscar doorstop in my hand, I could hear myself saying, "This is not *my* original story. It is Jerry Wald's. What is more, it is scarcely original. What is worse, there is not a word of truth in it, because there *were* no American troops in Burma, not even Errol Flynn."

Then I would call Jerry out of the audience, hand him the Oscar, and walk offstage to the sort of reverberating cheers that would have to greet any such unprecedented display of "integrity."

ACADEMY AWARDS NIGHT. March, 1946.

Helen Clare and I had seen the sneak preview of *Objective Burma* the year before in a little theater in—was it Cucamonga? (Well, it might have been Eagle Rock at that.) And when there is a sneak, the writer gets invited to The Executive Dining Room, where he eats in the presence of The Vice-President-in-Charge-of-Production, but his wife does not. So she met me at the theater, and I arrived there in a caravan of black studio limousines that looked like hearses, and we enjoyed the picture immensely.

Especially did I enjoy the night-attack sequence (which took place mostly in silence), because it was a faithful reproduction of one the Lincoln Battalion made from the top of Hill 666 in the Sierra Pandóls (Catalonia), where my friend and commander Aaron Lopoff received his fatal wound. I was grateful to Lester Cole and Ranald MacDougall (who wrote the screenplay) for leaving that sequence in, even though they had taken out most of the other things I had in the original.

When the night finally arrived for me to receive my Oscar and make my Jerry Wald speech, I was not accompanied by my superiors in The Industry, and the event became a sort of celebration of Helen Clare's birthday, which had taken place the day before. We rode to the Awards together, with two huge gold tickets clutched firmly in our hot little hands; and even when you drive up in a 1940 Chevrolet coupé (in 1946), the attendants at the door of the theater will park it for you (with an odd expression on their faces) and the fans in the bleachers on the sidewalk will stare at you to see whether you are Somebody, though they have a very good idea—from the year and make of your car—that you are not.

When Helen Clare and I stepped out of our vintage automobile, the most we heard anybody say was, "There's Virginia Bruce," a statement which always made my wife wince, not only because she did resemble Bruce (and the lady was a sappy-looking blond), but probably because Bruce had once been married to the long-dead John Gilbert and was long gone from Hollywood herself and had never been much of an actress in the first place. My wife would much rather have been mistaken for Tallulah Bankhead or Greta Garbo or even Katharine Hepburn, any or all of whom she could mimic to fine effect, with or without one dry Martini.

Nobody asked us to speak into the microphone in the lobby of Grauman's Chinese Theater, but I felt at ease in Lester Cole's tuxedo (we were the identical size, looked something alike, were born a few days apart, and were even temperamentally similar— which may account for the fact that we never got along too well with each other), and my wife's specially purchased evening gown was a knockout.

We sat patiently through all the technical awards, but the tension mounted by the moment. Each nominee knows in advance that the Academy Awards mean nothing, that endless politicking goes on to "win" first the nominations and then the awards themselves, that votes are bartered and swapped, that enormous money is spent in advertising, and that pressure is brought to bear on studio employees to vote for the product of their own employers. But the Awards themselves are always exciting to the putative winners, and the atmosphere of anxiety in the auditorium does strange things to a man.

When Miss Bette Davis (to our surprise) came onstage to announce the nominations and winners in the writing category, we not only took her casting in the role as an omen and a tip-off, we *knew* that we had won, and my mouth became as dry as it had ever been in combat in Spain. I poised on the edge of my seat, ready to run—in either direction—and my bowels were in the same sort of uproar you suffer only during an artillery barrage.

Miss Davis (how *clever* of Jack Warner to have his biggest star announce one of his own pictures, one of his own writers as winner!) unashamedly put on her horn-rimmed spectacles; I did not hear the names of the three other nominees in the "original story" category—only *The House on 92nd Street* by somebody or other—and then subtly accented by the lady, but unmistakably so, *"Alvah Bessie,* for *Objective Burma."* The man handed her the envelope, and she calmly tore it open, smiling widely. . . .

For a moment, the lady's voice faded from my consciousness, and I suddenly sat bold upright, rooted with horror in the midst of that overstimulated assemblage. Miss Davis' presence on that stage might indeed be an omen, but it was an omen that could be read either way, for the lady was nothing if not unpredictable. I suddenly recalled that memorable conference held in her dressing room on the set of *The Corn Is Green* in 1944. My two sons, Dan and Dave, were paying a summer visit from Connecticut, and while they did sit still long enough to watch her play a scene from this Emlyn Williams play, they found it (and her) a complete bore and spent all their time (when they came to the Burbank lot) fighting World War II from the mock-up of the B-17 bomber that had been used in *Air Force.* (They were *both* John Garfield.)

That was the time elections had come around again in the several states, and Governor Tom Dewey of New York, whose political career was to be blasted as much by that widely repeated description of him ("He looks like the little man on the wedding cake") as by his monstrous and inordinate ambition, had rigged things in such a way that New York servicemen who were out of the state (or States) would have one hell of a hard time casting a ballot. This caused considerable indignation throughout the country; protest petitions were circulating, and Vincent Sherman (Davis' director) and I took one to her in her dressing room on the set.

CAMERA COMES TO

MED. SHOT. INTERIOR. DRESSING ROOM
—where BETTE DAVIS is SITTING at her dressing table between takes, recuperating for the next sequence in her role as the strong-minded teacher who pushes, prods, coaxes, coaches, and inspires

a Welsh mining lad into Oxford. Now SHERMAN and NARRATOR
ENTER and PLACE the petition in front of her on her dressing table.

DAVIS

(glancing up)

I never sign these things.

An argument ensues and rages for a few moments.

DAVIS

(looking in mirror)

I'm on *your* side. I think it's perfectly scandalous. But I'm
in no position to sign petitions.

SHERMAN

You're in a *perfect* position to sign it. Some of the most
prominent—

NARRATOR

(self-consciously)

There's nothing subversive about it. Nobody could possibly
criticize you or do less than pay you homage for—

He intended to say ". . . exercising the sort of good citizenship
that Warner Brothers advertises on its outdoor billboards," but
she interrupts him.

DAVIS

I once signed a petition to every member of Congress, and
I've never heard the end of it.

SHERMAN

What petition was that?

DAVIS

(turns slightly from mirror)

I am the president of the Tailwaggers' Society of America
and I'm opposed to vivisection.

SHERMAN and the NARRATOR display astonishing tact and some
bent for the diplomatic service by not so much as cracking a
smile, but they do point out, respectfully, that this is scarcely
the same sort of thing; that vivisection is, at the least, controversial but that nobody could defend the little man on the wedding
cake's action by any stretch of the imagination. The two men
have the lady licked, and she knows it. They have her, figuratively
at least, backed into the corner of her dressing room. She has

no cogent answers to their arguments. Now she RISES from her dressing table, FACES the two men.

DAVIS
(articulating every syllable)
Gentlemen, the audience is at an end.*

It was. More than that was at an end, in fact, for as Miss Davis' voice flooded back into my consciousness and the stiff collar of Lester Cole's tuxedo shirt wilted, I clearly heard her say, ". . . and the winner—*The House on 92nd Street,*" and I sank back in my seat and wondered whether I had ever really liked Bette Davis at all. We had come to the Awards ceremonies as pariahs, in a 1940 Chevrolet coupé, and without a job—and we had figured on winning this skirmish, on winning a distinct victory over Jack L. Warner and his Steve and his Blaney Matthews.

But everything that happened after *that* became what we called in Spain "a holding action"—until not only the skirmish but the entire battle was lost.

DISSOLVE TO

TEXARKANA. Winter, 1950–1951.
The autumn is mild in this part of Texas, which is about 160 miles from Dallas, but the winter is brutal. There are snow, ice, and sleet and wild winds that howl across the low hills and drift the snow around the institution. It looks lovely under the flood-lights at night when you cannot sleep and stand next to the small radiator (that is lukewarm) and look out the barred window into the yard.

Across the yard, sometimes, you can see the lighted window of a small room where (before midnight) prisoners about to be released are "dressed out," and the sight does nothing to add to the "adjustment" of the prisoner who has months—or years—to pull before his own release. The NARRATOR is technically

---

* For some very shrewd and honest insights into this great star, written by Queen Bess herself, see *The Lonely Life,* by Bette Davis, New York, G. P. Putnam's Sons, 1962.

a short-timer, and although the phrase applies equally to men who will soon be released and to men who have a long time to pull, he *is* going to be released come spring. But to a man in prison in the winter of 1950, the spring of 1951 seems years and years away.

Once Herbert Biberman had left the institution—and despite the disagreements of the "fall partners"—time did not drag, it crawled. All the symptoms of a disease endemic to such prisoners, and known as "shortitis," were present: in the NARRATOR's case, it manifested itself not only through insomnia, eructation, and flatulence, but also in loss of appetite, a constant sense of impending disaster, the development of various nervous tics, including a pain in the right thigh that became progressively more pronounced throughout the working day and was so excruciating at night that he sat up in his cot and massaged his thigh for an hour before he could even attempt to sleep.

The typewriter—following the contretemps over the book of verses—had been taken away from him and now could be used only for the warehouse clerical work he was required to do and (a concession) the writing of letters to the people with whom he was permitted to communicate: his wife, his daughter Eva and sons Dan and Dave, his surgeon brother in New York, and his aging mother.

I rarely spoke to Mister Portly or Mister Heel except when I was spoken to, and most of my time off was spent with Del or a young fellow named Jimmy, who had adopted me as a substitute father (just as my older son Dan had hitchhiked to New York the previous summer seeking to find a surrogate father in his doctor uncle) and who came to my cell every night with problems.

Jimmy was a car thief, but he had an open face of so angelic a mien that no one could have considered him dishonest for a moment. He was from Nashville and was working his way through high school by correspondence; I tried to help him with his history, composition, and literature, but failed miserably when it came to geometry and algebra. (I had done very badly,

I was told by a trusty who worked in the hospital office, on my "achievement" test.)

But Jimmy spent less time on his schoolwork than in telling me the story of his life and how he had got into trouble and in pumping me for explanations of the Korean conflict, World Wars I and II, Spain, "The Hollywood Ten," politics and economics and the nature of the female sex (psychologically, that is, for he was acquainted with its physical attributes). A warm and somewhat tender friendship therefore grew between this young man of twenty-two and myself (who was forty-six). So, I had developed three friends in the joint by that time: Del, Jimmy, and a bear-shaped fellow named Bob, who had gone AWOL from the Army in Michigan because he too wanted "no part of that *Ko*-rea" and had drawn a five-year sentence and been transferred from the Army installation at Fort Leavenworth.

To these three, I smuggled books that had been sent as gifts by various publishers in New York who were sympathetic to "The Ten." One of these was James Aldridge's *The Diplomat,* about which the educational supervisor had said, "I have read it and you may read it, but if I hear of you lending it to any other inmate, you'll be in serious trouble, so see that you give it back to me to hold for you when you've finished it."

This prison official was a pathetic individual who looked exactly like a toad (*Bufo americanus*), and his only claim to distinction lay in the fact that he was a Harvard graduate. He had hoped, the grapevine said, to teach at Harvard but had disgraced himself in some way or other (rumor had it that he was queer, but when you pointed out that he was married, you were told, "So what? He's a switch-hitter."). In any event, the best job he had ever had was the one he held in the institution, and his salary even permitted him to take off for New York during his vacations and see the plays.

In addition to supervising what education there was in the joint—occasional classes for illiterates—he had charge of selecting the Saturday-night movies we attended. Usually we saw musicals, which seemed to alternate invariably between the masculine

Esther Williams swimming in a variety of swimming pools in a variety of swimsuits (and sometimes evening dresses), and they were a crashing bore, and the very masculine Gene Kelly dancing in a variety of locales, which really were a delight. The only time the educational supervisor showed any taste and some curiosity about his charges was the night he showed Laurence Olivier's film version of *Hamlet*. He was astute enough to preface the screening with a short speech in which he told the crowded auditorium (Negroes to the right, whites to the left of the center aisle) that the play had been written somewhere around A.D. 1602, it was all in poetry (which most of them had never heard spoken or even read), and anyone who wanted to leave might do so at any time.

That performance was a revelation: no one left the auditorium during the more than two hours it unrolled on the screen, and it was the only film shown during my tenure that was greeted with spontaneous applause when it was over.

I recalled having been told by Walter Hampden (before he decided that I was not tall enough to play classical drama) that he had presented *Hamlet* in mining camps in Colorado before men just as illiterate (so far as the classical drama was concerned) and had enjoyed a similar reception. Paul Robeson had reported an identical experience with *Othello* in Welsh and British mining towns. What is more, the men discussed the film for more than a week after it was shown, debating about what had happened and echoing, in their own terminology, arguments that have been raging in Shakespearean circles for more than three hundred years.

CAMERA COMES TO
TWO SHOT.

FIRST INMATE

Naw, he ain't off his rocker *at* all. He's just makin' like he's nuts to find out what cooks at the court.

SECOND INMATE

What was wrong with that broad Ophelia, anyhow?

She had hot pants for Hamlet and he wouldn't give her a tumble, so *she* went off her rocker. *Frus*-rated.

Any guy that wouldn' wanna lay a doll like Jean Simmons, he *musta* been nuts!

Their innate sense of taste during the showing itself was practically impeccable, for they laughed not only in the right places, despite the antique language and the poetry, but in places Olivier would not have appreciated—for example, when he started climbing the scenery or luxuriating in gestures that were not germane to the action. They also rejected the production's somewhat Freudian interpretation of Hamlet's relationship with his mother by stamping and whistling when Olivier pushed the big-breasted Queen Gertrude back onto her bed and leaned over her and her exaggerated cleavage heaved and she panted and rolled her eyes as he said, *"Come, come, and sit you down; you shall not budge;/ You go not till I set you up a glass/Where you may see the inmost part of you."*

(While he was still in residence, Herbert Biberman's stock in the institution rose enormously when word got around that his wife, Gale Sondergaard, was appearing in one of the films we were to see. But when the film was shown, Gale was playing an aged woman confined to bed, and the cons went around muttering to each other, "Didja see the old broad Beeberman's married to?" It did no good to explain over and over that Gale was a youngish and handsome woman who generally played character parts and that the decrepitude they had observed was strictly makeup plus her ability to project that age.)

To be completely honest, the presentation of *Hamlet* was not the only time the educational supervisor tried to practice the role he really should have played more often. He did institute a music-appreciation class, which lasted for a few weeks, and a small group of handpicked inmates attended it regularly, listening to recordings of Beethoven, Bach, and Mozart, as well as the original Broadway cast of *Carmen Jones.*

One special treat, the supervisor told me, was a full-length recording of a play he had seen in New York during his vacation, and I received a special invitation to attend its playing in the prison library. This recording ended my attendance (and his invitations), because it was T. S. Eliot's *The Cocktail Party*, and when he asked for discussion, I said I thought it stank on ice and detailed my objections to Eliot's High Church sentiments, his dramaturgical weaknesses, and his basically reactionary attitude toward people. The educational supervisor disagreed.

And he was away the week before Christmas, when I received a copy of a new translation of *Don Quixote* from my wife, prior to her arrival with my daughter for their scheduled visit. The control room told me the book was there—and that they had no intention of giving it to me.

"Why not?" I asked.

"This *Don Quicks-oat*," said the captain. "Never heard of it. Books gotta be passed by the supervisor."

"It's one of the world's great classics," I said. "You'll find it in every library in the world."

"All new books gotta be read and approved."

"It's not new. It was written in the first decade of the seventeenth century," I protested.

"You don't think I'm gonna *read* it, do you? It's over a thousand pages long!"

So I did not get it until the educational supervisor returned and assured the control room that it was perfectly all right for me to have it.

I did get a lot of Christmas cards, however, the only exception to the rule that said you could receive mail only from immediate relatives.

There must have been close to a hundred cards, and since we were not allowed to tack them (or anything else) on the walls, I used to stand ten or twenty of them on my small metal table and change them every day.

And on one evening just before Christmas, Jimmy, the car thief, came diffidently into my cell and said, "Mind if I look at your Christmas cards, Bess? I didn't get any."

My eyes must have filled with tears when he said that, for I remember nodding, and he came into the cell and stood in front of the little table and looked at them. I looked at him.

He grew white around the gills. He pointed to one card that had a photograph of a family on it—a man, his handsome wife, and their two daughters—and he said, "Who's *that?*"

"A friend of mine," I said. "A lawyer; those are his wife and daughters."

Jimmy stared at me, and the friendliness and warmth of the many months we had spent together froze instantly. His lips were pressed tightly together. He was pale. Between his teeth he said, "You . . . got . . . nigger . . . *friends?*"

"I have friends of all colors."

"Yeh, I remember," Jimmy said. "You *tol'* me you knew that Robeson." (I wondered why he had not become so agitated when I had talked to him about Paul.)

There was a pause, then Jimmy suddenly began to shout. "Hey, fellas, come looka *this!*"

CAMERA COMES TO

INTERIOR. CELL. NIGHT
—as JIMMY POINTS at the card on the table and a few of the MEN in the cellblock COME SWIFTLY IN. The NARRATOR MOVES BACK-WARD, unconsciously, toward the window.

JIMMY
(shouts)

Looka the nigger that's his *friend!*
The other CONS look. They TURN TO look at the NARRATOR. They SHOW THEIR TEETH, but there is no mirth or good humor in these grimaces. (They know the Narrator's feelings about race preju-dice, but they have never before said a word on the subject.) Now, as they SPEAK, one at a time, they reveal the unmistakable rage and fear that is a concomitant of any sort of racism.

FIRST CON
(gently)

Whata ya know?

[150]

SECOND CON

Good friend a yourn?

NARRATOR

I know him fairly well.

FIRST CON

Like him, huh?

NARRATOR

Very much. He's a fine man.

JIMMY

Looks like a baboon t' *me*!

THIRD CON

Goriller.

SECOND CON

You *like* these people?

The NARRATOR now—for the first time since Spain—feels active fear. The phrase *L'attaque, toujours l'attaque!* flashes through his mind.

NARRATOR

(trying for quiet)

I know Negroes I like and others I don't. I've met white men here I do and don't care for and Negroes I do and don't. I've been around the world a little, and I never noticed that the color of a man had anything to do with the kind of guy he was.

FIRST CON

You gotta daughter?

Here it comes, NARRATOR thinks. He NODS.

SECOND CON

How'd you like f'r *her* to marry one-a them?

NARRATOR

(too quickly)

That would be *her* business, wouldn't it?

FIRST CON

(quietly)

Any daughter-a-mine'd marry a nigger, I'd kill her.

JIMMY

Kill the nigger first!

[*151*]

NARRATOR is wondering where in hell the screw is, the former landscape gardener who was supposed to be on duty. The screws were always around when you didn't need them, but this would have been an excellent time for our friend to appear and make his nine o'clock count. He TAKES A DEEP BREATH. He figures there must be some way out of this cul-de-sac, but he doesn't know what it could be.

> NARRATOR
> (not thinking)
> Look, let me get you guys straight. You don't like these people?

> JIMMY
> Hell, *no*!

> NARRATOR
> You think they're repulsive?

> THIRD CON
> Yair!

> NARRATOR
> Then explain something to me, will you?
> (pause)
> How come there're so many *light*-colored Negroes?

There is an almost audible silence in the cell. That was infra dig, the NARRATOR is thinking, but he is scared stiff. FIRST CON, in the doorway, MOVES out into the corridor, then, slowly, one at a time, as though someone had given them a signal, they ALL LEAVE without a word.

I took another deep breath; then, after a decent interval, I closed the door of the cell (you could not lock it) and sat, exhausted, on the cot. What happens now? I wondered.

Nothing happened. No reference was ever made to the incident except (obliquely) one morning late that spring, when the joint was jammed and they had to put up double-decker bunks in some of the dormitories and we were eating in two shifts.

Standing at the grille, waiting to be let out to breakfast after the whistle blew, I said casually to the inmate known as Snake, "What's holding us up?"

He smiled and gestured toward the corridor. "The *colored* gentlemen go first this morning."

The night that Jimmy said, "Mind if I look at your Christmas cards, Bess? I didn't get any," I wrote a sonnet that didn't (on the face of it) seem to have anything to do with the situation that had arisen—and had not really been resolved. Someone, however, once said that poetry is the expression of emotion under pressure, and if you accept that definition, the connection becomes more obvious:

> The highways that are open to the mind
> are not confined to those on any chart;
> they are as various as any art
> might compass, and the traveler will find
> that some run straight to where he wants to go,
> while others spiral, circle, wander wide;
> some imitate the motions of the tide
> while others speed—or make the journey slow.
> There is no road that I would rather walk
> than that which leads from where I am confined
> into those tilted uplands of the mind
> that are not even known to those who talk
> of freedom, and who always have been free.
> Who knows not prison, knows not liberty.

There was a sequel to that frightening night in my cell about which the other cons never learned, and it went a long way to temper my bitterness about the South. There was a young fellow from Alabama who came into the warehouse once in a while on some errand or other (he later replaced me as clerk), and we became fairly friendly. I cannot recall his name, but I do recall something about him that will never be forgotten: he did not have the slightest prejudice against Negroes. This astonished me, and I asked him how he had managed to rid himself of the race hatred that is *so* blatant in the South that at dinner one night, a mild-looking fellow sitting opposite me, talking about a Negro prisoner, said "We're goin' out the same day, an' Ah'm gonna *kill* me that nigger," and no one batted an eye.

The young man from Alabama looked rather sad and said, "It was easy." His eyes sought the distance, and he said, "Fer's long 's Ah kin remember, Ah was in love with a little gal that lived a piece down the road. We practically grew up t'gether, an' Ah was crazy about that gal.

"Well, suh, when we-all was all growed up, Ah still loved that gal an' asked her t' marry up with me, an' she laughed raht in mah face. Ah *was* amazed.

"Ah said, 'How come, Amy-Lou? Ah love you an' Ah want t' marry with you,' an' you know what *she* said? She said, 'You ain' nothin' but po' white trash, boy, an' Ah wouldn' even innerduce you t' mah fam'ly. Yore *beneath* me,' she said."

He looked at me. "Her sayin' that made me think, sorta. Ah figgered, Ef she don' think Ah'm good 'nough fer *her,* mus' be somethin' wrong with *me*—not her an' the other colored folks Ah allus been tol' ain' even *human.*"

By the time Christmas week arrived, my moustache had grown thick enough so that I was certain my six-year-old daughter, Eva, would recognize me. I was even delighted that the joint did not look as oppressive as it might, for there was a Christmas tree, nicely decorated, in the dining room, and there were red and green paper streamers festooning the room. I had even managed to make Eva a sort of present—a jewel box (constructed from square-splint wooden matches) that had taken more than fifty hours of hard labor at night to build, with no tools other than a razor blade, a piece of sandpaper one of the inmates had snitched from the carpenter shop, and several tubes of LePage's glue purchased in the commissary.

She and her mother came from Los Angeles by train, and the day before their first scheduled visit to the prison, the captain's office told me that they had arrived in Texarkana. That night it was impossible to sleep. I kept looking out the window of the warehouse the next morning, leaping from the typewriter desk to the loading dock outside, to see whether I could spot their taxicab arriving at the tower, but I did not see them when they finally pulled up.

The telephone rang, however, informing me that I had visitors, and I was instructed to go up to my cell, where I was provided with a white shirt instead of a blue one and was then directed to the control room, where I was searched (the jewel box had been inspected the day before and held there) and given the following instructions:

"You will go into the visiting room. It is permitted to embrace once on meeting and again at the end of the two hours. You may not hold hands, and you must speak at all times in an audible voice. An officer will be present in the room. There will be no smoking."

Then I walked, almost on tiptoe, into the same room in which we had been received and processed in July, and Helen Clare was standing in the middle of the room, a smile on her face and her arms extended. I saw my daughter on the couch: she was wearing a short overcoat trimmed with imitation fur; she had a white imitation-fur muff, into which her hands were thrust, and there was a small head of Rudolph the Red-Nosed Reindeer on the muff, a symbol of the song that nauseated us day and night that week as it emanated from the Texarkana radio station, sung by a hillbilly. She wore a hat with white fur trimming, and she was lying face down on the imitation-leather couch.

I saw the officer sitting at the desk a few feet away, pretending to pay no attention to what was going on—and my wife's purse was on his desk, where it remained for the length of the visit—and after we had embraced and kissed (once), I walked to the couch and touched my daughter on the shoulder.

"Hi, Eva," I said.

She did not reply.

"Here's Father," I said (she has always called me Father) and touched her again, rocking her gently. She pressed her face further into the corner of the couch, and when I tried to turn her head to face me, she pressed it even further down and held her body rigid. I looked at Helen Clare.

"She was fine all the way here on the train," she said quietly. "She was wonderful, even in the Grim Hotel." She laughed. "That's right, it's called the Grim Hotel, *G-r-i-m*, not two *m*'s. . . .

[155]

And all the way out in the cab. But when we got to the front gate, she said she was sleepy."

She remained asleep throughout the two-hour visit, and after the first fifteen minutes, we gave up trying to get her to turn around and look at us. But we kept glancing at her and hoping she would wake up of her own accord, and we found that it was utterly impossible to say anything that meant anything or that either of us had planned to say for months.

So we passed the time of day. She told me about friends in Hollywood, mentioning only their first names. She reported at firsthand on the terror that had been created in that two hundred square miles of small town by the passage of local ordinances requiring the immediate registration of anyone who had even been called a subversive. She conveyed the regret of many people that our paroles had been denied despite the hundreds of individual letters that had gone to George Killinger, chairman of the Board of Parole; the petitions signed by more than twenty thousand individual Americans; and the documents that had preceded us to prison: some thirty briefs *amicus curiae* from organizations representing millions of people; sixteen articles in American law reviews upholding our position (or, at the least, demanding that the Court review the case on its constitutional issues); and the Supreme Court decision, in *Blau* v. *United States*.*

Sitting watching Eva and wondering whether she would wake up before I was removed from the room and she and her mother had to go back to the Grim Hotel in Texarkana, I recalled trying to explain our case to this six-year-old before I left for trial and instant imprisonment. And I recalled two things she had said: "Who is on our side?" was the first. I tried to tell her that there were literally millions of people on "our side," but children cannot understand why, if millions support your position, you must still go to prison (and neither can many adults).

* To this day the Supreme Court has yet to accept a First Amendment case and rule unequivocally on the constitutional issue involved. So to rule— and uphold a witness's refusal to testify—would put the House Committee on Un-American Activities and all its counterparts out of business overnight.

So I tried to tell her in terms of individuals she knew, and one of them was Paul Robeson, whom she had met and heard sing; and when I mentioned Paul, she smiled for the first time and said, "He's *big*! People will be afraid of *him*!"

But she did not wake up that day, and the next day, when the second visit was scheduled, the control room informed me that there would be no visit. "Your little girl is sick. Your wife called. Said it's nothing to worry about."

I requested permission to speak to Helen Clare on the phone —she was only five miles away; permission denied. They said they would inform me if there was any change in my daughter's condition, and I could get no statement out of them the next two days other than, "She'll be all right; your wife says not to worry."

So I tried not to worry; and on the fourth day, they reappeared, and this time Eva was awake and consented to sit up, across the room, and stare at me. Her mother told me that the child had come down with a raging fever, and the house physician at the Grim Hotel (which lived up to its name in all departments) had expressed the opinion that she had polio and had done a spinal tap. My wife had been close to hysteria for the two days it took to get a negative report.

That day and the next, I was permitted to show Eva the dining room with its Christmas decorations and the tree, and she said it was very pretty but asked no questions about the place, my activities there, or the other men she saw passing through the corridor from time to time.

On the day they left, I stood in the visiting room and watched their taxicab move up the driveway outside the administration building and come to a halt till the guard in the tower got word to wave it on (like an airplane asking clearance to take off), and then they were gone.

The screw on duty said, "You can go now," and I walked into the corridor past the control room.

Another guard there apparently saw me pass, for he came out of the room after me and said, "Hey!" When I turned to look at him, he drew one finger across his upper lip and said, "Take it off." *

DISSOLVE TO

SAN FERNANDO VALLEY and HOLLYWOOD. Spring, 1946–Fall, 1947. The NARRATOR, his wife, and their two-year-old daughter are living in the most beautiful house they have ever inhabited in their lives. Situated on a full acre of land on Laurelgrove Avenue in the Valley, this is a ranch house belonging to the actor Alan Baxter, who specializes in playing frozen-faced gangsters when he is not playing frozen-faced Army officers or detectives. He rented the place to them on the recommendation of the former tenants, MORRIS CARNOVSKY, his wife, and child, who were old friends from New York and Group Theater days. Baxter had thousands of dollars' worth of exotic flowers planted around the house and grounds but the NARRATOR had developed a healthy hatred for gardening of all kinds when he lived in Vermont during the Depression and it was necessary to be a (vegetable) gardener or gracefully starve to death. (He had always rationalized this hatred for gardening by claiming that the Jewish temperament did not lend itself to farming—and he maintained that position until the birth of the new state of Israel, when it became patently absurd.)

So, after the exotic flowers began to fade from neglect (and the ministrations of competing weeds and predatory insects), he was forced to hire a gardener to save the lives of the surviving flora. This was a drag, but no more of a drag than the fact that he was living in a grand house without a job. . . .

Then, on March 1, Eva's second birthday, the Narrator got a job as well as a gardener. The former arrived in the form of

* The most perceptive remark Eva ever made about that visit (until she was nineteen) was reported to me by letter after their return home. All the way from Los Angeles to Texarkana and back, various gentlemen had tried to pick up the handsome Swedish blond and her little blond daughter, invariably opening the conversation by asking the little girl, "And what are *you* going to be when you grow up?" To one and all she had said, "I don't know." To the last aspirant, just outside Pasadena, she replied, "I don't know what I'm going to be when I grow up, but I know what I'm *not* going to be." "And what is *that?*" said the gentleman, and Eva answered, "I'm not going to be one of those *disturbing writers.*"

[158]

a contract from an outfit called A. & S. Lyons, which was really a talent agency but now fancied itself a producer of motion pictures. The offer came through the machinations of Robert Rossen, who was becoming important in The Industry.

Rossen was about to become a writer-director, but he was apparently interested in keeping a finger in the Lyons pie, which consisted of a novel called *Prelude to Night*, by Dayton Stoddard, which the agency wanted Rossen to adapt himself. Since he was already busy preparing a film he was to direct, he made a deal with Lyons, whose terms involved hiring me as screenwriter, with Rossen to be responsible for what I did (Lyons did not know me from Adam) and, quite possibly, to serve as director.

It was quite a respectable novel and appealed to my radical insights, for it concerned a young fellow of Greek-American background who determined at the age of fourteen to become a millionaire—and made it. He was to be played by Zachary Scott (who had achieved some notoriety playing opposite the indestructible Joan Crawford in her Warner Brothers film, *Mildred Pierce*), and the role called for the stereotyped "charming heel" whom the audience could identify with and hate at one and the same time. In the novel, the man is completely ruthless, and he acts effectively on his drunken and ineffectual father's advice, which went like this: "If you want to become rich, find out what people need and get a corner on it. Then sell it to them at your own price."

That is what our antihero does. He gets a corner on produce, and he also corners a number of attractive and well-to-do women, bedding them, milking them, discarding them—or marrying them and then discarding them—in his relatively short climb to affluence on Wall Street. Of course, he gets his comeuppance, in a wonderful scene in which he falls off his yacht while his closest friend stands by impassively and watches him drown. I don't remember why our antihero could not swim.

Rossen had pitched me so effectively to A. & S. Lyons that my salary rose immediately from the $425 a week that Warners had reluctantly parted with a year earlier (when I was "unhappy") to $600 a week, and when I expressed a desire for some immediate cash, a secretary promptly arrived at the Laurelgrove ranch house with an envelope containing $1,000 in $100 bills, to be deducted from my salary at $100 a week. Then, after consultation with Rossen, I went to work on the treatment of the story. He asked to see pages once a week, and I visited him at his home in Brentwood, where we discussed what I had done and he—making like the producer he has since become—produced ideas of his own.

When the treatment was finished, typed, and mimeographed, a story conference was held in the boardroom of A. & S. Lyons in Beverly Hills, at which were present one Lyons (A. or possibly S.), who wore elevator shoes; his story editor, a mousy little man named Brown; the moneyman for the picture, Joseph Justman (who had made *his* pile in produce, oddly enough); Rossen; and me, the screenwriter. I did not utter a word during the entire conference. The meeting was opened by Lyons, who said that he did not care for the treatment; then he turned it over to Brown, who detailed the reasons Lyons did not like it and spoke for nearly half an hour. I sank deeper and deeper into my hardwood captain's chair at the board table, but Rossen maintained an utterly impassive face until Brown had finished ticking off a long list of things that were wrong with the treatment (including its radical content, which stemmed, of course, from the novel, not the hired writer). This list was written out on numerous typewritten pages, and the bare recital of objections depressed me more and more, for I was convinced that the majority were correctly taken.

CAMERA COMES TO

MED. SHOT. BOARDROOM

—as BROWN FINISHES his tabulation and ROSSEN RISES mildly from his captain's chair, his round face still impassive.

ROSSEN

(to Brown)

Are you through?

BROWN NODS and ROSSEN TURNS to A. (or S.) LYONS, who seems to be of normal height when he is sitting down. Suddenly ROSSEN's face becomes transfigured: it becomes red!

[*160*]

ROSSEN

(pointing at SCREENWRITER)

That man is the best goddamned screenwriter in Hollywood today!

SCREENWRITER GASPS, then is silent.

ROSSEN

(continuing)

You're paying him a measly $600 a week, and he's worth four times that much if he's worth a cent! *I'm* telling you!

LYONS

Well, I—

ROSSEN

(voice rising)

Don't interrupt me! I didn't interrupt your stooge when he was talking.

(pounds table)

How *dare* you call us here to waste our time and insult my writer with these ridiculous ideas!? I *like* what he's done. It's great! Do you *hear me? Great!* and *that's* the way the treatment's going to stay and that's the way the screenplay's going to be written and if you don't like—

LYONS

(stuttering)

Well, I . . . only . . .

ROSSEN

I wash my hands of the whole thing!

(washes his hands)

You can get a couple new boys and see what kind of a shitty screenplay you'll get *then!*

LYONS

(apologetically)

You got us wrong. It's just a few things we—that is—

ROSSEN

Take it or leave it.

LYONS

We *like* it, *honest* we like it. We just thought—

ROSSEN

You leave this thing in my hands, I told you, and you'll have an Academy Award picture and you'll get down on your hands and knees and thank me and my writer here that—

LYONS

All right, all *right*, it's only that—

There are SMILES all around as ROSSEN MARCHES OUT of the room, with SCREENWRITER at his heels.

CAMERA TRUCKING TO

CLOSE TWO SHOT. ROSSEN. SCREENWRITER

—as they CLIMB INTO the car for the drive back to Brentwood. They are silent for some time. Then ROSSEN TURNS to the WRITER.

ROSSEN

Everything they said was right, of course.

SCREENWRITER

It *was*?

ROSSEN

Of course.

SCREENWRITER

I'll do another treatment.

ROSSEN

You'll do no such thing. You'll just start screenplay and incorporate some of the things they want, but we'll be working on it together, so stop worrying.

I stopped worrying and started screenplay, sending the pages to Rossen weekly. He sent them on to Lyons, and every week I got either a message or a telephone call from A. (or S.), the one with the elevator shoes, saying it was "great" and they "loved it," until the last four or five weeks, during which time I heard nothing from anybody, including Rossen.

The entire job lasted about nineteen weeks, and the film was eventually made and released under another title (with Zachary Scott) and was duly panned, but it did not have my name on it —or Rossen's—for the simple reason that the producing company decided that the whole thing was simply "too radical" (maybe

Justman's shoes pinched). They had hired other writers and a new director, and the writers promptly wrote me out of the screenplay. This is a simple thing to do: you merely write enough new dialogue and create enough new scenes to guarantee that the original writer does not have a third of the final screenplay to his credit. (Nor did I ever see the film.)

We had moved by this time (because Alan Baxter was returning to Hollywood now that the war was over) to a little imitation English house in Hollywood that sat in a tiny imitation park on DeLongpré Avenue, but it had one genuine distinction: our next door neighbors, the enormously talented, gracious, and charming Dame May Whitty (who was in her seventies) and her aged husband, Ben Webster, the Shakespearean actor. The old man had long since retired from the boards, but he maintained an avid curiosity about the world in which he lived, which sometimes prompted him to peek into our living-room windows when he thought no one was looking. Dame May not only was still active on the screen but was a staunch supporter of at least one organization to which I was devoted. This was the Spanish Refugee Appeal (SRA), and Dame May (who never vanished when there was a good cause to support) was a regular speaker at the large mass meetings that SRA held at regular intervals in Hollywood to raise money for refugees in France, Mexico, and the Dominican Republic.

Then we moved again, to a triplex apartment on Olympic Boulevard that was owned by Edward Dmytryk. He had gone to England to direct a film, and my sons came out from the East again and lived in the basement playroom, which was decorated with fishnets, tennis and badminton rackets, rifles and pistols, foils and sabers, weights (which Dmytryk lifted—he is a short man) and punching bags. They had a ball.

I might have had a ball myself, for there was a study furnished with built-in desk and bookshelves, a couch with heavy square bolsters (the couch had a tiger skin draped carelessly across it), and a huge leather armchair such as I had never had before or since. It would have been an ideal place to work, if there had been work to *do*, but there was none. For months. The $4,000 we had in the bank and the war bonds we had accumulated at Warners started to go down the drain, and my agent reported that he was running into something called a "list," on which I had apparently been placed.

It was not until December of 1946 that another assignment came along, at Columbia, to work on a thing called *Double Crossroads*, which my agent had talked its producer into giving me because the story concerned Spain and I was supposed to be an authority on Spain (as well as a writer). I can remember little about this job except that its central character was alleged to have fought for the Spanish Republic (like myself), but you would never have known it from the way he talked and acted. I also remember that the job lasted only three weeks, then the script was shelved. Another did not turn up until Bastille Day, July 14, 1947, and $4,000 in cash and another $4,000 in bonds evaporates rapidly when you are supporting a wife and three children, two of whom had moved to Santa Monica with their mother (my first wife).

Both the Columbia job in 1946 and the one that finally came in 1947 paid me my "established" salary ($600), and the latter (for Allied Artists) was the last screenplay I wrote for Hollywood under my own name. So, in a way, the word "Bastille" came to have prophetic overtones, though I did not know it at the time. It was not as though there were not any number of portents, of alarums and excursions in the air. Anyone who was even half-awake politically knew that the atmosphere in Hollywood was changing and had been changing for some years.

As far back as 1938, when the Un-American Activities Committee was founded under the chairmanship of Martin Dies of Texas, its chief investigator, a man named Edward F. Sullivan, had announced that "all phases of radical and Communist activities are rampant among the studios of Hollywood." Sullivan had been associated, since 1933, with the Nazi-inspired Ukranian Fascist movement in the U.S.A. In 1934, he addressed a meeting of German-American Bund members and uniformed American storm troopers in New York City. In 1936, he was a featured speaker at a meeting in Asheville, North Carolina, which was attended by leading anti-Semitic and pro-Nazi propagandists and at which the Roosevelt Administration was denounced as a "Jewish Communist plot." Sullivan also had a long police record, involving everything from public drunkenness to larceny, and the Senate Civil Liberties Committee later brought out the fact that he had been employed for a time as a labor spy by a "strikebreaking, labor espionage agency."

When the ineffable John E. Rankin of Mississippi took over the Dies Committee (which was about to expire) and made it a permanent committee of the House in 1945, he began a cautious "probe" of Hollywood, which got plenty of headlines, but there were no official reports on it by the Committee itself. Gerald L. K. Smith took full credit for the investigation, and no one on the Committee itself denied it to him.

In the next two years, under the leadership of Rankin and J. Parnell Thomas of New Jersey, the Committee was in full cry, and Hollywood was not the sole recipient of its wrath. A constant drumfire of attack was leveled against the New Deal and its late leader, Franklin Delano Roosevelt and against his successor, Harry Truman of Missouri. Smith himself was called before the Committee—in order to give him a forum—and, under questioning by Thomas, denounced the "New Deal bureaucracy" as "the only effective fascism that has really imperiled our people." Roosevelt was called "very much an imitator of Hitler." Frank Sinatra was termed "a sort of a Mrs. Roosevelt in pants" (Thomas).

On the more serious side, the Committee's attack on the progressive measures of the New Deal that had begun with Martin Dies in 1938 continued unabated until 1947. The Committee successfully defeated Frank Murphy for reelection as governor of Michigan; it demanded, at various times, the resignation of such Cabinet members as Frances Perkins, Harold Ickes, and Secretary of War Stimson.

In 1944, Rankin had denounced the Fair Employment Practices Committee as "the beginning of a Communistic dictatorship the like of which America never dreamed"; in 1945, the same attack was made on the Office of Price Administration, and the Department of Agriculture was accused of broadcasting "pro-Russian propaganda." The governments of Roosevelt and Truman were alleged at all times to be full of Communists and fellow travelers, and on June 11, 1945, Rankin insisted that Truman "clean out the Reds" in the government.

Then demands were made that the President turn over to the Committee the personnel files of all war agencies; the State Department was denounced for harboring "more than two dozen" officials having Communist affiliations; when Chester Bowles announced a price ceiling for the 1946 cotton crop, Rankin insisted that Bowles was a Communist; Representative Mundt called on the government to conduct a screening of all United States personnel assigned to the United Nations; the radio programs of various government agencies were alleged to be putting forth the "Communist Party line"; and when Thomas became chairman, an official report of the Committee (January 2, 1947) recommended that Congress create "an independent commission with authority to investigate and to order the discharge of any employee or official of the Federal government whose loyalty to the United States is found to be in doubt."

President Truman folded up and on March 22, 1947, issued Executive Order 9835, which subjected two million Federal workers to a loyalty purge, to be financed by an appropriation of $25,000,000. This was the nodal point that determined everything that followed, and the attack on Hollywood was only one small part of the hurricane of suspicion, hysteria, fear, and witch-hunting that scourged the country from 1947 to well into the 1950's.

It was widely rumored in the spring of 1947 that another investigation of Hollywood was imminent. It was known that investigators came to Hollywood in May and questioned various film personalities—including Jack L. Warner—in executive session at the Biltmore Hotel. Nobody knew what had been said, but it was alleged that Warner had "named names."

A few days later, Thomas himself announced that his outfit had uncovered conclusive proof that the Roosevelt Administration had compelled "patriotic" film stars to appear in "pro-Russian" films (against their will, of course); that the industry had become a "Red propaganda center"; that Roosevelt, acting through Joseph E. Davies, former ambassador to the USSR, had "forced" Warner Brothers to produce a film version of Davies' book *Mission to Moscow*; and that Davies himself had indeed been a "liaison man" between Roosevelt and Hollywood.

The Motion Picture Alliance for the Preservation of American Ideals was openly calling for an investigation of Hollywood in spite of—or perhaps because of—the fact that it had been resoundingly condemned in public meetings by representatives of most of the studio unions as being not only anti-Semitic and anti-labor but Fascist into the bargain.

But these things had to be put out of mind in favor of the Allied Artists job, a story called *Smart Woman*, which had been written by Adela Rogers St. Johns, a veteran Hearst sob sister and successful screenwriter. She had sold it to Constance Bennett, one of the daughters of the celebrated Broadway actor Richard Bennett. Miss Bennett had employed two writers to make a screenplay for her. They made a mess of it. So, being an excellent businesswoman, she decided not to waste any more of her own money on the thing and took it to Allied Artists, which agreed to put up the money for production and assigned a little fellow named Hal as producer.

Hal looked like what he was reputed to have been—a member of the original Dead End Kids. He also talked like one and behaved like one, but he had a flair for what is admiringly called "showmanship" in Hollywood, when what they mean is vulgar sensationalism; and wherever he is today, he probably still has it.

How I got assigned to this screenplay, I do not know, but my agent probably sold me to Hal, and Hal was delighted to let me know that he approved of me, of my having fought in Spain. He was, he said gratuitously, something of a radical himself.

The story was a lulu, and I hope no one ever saw the film. In it, Miss Bennett is a criminal attorney whose job it is to defend gangsters and save them from their just deserts at the hands of an outraged society. She is opposed by a crusading young special district attorney (played by Brian Aherne) who has been brought in to "clean up" the corrupt city. Naturally, they find themselves on opposite sides of the same case, and just as naturally they fall in love with each other—and you can write the story yourself from here on in.

But you cannot write the story behind the story, as the newspaper boys like to put it, because you will not believe it even after you have read it.

There were a few conferences (story conferences, that is) with Miss Bennett, who lived in a lovely, well-appointed house with her Air Force officer husband, and she even had Hal and me to dinner on one occasion. And not once did she ever express—at least to me—any objection to anything that was in the "original" or the screenplay that I was attempting to develop from it. She expressed nothing but pleasure in her role—the opportunities it offered her to give a good performance, the tough, biting quality it was expected to have upon the screen, and so on.

To study for her role, the three of us (Bennett, Hal, and I) went down to the Los Angeles courts to watch a real-life female criminal attorney in action. This woman was famous for defending sex offenders, and her appearance—and behavior—in court was startling to everyone but the judge, other attorneys, and court attachés who dealt with her every day. She appeared in an enormous picture hat, wearing a purple silk gown (cut low enough to reveal some admirably firm cleavage, even though she was in her forties at the time). Her arms were burdened (and jangled) with innumerable gold and silver bracelets; her fingers were heavy with costume-jewel rings (admirably called *Schmuck* in German, though it means something else in Yiddish); her face was so made up that anyone would have thought that it was she and not Constance Bennett who was about to appear before the movie cameras; and she reeked of a perfume that could be smelled before she even entered the courtroom.

The case she was defending involved a miserable-looking creature who sat at the counsel table with her, his head hanging almost between his legs. He was accused of incest with his twelve-year-old stepdaughter, and—much to our astonishment—his wife (the mother of the child) was permitted to testify against him.

This woman sat on the stand and testified that the three of them lived together in a trailer and that late one night her husband had come into the trailer (and she admitted he was drunk), had gone to the cot in which her twelve-year-old child was sleeping, and apparently had entered her, for, said this woman, she could see him "going up and down on her."

At one point in the woman's testimony, the defendant spoke to his attorney in a low voice, and she, waving one bangled arm in obvious annoyance, said, loud enough for everyone in the courtroom to hear it, "Shut up! You know you're guilty as hell!"

This did not seem to faze anyone (except the three of us), and it looked like an open and shut case of statutory rape, good for anywhere from one to fifty years in prison—until the purple, scented criminal attorney got to work.

She did not deign to cross-examine the man's wife; she merely made a speech. The speech was corny; her gestures were flamboyant; her voice, loud and even strident; but the burden of her argument was that it was impossible to believe the chief—and only—witness for the prosecution. Why? Because, as the woman testified, she had seen the man come in; she had seen him approach her daughter's cot; she had watched him "going up and down" on her—and she had *not said one word or performed one act* to stop the man!"

"What sort of mother," cried the attorney for the defense, "would do a thing like *that*? What sort of woman could it be who would not spring like a *tigress* to the defense of her only child?" Obviously, it was impossible to believe a word the woman was saying.

And despite the evidence, despite the statement "Shut up! You know you're guilty as hell!" the man was convicted—*not* of statutory rape but of contributing to the delinquency of a minor, which would cost him, at most, one year in the county jail.

We stood and watched the criminal attorney as she was congratulated by various people, presumably friends and colleagues, including one sharp-looking fellow who was reputed to be her husband. She bowed and smiled and waved like a movie star, and her perfume was so overwhelming that I became slightly ill.

Her reputation and her fees were obviously justified by her performance before the bench, which explained why anyone accused of a sex crime in Los Angeles in the late 1940's immediately called her office and retained her services.

Miss Bennett expressed our common disgust over what we had witnessed and said she was delighted that in the film she would not be called upon to defend such a case. It was better to defend murderers and hoodlums than the low-down specimens of humanity that her real-life counterpart had developed into such a lucrative specialty.

That real-life sequence, however, was far more credible than what happened behind the scenes of *Smart Woman.* For although Miss Bennett had nothing but praise for what I was doing with the screenplay (when I saw her), she complained daily to the producer, Hal, as we drew closer to the end of the work, that she was not satisfied with it at all. Perhaps she had got wind of the impending investigation of Hollywood by the House Committee on Un-American Activities, and certainly in the few conversations we had with her, it was obvious (to me at least) that she was a dedicated reactionary. Perhaps she had decided to investigate her writer herself, and had called up the Motion Picture Alliance for the Preservation of American Ideals to find out about him. Perhaps she had merely talked to her "original" writer, Adela Rogers St. Johns, who had served with me on one or two committees of the Screen Writers' Guild and therefore could be presumed to know more about me than the star herself.

In any event, in order to understand what happened next, it is necessary to suffer through one scene of the story:

The crusading young special district attorney (CYSDA) has, of course, discovered in no time at all that the front man for the gangsters who control the city is none other than the district attorney himself. He therefore confronts him in the steam room of a Turkish bath (such scenes were popular in those days). There is one other man in the room, a little fellow who is wrapped in a sheet, lying in a chair with an ice bag on his bald head, recovering from a hangover. His eyes are closed.

The CYSDA says to the DA, "I know you're a small potato in this town, but I also know enough to ask for an indictment against you tomorrow morning unless you give me the names of the key men who control the rackets."

The DA rises in high dudgeon (also in a sheet) and says, "You can't talk to *me* like that! I've been the district attorney of this county for the last twenty years!"

This last sentence is all that our little fellow with the ice bag has heard, and he too rises like a Roman Senator and says, "So *you're* the district attorney, are you? Well, I've got a bone to pick with you."

"Don't bother me," says the corrupt DA. "Can't you see I'm busy?"

The little man with the ice bag says, "The woman next door to me keeps chickens. I came down to your office to complain about it and your stooge gave me the brush-off."

"That's scarcely in my department," says the crooked district attorney, waving one hand disdainfully.

"Is *that* so!" says the little man with ice bag. "Well, I *voted* for you, didn't I?" He shakes one finger at the DA, holding his sheet around him with the other hand (a little humor there, you see). "I can tell you *this*! I won't vote for you again, and neither will my wife or my mother-in-law!"

He marches out of the steam room holding his sheet around him—though it slips, momentarily, at the door.

The star called in our producer and told him that this particular scene was one of the most vicious pieces of Communist propaganda she had ever read. He was baffled, so she elucidated.

She said that what I had done was to discredit the elected representative of the people—the district attorney. The producer told her that the DA was the *heavy*. She didn't care, she said; that character had to come out! If he comes out, said the producer plaintively, you don't have a picture! The star still didn't care; she still insisted it was Red propaganda.

The producer was dumbfounded; he pointed out that so far from being propaganda, it was the oldest tradition in American politics: you treat me right or I don't vote for you.

The scene comes *out*, said the star.

Then a light dawned over the producer's small head. He pointed out to the star that I had not created that scene at all; it had come right out of the original story she had bought herself!

The star was adamant. *The scene comes out*, she said, *and he goes off the picture.*

So the scene came out, and I went off (but not before I had conveniently finished the screenplay). And one bright day, when I was living in one of Edward Dmytryk's apartments on South Crescent Drive in Beverly Hills, I opened the door when the bell rang, and a handsome middle-aged man said, "Alvah Bessie?" and when I nodded, he handed me an appropriately colored sheet of paper (blush pink), neatly folded, which read:

BY AUTHORITY OF THE HOUSE OF REPRESENTATIVES OF THE CONGRESS OF THE UNITED STATES OF AMERICA

To ROBERT E. CLARK, United States Marshal

You are hereby commanded to summon ALVAH BESSIE to be and appear before the UN-AMERICAN ACTIVITIES Committee of the House of Representatives of the United States, of which the Hon.

J. PARNELL THOMAS of New Jersey is chairman, in their chamber in the city of Washington, on October 23, 1947, at the hour of 10:30 A.M.

then and there to testify touching matters of inquiry committed to said Committee; and he is not to depart without leave of said Committee.

Herein fail not, and make return of this summons.

DISSOLVE TO

FEDERAL CORRECTIONAL INSTITUTION. Texarkana, Texas. January–APRIL, 1951.

Spring was slow in coming to Texas. It generally is, but it seemed slower than usual once my wife and daughter had returned to Los Angeles and the realization dawned on me—and kept dawning day and night—that I had five months more to pull. I kept a calendar in the steel drawer under my cot, and every night, at the start of my prison sentence, I had crossed out the day through which I had just lived (like in the movies). But now, each morning when I woke, I was compelled to go to the drawer, take out the calendar, and cross out the day before it had even begun, out of some unconscious belief in sympathetic magic.

The work in the warehouse was dull: endless receiving reports, inventories, bills of lading (in quintuplicate). The prison farm raised its own pork (which was the basis for a ghastly dream I had one night, after I had passed the slaughterhouse on the truck and heard the pigs screaming as they were killed: I dreamed that *I* was slaughtered—by the Fascists—and cut up in quarters with a butcher's cleaver and that the quarters were strewn in an empty field as an example to anyone who might be inclined to follow my subversive example); and the farm also grew countless vegetables, although the crop, in summer, seemed to consist entirely of bell peppers and okra. The clothing we wore was manufactured by women prisoners in Alderson, West Virginia, and other joints. Thus, there was not a very large variety of bills to occupy my time.

For a while I amused myself by studying the invoices that came with the few foodstuffs the institution did buy: whitefish from Shreveport, Louisiana; beef that seemed to be embalmed in formaldehyde; eggs; and milk. As the months wore on, it became apparent that the institution was buying cheaper and cheaper cuts of beef; and when it arrived in trucks and was carted into the freezer, it not only looked embalmed, it smelled that way too.*

The duller the work in the warehouse became, the harder I worked at night, manufacturing cigarette boxes, powder boxes, and other small items out of square-splint matches and LePage's glue for various friends who might like to have such souvenirs— when I was free. I never made picture frames (as did most of the Mexican-American prisoners), because they didn't look right to me, or any of the elaborate mosaic-type designs these men

* It cost the institution about sixty cents a day per inmate for all expenses: food, clothing, medical attention, and so on.

executed—with far greater skill than I had developed in my first five months in residence.

I also had endless conversations with fellow inmates on such fascinating subjects as drug addiction, prostitution, counterfeiting, safecracking, and a wide assortment of other criminal activities, and I began to compile a dictionary of criminal (and prison) slang and notes on the life histories of those inmates who confided in me.

For example, if you asked a young man who was a pimp, a dope fiend, and a "retailer" for a counterfeiting gang how he had managed to wind up in the cell next door, he smiled and said, "It's easy. You start off with the wrong gang, and they give you a weed to smoke. You get high on pot, and after a while somebody else will say, 'You like that? You ain't seen nothin' yet'—and he'll introduce you to horse. And the first thing you know, you're mainlining it.

"Then you got a habit, an' a habit's an expensive thing to keep. Costs, after a while, maybe thirty, forty bucks a day. There ain't no easy way to get that kind of loot, so you steal an' you take a girlfriend that's hooked on you—below the belt, I mean [he grinned]—and you hook *her* on H; when she's hooked, you put her on the street an' say, 'Now you go to work or you don' get your fix,' an' she goes to work."

It always astounded me (though I tried not to show it) that these men saw nothing wrong in this. They reserved their sense of morality—of what was "right" or "wrong"—for the cops, who never gave them a chance to go "clean," even when they wanted to, and harassed and shook them down as soon as they were released, sometimes planting the stuff on them if there was no other way to pick them up again. They were also very bitter about rich addicts, who never were arrested and supported habits just like theirs without the slightest danger to their reputations or their liberty. "Why," one of these men told me, "I can name you any number of Hollywood stars that *you* know [and he named them] who're hooked the way I am, and nobody pays *them* no nevermind. They got the loot. With loot you can do anything. You can even get away with murder."

We had endless arguments about addiction, in which I insisted (perhaps out of ignorance) that addiction resulted in physiological changes that set up a craving that could not be controlled. They laughed at me and said it was "all in the head," and there must have been some merit to their argument, because there were men there who had been "clean"—who had been off the stuff—for as long as three years; but still their sole topic of conversation, night and day, was the fix they were going to get the moment they were out.

But whether it was dope that warped their sense of moral values or merely the society we all inhabited, I do not know. There was one occasion, for instance, when the young man who was pimp, dope fiend, and "retailer" came into my cell with two other cons in a state of high excitement and said, "We want you to settle an argument for us."

"Why pick on *me*?" I said. (I was trying to reread Plato at the time and was already annoyed by the radio and the guys playing dominoes in the corridor.)

"You're an old guy," they said, "an' you been aroun' an' seen a thing or two."

"Okay," I said. "What's the beef?"

"We wanna know if you think it's right for a pimp t' beat his whore," said a young fellow.

I looked at them. They were dead serious. Their faces were as intent upon my answer as though they had asked me to explain the quantum theory or foreign exchange, and they confidently awaited an explanation and expected to understand it.

"Do you think it's right for anyone to beat *anyone*?" I asked. There was a pause.

"What does it prove?" I asked. "That one man's stronger than another? That a man's stronger than a woman?"

"You got a wife," said one of them. "What'd you do if while you was in here, she stepped out on you?"

"If I knew about it, I'd be hurt, I suppose."

"You wouldn' lam the living shit outta her when you was out?"

"No. . . . She's a grown woman. She's got the right to do what she feels like, hasn't she? Same as you?"

The fellow scratched his head. "Women gotta be kept in line," he said after a while.

The young fellow who had asked the first question shook his head. "I forgot," he said apologetically. "You're supposed to be a Red, ain't you?"

"I'm supposed."

"You *really* think men an' women're equal, don't you?"

The talk (not among the addicts, to whom women generally meant nothing at all) was of women, day and night. You picked up scraps of conversation without even listening that testified to their obsession, and the Mexican-American prisoners made explicit gestures with fingers, mouth, and tongue. It amazed me for a while (but then I thought, You're an old guy; you're forty-six, you're forty-seven) that I had practically no desire while I was in prison, and I ascribed that to the potassium nitrate they were alleged to mix into our food (as they are alleged to do in the Army too). But I doubt that that had anything to with it, for I had never seen any lack of desire in the Army men with whom I served (in Spain), and there was certainly no lack of it among the men in Texarkana.

But neither was I approached by any prisoner for the sort of homosexual gratification that is said to run riot in such places, and the only men who practiced it—who were obviously queer when they came in—were promptly segregated by the administration in a separate unit, where, no doubt, they could practice on one another.

Masturbation seemed to be the standard operating procedure in the joint, and there was a wonderful story about a con named McCree (I'll call him that, anyhow), who was serving five years for cashing Navy checks when he was a clerk in service in California. McCree was a character (he looked like something out of a British film) and was, of course, known as Mother, for he was alleged to be the prison fellator, whose services could be had for a song—well, for a pack of cigarettes, let us say. (I never heard of anyone employing him, for as Oscar Wilde said about a young man at his trial, he was a dreadfully ugly boy.)

He also ran a thriving business of a semilegitimate nature: for a pack of cigarettes or a chocolate bar, at stated intervals, McCree would get you extra handkerchiefs and socks (for which there was no need, since there were two large tin cans off the shower room that were filled with them every day). He could also produce any newspaper or magazine published in the United States (or so it seemed) and would sweep and swab your cell and make your bed if you were too lazy to do it yourself and the hack was not looking.

It was the landscape-gardening screw who told the story about McCree, and it swept the joint like wildfire.

After lunch each day, you had about half an hour in which to rest, and I never failed to close the door of my cell and lie on my back on the cot. (And it never failed that the moment I started to fall asleep, the siren blew for resumption of the day's labor.)

One day after lunch, the screw was making his regular count in McCree's cellblock; noting that his door was closed, he stopped and looked through the small glass pane to make sure that he was there. What he saw made him open the door and step into the cell and look down at McCree, who was lying on his back on the cot. "McCree," said the screw, "what're you *doing?*"

"Five years," said McCree and kept right on doing it.

By the end of March, it was beginning to get warm. I was scheduled for release at midnight of April 29, and in that last month the days grew exceeding long and the nights seemed endless. I spent many of them awake, standing next to the window smoking and watching the light on the grass between the buildings. [*They are the floodlights (not the moon)/that make the nights so white in Texarkana./When I awake at night, I always take/the one to be the other.*]

And every time the airliner crossed the sky at 11:06 P.M., flying north from Dallas, I remembered a poem I had written while I was still in quarantine, called "Pilot's License":

My number here is fifty-eight five three.
I used to have another number,
engraved on a silver bracelet

given by my wife and worn on my right wrist—
a childish life ambition, if you will,
conceived one day in 1910, when I was six
and saw a man named Orville ride the air on linen wings—
achieved exactly thirty-five years later.
   3, 1, 3, 6, 8, 4, the number.
   At night, sometimes, when I cannot sleep,
   I practice landings, rather than count sheep.

It is quite possible—
the muscle tone returns, the feel, the sense . . .
the left hand on the throttle,
balls of the feet on rudder pedals,
right hand lightly on the stick,
the thumb on top, the fingers loose, relaxed. . . .

All right: the square approach is made,
the ship's at gliding angle, trim tab set;
the engine idles and the prop
turns over slowly, the exhaust
pops once or twice (clear the engine). . . .
Now the ship settles in a groove,
yawing neither right nor left . . .
constant air speed . . . constant rpm . . .
constant rate of sink. . . .

Now you flare out—
   gently, gently hold her off
   (the lovely dialectic of the thing,
   that when you want to land
   you do your best—to stay aloft!)—
   she floats just off the ground,
   a sudden gust that lifts the starboard wing
   corrected now with rudder, not with stick . . .
   wait . . . wait . . . the grass-blades swell
   like hairs under an adjusting microscope;
   she wants to sit . . . hold off the nose,
   up nose . . . down tail . . . as gently as a feather

if your luck is holding, with a sigh
the airborne creature feels the earth take hold
and sinks to rest upon it. . . .
  3, 1, 3, 6, 8, 4 . . . the number!

If freedom is the opposite of prison,
then flying is the ultimate of freedom—
and at the very selfsame time
(nature is the proof of dialectics)
rather than divorce you from the earth,
binds you more closely, watching from on high
(O temporary bird!),
to the tiny houses and their tiny people
tortured by their deathless, mighty,
everlasting struggle to be free.

  At night, sometimes, when I cannot sleep
  I practice landings, rather than count sheep.

Takeoffs are much harder to accomplish,
lying in a prison bed in Texas.
                    My number here
              is fifty-eight five three.

Though it was relatively easy to fly in prison, it was much more
difficult to keep my feet on the ground. I was suffering from all
the most uncomfortable symptoms of "shortitis," and the prognosis was grave.

Before I was denied parole the previous November, I had a
parole adviser (the Reverend Stephen H. Fritchman, pastor of
the First Unitarian Church of Los Angeles) and a "parole employer"—a fellow writer who was probably as subversive as I
had been myself but who had kept his nose so clean that he was
able to help sell a story for me under still another writer's name
three months before I went to prison. I had speculated (before
parole was denied) on what work he intended to give me—and
I discovered on my release that he had none; it was simply a

formality, but no doubt he would have tried to find me something.

But what was there to find for such a character? Dalton Trumbo and John Howard Lawson, who were imprisoned a month before the rest of us, had already been released. I did not know what Jack was doing, but I had heard that Dalton had gone to Mexico. The political atmosphere had deteriorated while we were in prison (and was to deteriorate still further with the meteoric rise of Senator Joe McCarthy); people suspected of subversive ideas were being fired right and left, and a subsequent investigation of Hollywood, after we went to jail, had resulted in the blacklisting and firing of scores more: writers, directors, backlot workers, actors, story analysts. Into the bargain, the previous September, Congress had passed over President Truman's veto the McCarran Internal Security Act, which required the registration of anyone who could for any reason be tagged subversive and provided detention camps for their imprisonment in the event of a "national emergency." (These camps are still on a standby basis.)

I tried not to think about the future that last month of my government-paid vacation. Instead, I concentrated on the new job that had been given me and wondered about it: along with other prisoners soon to be released, I was given a lawn mower and told to keep the grass short in front of the warden's office in the administration building and at the village a quarter mile down the road, where the officers lived with their families. It had a salutary effect on my health. I had not pushed a lawn mower in many years—and certainly had never pushed one for five to eight hours a day at any time, and I began to develop muscles I never knew I had. I also got very tanned (I took off my shirt and undershirt when none of the screws was looking), and it occurred to me that it was prison policy in this particular joint to return the inmate to his hometown looking like a million dollars, perhaps so people could say, "You never looked better in your life," and you could reply, "I never felt better," and then you could all do a double take.

[180]

I used to hope that the warden would come out of his office and talk to me. He never did, and on the few occasions I saw him, he acknowledged my presence and my greeting by no more than a nod. In addition to the lawn mowing, I was occasionally told to swab the deck in the corridors of the administration building, and then I could peek into the warden's office in the hope of seeing him there. He never was.

But there was no dearth of custodial officers at any time, and this was the time that Mr. Griffin, the punch-drunk ex-Marine, who had been a perfect gentleman for nine solid months, took it into his head to provoke me.

The joint was jammed. Built to hold three or four hundred prisoners, it had close to a thousand men crammed under its roof. Double-decker bunks had been set up in the dormitories, and we were feeding in two shifts at every meal. That meant that we had to get up earlier than usual, and sleep was difficult those last weeks. All my life I have had a habit of sleeping on my belly; and at some time during the night, I must pull the covers up over my head, because they are always there when I wake up.

Mr. Griffin was assigned to my cellblock that month, and he made his count at least twice during the night. He would come into the cell and rip the covers off me, and I could not get to sleep again for an hour or so. One night he did it three times, and when the whistle blew for breakfast and one of the inmates, a jeweler from Memphis who greeted every whistle for the ten months I was there with the invariable cry of *"Hot* coffee! *Hot* coffee!" had shouted, *"Hot* coffee! *Hot* coffee!" once again, I staggered to the grille that led into the corridor and waited for Griffin, on the other side, to open up.

I said, "Mr. Griffin, isn't it bad enough we have to get up an hour earlier without you waking me up three times a night?"

He stared at me. Finally, he said, "I'm paid to count men, not blankets."

"Where did you think I'd *be?"* I said. "I'm going out in three weeks."

He stared at me and licked his lips. "You don't like it," he said.

It was a statement, not a question. I did not reply. He pointed a finger at me. "Say one more word about it—say-one-word-more— and I'll take away your good time!"

I was silent, but I was boiling. I *hoped* my more than ordinarily mobile face was not showing what I felt, for the words "silent contempt" sprang into my mind immediately. I wanted to turn away, but there were nineteen men lined up behind me and it would have been a confession of defeat.

The whistle blew, and that night when I was talking to Del, the charming confidence man who occupied the cell on my right, I burst out in bitter rage—against myself.

"You know," I said, "I didn't hesitate to tell the Congress of the United States where to get off, and here I am scared stiff to talk back to that prick Griffin!"

"So what?" he smiled.

"So I *thought* I had some principles," I said. "I don't like to be pushed around any more than any other American, and here I let myself be pushed around by that shit!"

"Screw principles," said Del. "You want to stay here a couple extra weeks?"

"Hell, no."

"Then shut *up*," he said.

DISSOLVE TO

BEVERLY HILLS. October, 1947.

There was almost a feeling of relief now that the subpoenas were being served, and everybody was wondering who had received them and was calling everybody else on the phone to inquire. People who had been served were proud of the distinction; others were disappointed until their pink papers arrived. For the contempt in which the so-called Thomas-Rankin Committee was held was widespread and deeply rooted and people felt that it was time for a showdown.

I had a conversation at that time with my last producer, Hal. He had professed anger and disgust at Constance Bennett's insistence that I be taken off her picture, and we both had a good laugh over the fact that she did not insist until the script was

[*182*]

finished (though she subsequently had it rewritten by two other writers).*

"Hell," he told me, "you're the greatest writer in Hollywood," by which I suppose he meant that I was the best he had encountered in his limited experience in making B's. (*Smart Woman* was his first A.) "You and I will be making pictures," he said, "when Connie Bennett's in her grave. In fact, I've got one for you to rewrite right now, so why not come to the office and talk to me about it?"

"Will it make any difference to you," I said, "that I've received a subpoena to appear before the Thomas Committee?" (I figured I might as well tell him, for the news would be out in all the papers in a day or so anyhow.)

Long pause. "Have you?" he said.

"Yes."

Short pause. "Why should it make any difference to me?" Longer pause. "When are you due in Washington?"

"October 23, but we may have to be there earlier."

No pause at all. "When you get back from Washington, get in touch with me."

I had a faint suspicion that he had changed his mind about the script, but then I decided I was being unjust to the little man, for he surely realized that there was a lot of preparatory work to be done before appearing before a congressional committee—finances to be arranged, lawyers to be consulted, travel plans to be made—and any work attempted in the midst of such a hullabaloo would be certain to suffer.

So it was just as well. Into the bargain, my wife and daughter and I had received an invitation from Dalton Trumbo to visit his ranch in the Tehachapi Mountains for a week, and we packed our bags and merrily drove the ninety miles over the Grapevine.

---

* In January of 1948, Hal tried to get me to take my name off *Smart Woman* and even cried in my living room, claiming that I was "ruining" him. I was not moved, and the case went to arbitration before the Screen Writers' Guild, which has jurisdiction over disputed credits and which awarded me first credit over the two other writers Hal had hired to "write me out." The fight was scarcely worth the effort, for the picture stank.

If the fact that *Smart Woman* arrived on Bastille Day, 1947, could have been considered a sign (in retrospect), what happened on the Grapevine might have been another if we had been perceptive enough to notice it.

We were tooling along at seventy miles an hour over this highway (99) and were about ten miles from Lebec, when I said, "This road has a bad reputation. Crashes every ten minutes, according to the papers. I don't see why." I gestured at the four-lane well-banked highway, which, at that point, was running straight as a string toward the San Joaquin Valley. Then it happened.

A small car behind us decided to pass precisely as a Greyhound bus, coming toward us, roared by on its way to Los Angeles.

I saw it in the mirror and shouted, *"Christ!"* I stepped on the brake, throwing my three-year-old daughter into the windshield despite Helen Clare's best efforts to hang onto her. She got a bad bump on her forehead and after we had ascertained that it was nothing worse, I jumped out of the 1943 Hudson and ran back down the highway.

It had been deserted a moment before, with the exception of the bus and coupé behind me, but then cars seemed to be arriving and pulling off the road every moment, and there were at least four other men to help extricate a badly injured and unconscious woman from the wreckage of her car. The bus was off the road but still upright; the coupé had been hit so hard that its engine had been torn out and lay a hundred yards away. The rest of the wreckage was smoldering, and we worked as fast as we could to disentangle the groaning middle-aged woman, whose shattered thigh bones could be seen through her torn flesh. (I thought of Spain.)

After the ambulance took her away, we moved slowly (at thirty-five miles an hour) toward the turnoff at Lebec and drove the additional ten miles to Dalton's ranch in Frazier Park. There was scarcely a house to be seen, and we were silent. Then we spotted the long, low ranch house and what looked like a vast, raw depression next to it. I noticed that there was a meadow as level as a billiard table and decided that it would be possible to fly a lightplane up sometime and land it on Dalton's front lawn. (I never did.)

Dalton came out of the house when he heard us and ushered us into what had looked—from the outside—like an unpretentious residence that suited its surroundings admirably. He was aware immediately that we were shaken by something and said, "Don't worry about the subpoena—we'll lick them to a frazzle," so we told him about the accident, and he said, "You need drinks."

He produced the drinks from behind a bar and showed us around the house. Inside, it was as richly appointed as the $100,-000 Beverly Hills mansion he inhabited in town; he had even brought the silver horses that used to stand on the sideboard, and they were on the mantlepiece.

In his small study, we sat and drank, and I said, "This is quite a place," and he said, "Isn't it?" He showed us a photograph on the wall. "This is the way it started ten years ago," he said. "People called it Trumbo's Folly, and I've certainly sunk every cent I've earned into it."

It had started with the small study (a shack, really) in which we were sitting, and he had built onto it until it sprawled over the landscape in the shape of an H. There were floodlights outside to light the giant pine trees at night; the vast depression next to the house was explained by the presence of bulldozers at work: they were diverting a mountain stream, building a dam, and creating an artificial lake so that the three Trumbo children and Dalton's wife, Cleo, could swim (Dalton rarely swam or, for that matter, went out in the midday sun, claiming he was allergic to it).

In those days, he was a strange and fascinating man (he still is—and today he wears a white Grenadier Guard's moustache) who preferred to work all night and sleep all day. (Nowadays he works all day *and* night.) And he used to work in the bathtub a good deal of the time, sitting crossways (and cross-legged) at a specially built writing table that spanned the tub, the water running in and out to maintain an even temperature and a huge coffee cup on his table that was always full.

The only member of what subsequently became "The Ten"

to come out of the working class, Trumbo has never forgotten the fact. He was born in Colorado and, as a young man, worked in Los Angeles as a baker (this occupation may have established his nocturnal habits), living near the Griffith Park area.

A legend even then—before he beat the Hollywood blacklist single-handed (with an Academy Award under the name of "Robert Rich" for *The Brave One* and other solo credits under his own name for *Exodus* and *Spartacus*)—Trumbo was known to have a contract that was unique in the annals of The Industry. It was signed by MGM, and its provisions turned every other writer in Hollywood sick with envy: (1) a salary of $4,000 a week; (2) complete choice of materials; (3) a minimum of one screenplay a year—or as many as he chose to write; (4) if story conferences were required, the producer had to come to Trumbo's house—he refused to go to the studio. And he had no "morals clause" in his contract—a neat little device that is more honored in the breach than the observance; for there are many screen stars, producers, and directors who are drunks, sadists, narcotic addicts (as my fellow cons pointed out), wolves, masochists, nymphomaniacs, lesbians, or male homosexuals. They live (and travel) all over the world with one another without benefit of clergy and the morals clause is rarely invoked—except in the case of political offenders like "The Ten," when it was used to break all the contracts that contained such a clause.

Legend has it that Trumbo had told MGM that he would sign a morals clause—if Louis B. Mayer would sign one too. They said, "Forget it."

"You should have seen this place in the old days," Dalton said, freshening our drinks. "In those days, when you drove up to the house, a liveried butler came out to your car with Martinis on a silver tray."

"No!" I said.

"Yes!" said Trumbo. "And I loved every minute of it."

"Do you really think we'll lick them to a frazzle?" Helen Clare asked.

He took a swallow of his drink and said, "Of course not. We'll all go to jail."

All the Trumbos were going into town for the week—Dalton, Cleo, Nikola, Christopher, and Melissa (who for some reason or other is called Mitzi), leaving the ranch to us.

"Make yourself at home," they said. "There's Heineken on ice, plenty of liquor, all the food you'll need." They took off, and we promptly made ourselves at home.

We knew that there was to be a meeting that week of all nineteen subpoenaed people at Edward G. Robinson's house (he was not subpoenaed, but some time later he voluntarily presented himself before the Committee—twice, in fact—to quash persistent rumors that he was not a good American), but since we were on "vacation" from *Smart Woman,* Dalton said we'd get a report on it when we got home.

The Los Angeles *Times,* which turned up in the mailbox down the road the next afternoon, had no news of the impending investigation, but diligent search turned up a two-paragraph item on page nineteen about the accident we had witnessed on the Grapevine. The woman was a trained nurse, on her way to Los Angeles. She had died. Her first name was Bessie. . . .

The report we received when we got home was appalling. The case was going to cost a fortune: there were a number of lawyers involved, and they more or less expected that we would all be found in contempt of Congress, indicted, tried, and convicted and that the issue would eventually go to the Supreme Court before a solid decision could be reached. This would mean a series of trials and all the expenses attendant on such an eventuality: lawyers' fees; travel expenses for witnesses who would eventually be subpoenaed—and *their* fees; money for the printing of transcripts; travel and living expenses for all nineteen witnesses and their lawyers to and in Washington and back (as things turned out for ten of us, that trip was taken several times); rental of an office to coordinate the publicity and paid advertising we agreed to put out; telegrams and long-distance telephone calls; salaries for research assistants (who dug out information about all members of the Thomas-Rankin Committee, their voting records and personal views); mailing pieces (printed and mimeographed); and postage—and this would go on for years for the simple reason that when you decide to challenge any official or division of the government, you are in for a long siege, quite aside from the law's delay.

Each of the nineteen witnesses was therefore asked—as a token down payment on the expenses that would have to be incurred—to contribute sums up to $4,000, which would be deposited in a fund administered by an executive committee of the group. Most of the nineteen were able to do this, but there were two of us who could not contribute a dime: Samuel Ornitz and myself. Ornitz had, in effect, been blacklisted years before and simply had no money at all. I desperately needed what money had been saved from the last "established" salary, and I desperately needed work. Therefore Ornitz and Bessie were the paupers of the group and were freeloaders for the three years it took to bring the case before the Supreme Court which refused to review it.

But before we went to Washington, each of us individually consulted one of the attorneys and was advised of his constitutional rights. Each of us, therefore, had to decide what course of action he would follow, and the disagreements that ensued would fill a separate volume. Some, of course, were members of the Communist Party and some were not, but there was little agreement at first—contrary to what is frequently alleged—between the Party members themselves. Communists and non-Communists alike, some wanted to say, "Yes, I'm a Communist, and what do you want to make of it?" Others wanted to say, "No, I'm not." Some agreed that the best course of action was to challenge the Committee all the way down the line and not *refuse* to answer questions, but to answer them in their own way. Some suggested invoking the Fifth Amendment, but others insisted that they would have nothing to do with it because a refusal to reply on the grounds that any reply might tend to "incriminate and degrade" them was tantamount to a plea of guilty.

The lawyers pointed out that there was nothing in the Fifth Amendment itself that implied such a confession, that the words "incriminate and degrade" do not even appear in the language of the amendment; but the consensus was no, and the ultimate decision—agreed upon by all nineteen witnesses—was to strike at the very mandate of the Committee and its right to exist, which meant reliance on the First Amendment and the protections it offers all citizens to speak, write, or assemble for any honorable purpose without fear of intimidation or reprisal.

Even so, two or three of the nineteen signed statements to the effect that they were not Communists—and deposited them, secretly, with their own producers—and one (Howard Koch) took a full-page advertisement in the Hollywood trade papers to the same effect (attacking the Committee anyhow), which did not prevent him from being blacklisted for years even though he did not get to testify with us.

The month that elapsed between the service of the subpoenas and our appearance in the Old House Office Building in Washington, D.C., was filled with almost daily press releases, almost daily meetings all over the West Coast and in Chicago and New York, en route to Washington.

The enthusiasm for our cause was enormous—or so it seemed to us—and it was gaining national and international publicity and the support of countless professionals in all fields of human activity. In Hollywood, five hundred people formed the Committee for the First Amendment and set to work protesting the hearings through a series of advertisements, pamphlets, and two nationwide radio broadcasts during the actual hearings themselves. These people made it plain from the start that they "espouse[d] no political party . . . represent[ed] no motion picture studios . . . [and were not] attacking or defending any individuals connected with the hearings," but were unalterably opposed to witch-hunts, the House Committee, and the investigation of The Industry.

There is no room here to print all the five hundred names, but one would be hard put to find any important person in Hollywood's motion-picture industry—with the understandable exception of most producers—who was missing from this list, which included four U.S. Senators (Harley Kilgore, Claude Pepper, Elmer Thomas, and Glen Taylor), as well as such luminaries as Thomas Mann, Humphrey Bogart, Lauren Bacall, Gregory Peck,

Katharine Hepburn, Eddie Cantor, Myrna Loy, Paulette God-
dard, Burgess Meredith, Danny Kaye, Walter Huston, George S.
Kaufman, Canada Lee, Moss Hart, Rita Hayworth, Leonard
Bernstein, Kirk Douglas, Henry Fonda, Benny Goodman, Paul
Henreid, Van Heflin, John Huston, Burt Lancaster, Vincent Price,
Robert Ryan, Irwin Shaw—and even Jerry Wald, Warner
Brothers producer. Thousands throughout the country later sup-
ported the Committee for the First Amendment with their names
and contributions.

DISSOLVE TO

WASHINGTON, D.C. October, 1947.
The Shrine Auditorium in downtown Los Angeles was jammed
with seven thousand people the night before we were to fly to
Washington. It was a send-off for the group that the newspapers
were already calling "the unfriendly nineteen," and Gene Kelly's
opening remarks (he was the chairman) brought down the house.
He appeared in a walking cast, and he said, "I'm Gene Kelly.
Now, first of all, about these crutches, so we can forget them—
I broke my ankle, Sunday, rehearsing a dance. I didn't do it on
purpose, or for dramatic effect, as has been charged.

"I'm here because of the Constitution of these United States
and the Bill of Rights—both of which I believe in and which I
believe are being subverted by something called the House Committee on Un-American Activities."

Most of our attorneys spoke at that meeting and some of the
nineteen themselves, as well as a number of motion-picture per-
formers; and from the atmosphere in the vast hall, you would
have thought we had the House Committee licked to a standstill
before we ever got into the ring.

There was word that night that the Committee for the First
Amendment had chartered one of Howard Hughes's Constella-
tions and would send a delegation to audit the investigation and
make a report on it. There was word—later proved to be a base
canard—that Hughes himself was sympathetic to the Hollywood
people, since he had been pushed around by a congressional
committee himself. (He had told them where to head in, but no

[190]

citation or indictment for contempt was ever issued against this weird and fascinating character.)

We flew in another TWA Constellation and stopped over one night in Chicago to speak at a couple of meetings, then in New York to speak at another. In Washington, we stayed at the Shoreham Hotel, which to my naïve eyes was a luxury caravansary, and I was awed by the quantities of good foods and good liquors that were delivered—almost every hour on the hour, it seemed—without any need on my part to pay one cent for the privilege of sharing in them.

We had regular consultations, both individually and as a group, with our lawyers; and one night, one of our attorneys, Bartley Crum, held a memorable conversation with someone in Hollywood named David.

DISSOLVE TO

LUXURIOUS LIVING ROOM in SUITE at the Shoreham Hotel. Night. In it are gathered the NINETEEN MEN who have been subpoenaed by the House Committee on Un-American Activities. Thirteen are screenwriters, one is a writer-producer, four are directors, and one is an actor. (Coincidentally, perhaps, thirteen of the nineteen are Jews.*) The Committee, in "advance-dope" stories to the press, has announced that they will all be "unfriendly" witnesses. They are represented by SIX ATTORNEYS, one of whom (BARTLEY CRUM) is in hot conversation on the long-distance line to Hollywood. The nineteen men and their attorneys have been in conference, but now they are listening to CRUM'S CONVERSATION, of which, of course, only one-half can be overheard.

CRUM

But David, you've *got* to be the chairman of the Committee for the First Amendment.

(pause)

Everyone's on it. You want their names?

(pause)

* So were three of the four producers that the Committee would later run through its wringer.

You know the names? Of course. You couldn't be in more distinguished company.

(pause)

Yes, I know you're an independent producer.

(pause)

Yes, I *know* about your father-in-law. What does *that* prove?

(pause)

Yes, I *know* you're a Jew.

There is a long pause as CRUM shows mounting agitation and something close to anger.

CRUM

(continuing)

David, *listen* to me! I was in Germany after the war. They did the same thing there in 1933 when Hitler came to power. They pilloried a handful of men—drove them out of the industry—and after that the motion-picture industry made *nothing* that wasn't approved by the Nazis.

(pause)

What's that?

(pause)

No, here's the point. I *saw* a man like you in Germany after the war. *He* was an independent producer. *He* was a Jew. *He* was a liberal too. *He* didn't want to be involved either.

(pause)

Are you listening, David? Do you know what *became* of that man because he wouldn't fight?

(pause, shouting)

I *saw* him, David! *He was a cake of soap!*

He listens for a moment, SIGHS, GESTURES toward the men in the room, SHRUGS, says good-bye, and HANGS UP.

DISSOLVE TO

ANOTHER SUITE. Shoreham Hotel.

The same lawyers are present as in the previous scene: CRUM, ROBERT W. KENNY, former attorney general of the state of California; BEN MARGOLIS; CHARLES J. KATZ; MARTIN POPPER; and SAMUEL ROSENWEIN, authority on constitutional law. They are in conference with their opposite numbers in the motion-picture industry: ERIC JOHNSTON, president of the Motion Picture Association of America and former president of the U.S. Chamber of Commerce: PAUL V. MCNUTT, attorney, former U.S. High Commissioner to the Philippines, former chairman of the War Production Board, and once national commander of the American Legion; and MAURICE BENJAMIN, attorney. KENNY, a soft-spoken man with a diffident air, IS SPEAKING to the producers' representatives.

KENNY

We're maintaining that the Thomas Committee aims at censorship of the screen by intimidation. This accusation is not merely rumor. There's ample reason for this in the public statements of its chairman.

JOHNSTON

We share your feelings, gentlemen. And we support your position.

KENNY

The subject with which we're chiefly concerned is the character of the statements attributed to J. Parnell Thomas by the newspapers. He was quoted as saying that the producers had agreed to establish a blacklist throughout the motion-picture industry.

JOHNSTON
(indignantly)

That report is nonsense! As long as I live, I will never be a party to anything as un-American as a blacklist, and any statement purporting to quote me as agreeing to a blacklist is a libel upon me as a good American!

CRUM
(crossing to Johnston, shaking his hand)

Eric, I knew you were being misquoted. I'd never believe that you'd go along with anything as vicious as a blacklist in a democracy.

KATZ
(dryly)

The witnesses we represent will be more than delighted to have that assurance from you.

[193]

Tell the boys not to worry. There'll never be a blacklist.
We're not going to go totalitarian to please this committee! *

That same week Crum, whose enthusiasm for the case was
boundless, came into our hotel room one day in a state of high
excitement. He said that President Truman was so outraged by
the Committee and its imminent investigation that he had urged
his President's Commission on Civil Rights to issue its report
earlier than scheduled and had also decided to invite us all to
luncheon at the White House. The report came out, it is true,
but the luncheon invitation never arrived.

Nevertheless, we ate well. When we did not eat in the Shoreham off handsome silver trays wheeled into the separate rooms
by uniformed waiters, we ate at a restaurant in downtown Washington that featured fish and a wonderful brew that could not
be purchased anywhere in bottles, was called musty old ale, and
was dream stuff.

But the man who came in as we were sitting at table was not a
dream. Call him a nightmare. We recognized him instantly as
he took a seat near the door, and we saw him every time we
ate there. He was tall; there was that bulldog face that had been
featured in countless newspaper and magazine stories—many
bearing his celebrated by-line (whether he wrote them or not).
Here in front of our eyes was the man who was reputed to be
the Mover and the Shaker, the Most Powerful Man in the United
States Today; who was certainly one of the most feared; who was
alleged to know Where the Body Was Buried and to have millions
of skeletons locked into his capacious oubliettes, ready to spring
forth at the pressure of a button on his desk.

He was accompanied by another tall and dark (and far more
handsome) man. We pretended not to see the Powerful One, for
the legend was at total variance with the actuality: he *minced* as
he walked, and my sensitive nose detected a perfume the moment he came in the street door that has reeked in my nostrils
for the past sixteen years.

* Gordon Kahn, *Hollywood on Trial,* New York, Boni & Gaer, 1948.

INTERIOR. CAUCUS ROOM. Old House Office Building.

It is October 20, 1947, the opening day of the hearings. We see the Committee for the First Amendment's delegation in attendance: dramatist Robert Ardrey; Bogart; Larry Adler; Bogart's young wife, Lauren (Baby) Bacall; Geraldine Brooks; Richard Conte; Philip Dunne; Ira Gershwin; Sterling Hayden; June Havoc; Paul Henreid; John Huston; Evelyn Keyes; Danny Kaye; Arthur Kober; Marsha Hunt, who had also spoken at the Shrine; Jane Wyatt; and others whose names and faces I do not recognize.

The scene in the room is a chaos, and I am coming down with the flu. Thirty-nine newspaper cameramen with hand cameras squat boldly in front of us, taking close-ups of the witnesses, friendly and unfriendly. There is a battery of nine newsreel cameras; there is a forest of floodlights; there are ninety-four newspapermen and women from all over the United States and Europe; there are rows of control panels and other broadcasting and recording equipment; there are uniformed guards to keep order in the jammed room. I spot Joe North of *New Masses,* whom I had known when he was a correspondent in Spain and who was its editor when I was its film and drama critic. A man I had known eleven years earlier on the Brooklyn *Eagle,* who has a yellow face and is named Oliver Pilat, passes me and mutters something to the effect that I am now about to get what is coming to me. (I guess I did.)

On the rostrum, the Committee is seated and, in addition to Thomas, whose face is as round and red as a beefsteak tomato (and who has to sit on a pile of telephone books so that he will be in focus), there are McDowell of Pennsylvania, Vail of Illinois, Nixon of California, and others who will later sidle or fight their way into political oblivion.

SEATED before the Committee in the witness chair is JACK L. WARNER, Vice-President-in-Charge-of-Production of the studio that bears his name and whose slogan is: "Combining Good Citizenship with Good Picture Making."

He is listening to testimony he had given in executive session in May, 1947, in Los Angeles. The Committee is reminding him of it, since he seems to have had the benefit of counsel in the interim and is being rather cautious. ROBERT STRIPLING, committee counsel, a thin, pale man with a Southern accent, IS READING.*

CUT TO

CLOSE SHOT. STRIPLING.

STRIPLING

"MR. WARNER: When I say these people are Communists, as I said before, it is from hearsay. It was from printed forms I read in the *Hollywood Reporter.*

"MR. THOMAS: But you got enough information to let them go?

"MR. WARNER: I could tell in their writings and method of presentation of screenplays. . . .

"MR. STRIPLING: And you let these six people go. Can you name the six? . . .

"MR. WARNER: Here are the names of people who in my opinion wrote for the screen and tried to inject these ideas, and I personally removed them. . . . The first one is Alvah Bessie. . . .

"MR. STRIPLING: Identify the films.

"MR. WARNER: Alvah Bessie, *The Very Thought of You.* Gordon Kahn, *Her Kind of Man. . . .*"

CUT TO

CLOSE TWO SHOT. BESSIE. KENNY

—as BESSIE TURNS TO attorney ROBERT W. KENNY, GRABS his ARM, tries to keep his normally resonant voice down.

BESSIE
(indignant)

He's *lying!*

KENNY

Sh!

BESSIE

But he—

KENNY
(finger to lips)

So he's lying.

* *Hearings Before the Committee on Un-American Activities, House of Representatives, Eightieth Congress,* Government Printing Office, Washington, D.C., 1947.

CLOSE SHOT. JACK L. WARNER
—in the witness chair as STRIPLING'S VOICE CONTINUES.*

STRIPLING'S VOICE

"MR. THOMAS: That is a familiar list.

"MR. WARNER: Julius and Philip Epstein, twins.

"MR. THOMAS: What are they doing?

"MR. WARNER: They are at MGM. I will give you my theory of what happened to those fellows when I finish. . . .

"MR. THOMAS: You did not do *Song of Russia*?

"MR. WARNER: No; we did not. The Epstein brothers worked on a picture called *Animal Kingdom*. As I recall, that was aimed at the capitalistic system—not exactly, but the rich man is always the villain. Of course, those fellows getting $2,000 or $3,000 a week aren't rich men. I don't know what you would call them. Both of those fellows work together. They are never separated. . . ."

CAMERA NOW PULLS BACK TO

MED. SHOT. CAUCUS ROOM
—as STRIPLING CONCLUDES his reading.

CHAIRMAN

We would like to know from Mr. Warner at this point whether he still believes as he did when he testified in California on May 15, I think it was, the testimony of which was just read? . . . On all these other names, you would make the same statement in relation to them?

WARNER

I would with the exception that I have looked up one or two of the men; it has been so far back. I was naturally carried away at the time with this testimony being taken. I was rather emotional, being in a very emotional business, to a degree. There are several names here, one or two that I mentioned that I haven't any recollection of at this time, after careful investigation, having written any subversive elements.

* *Hearings, ibid.*

CHAIRMAN

You had better name them.

WARNER

Guy Endore—it has been so long ago.

CHAIRMAN

Then you would take him off the list?

WARNER

Yes, sir. . . . As I stated, I hope fully here, I have referred
to Julius and Philip Epstein in this one particular picture.
The rest of the time, they were always on very good American films, and there is very little can be said about them.
As I said, they do it in a joking way. The rich man is always
the villain, which is as old as the world itself. . . .*

                                                    DISSOLVE TO

THE SAME. TWO DAYS LATER.

The witness before the Committee is a heavyset man named
JAMES K. MCGUINNESS, an executive at Metro-Goldwyn-Mayer. He
is being questioned by H. A. SMITH, a committee investigator.**

SMITH

Mr. McGuinness, do you know who Alvah Bessie is?

MCGUINNESS

I do.

SMITH

Who is he?

MCGUINNESS

Alvah Bessie is a former movie critic of the *New Masses* who
came to Hollywood. I think—yes, in the employ of Warner
Brothers. He was known amongst writers I knew on the
Warner Brothers lot as the party's hatchet man.

BESSIE TURNS TO attorney KENNY, GRASPS his ARM.

BESSIE

What's a hatchet man?

* Of the nineteen "unfriendly" witnesses, Warner managed to name only
eight who had worked for him, as well as a score of others who were
pilloried in later investigations.
** *Hearings, ibid.*

[*198*]

KENNY
(side of the mouth)
Somebody who kills people.
BESSIE
(hot)
But I never saw the man in my *life*!
KENNY
(looking at him)
He didn't *say* he knew you.

DISSOLVE TO

MED. SHOT. CAUCUS ROOM
—with a screenwriter and motion-picture critic for *Esquire* on
the stand. His name is JOHN CHARLES MOFFITT. He is quite fat
and waddles like a duck when he walks. He has a huge dossier on
the desk in front of him as he testifies. STRIPLING IS QUESTIONING
him.*

STRIPLING
Mr. Moffitt, then, without naming any specific pictures, could
you give us some example of the techniques that have been
employed?

MOFFITT
Well, I gave you one, of the confusion of the class war with
the war against Nazi Germany. There is also the campaign
against religion, where the minister will be shown as the tool
of his richest parishioner. . . . There has also been the party
line of making the returned soldier fear that the world is
against him, that the American principle is against him, that
business is against him, that the free-enterprise system is
against him. You will see picture after picture in which the
banker is presented as an unsympathetic man, who hates to
give the GI a loan. . . .

STRIPLING
Have there also been cases in which the legislative branch
of our government has been put up for ridicule or scorn
through certain scenes and themes in pictures?

* *Hearings, ibid.*

[199]

Yes, sir; there have. . . .

Moffitt, of course, was talking about *The Best Years of Our Lives,* which William Wyler, its director, on a nationwide broadcast five days later said he "would not be allowed to make today," thanks to "the activities of the Un-American Activities Committee." The reference to the subservient minister could easily apply to *Pollyanna;* and although Moffitt and Constance Bennett were obviously not in cahoots, it is certainly true that they thought alike, for the "ridicule or scorn" of governmental agencies or individuals applied directly to the screenplay I had supposedly subverted, called *Smart Woman.*

The first five days of the hearings were devoted not only to hauling Jack L. Warner and Louis B. Mayer over the coals for making such films as *Mission to Moscow* and *Song of Russia,* but to presenting the testimony of "friendly" witnesses who would light the fire for the barbecue of the "unfriendly" that was to follow. There was a spate of verbiage from such cinematic dignitaries and experts on Marxism-Leninism as Sam Wood,* the director; Ayn Rand; Adolph Menjou; Rupert Hughes, who said he could identify Communists by "smelling them, in a way"; Robert Taylor; George Murphy; Ronald Reagan; Gary Cooper; and Mrs. Lela Rogers, among others.

Every time a movie star appeared, the proceedings came to a chaotic halt as movie, television, and still cameras were focused, the floodlights grew even brighter, and they posed taking the oath to tell the truth the whole truth, etc.**

Our attorneys, Robert W. Kenny, Charles Katz, and Bartley Crum, got nowhere with the Committee in their efforts to win

---

* Mr. Wood's will (published after his death) forbade his daughter, actress K. T. Stevens, from accepting her inheritance until she had signed a non-Communist affidavit. (I have often wondered whether she did.)

** Ruth Montgomery of the New York *Daily News* reported: "More than 1,000 shoving, sighing women today mobbed the House caucus room to see film star Robert Taylor. The hearing room was jammed to capacity, with hundreds of curious lining the walls outside. A 65-year-old woman, scrambling on a radiator for a better look at the film star, fell and struck her head. The clothes of others were torn in the mad scramble to the door. . . . Wild applause frequently punctuated Taylor's testimony."

the right to cross-examine witnesses who made the most outrageous statements about the "unfriendly" nineteen who were now impatiently waiting to come to bat. (Katz was thrown out of the room, bodily.)

From these friendly witnesses, the Committee learned and broadcast to the world the indisputable fact that Hollywood was infiltrated by Communists, who not only wrote their subversive material into screenplays but directed actors in such subtle ways that anyone who was well-to-do would appear "decadent" and "corrupt" (by the way he cocked an eyebrow, for example). The Reds controlled the material that got onto the screen by carefully buying the books and stories of other Reds and of fellow travelers, rejecting good "American" material; they saw to it that fellow Communists were hired as actors, directors, writers, and even producers—and excluded non- or anti-Communists from The Industry. Their enormous dues in the Party went to swell the millions in its coffers and, no doubt, were siphoned to the USSR as well, which everyone knows is a notoriously bankrupt concern (when it is not enormously rich and subsidizing Communist parties all over the world).

The late Gary Cooper was pressed to name some of the scripts submitted to him as a star, "quite a few" of which he said he had turned down because they were "tinged with Communistic ideas." He said he couldn't remember or name any of them, ". . . because most of the scripts I read at night."

Ayn Rand (writer at Warner Brothers when I was there and later author of *The Fountainhead* and other unreadable reactionary novels) testified that she had escaped from the Soviet Union and claimed that *Song of Russia* (MGM) was Red propaganda because, among other equally cogent reasons, "There is a park where you see happy little children in white blouses running around. . . ." She said she had never seen such children around the time she escaped (1926), and when asked, "Doesn't anybody smile in Russia any more?" she replied, "Well . . . pretty much no." *

* This statement is only slightly less fantastic than testimony offered and accepted without question by the Committee, under the chairmanship of Congressman Rankin, shortly after V-J Day in 1945. Rankin had on the stand the former diplomat William C. Bullitt:

Pressed again about how she managed to escape, she switched her story in midstream and admitted, "No . . . strangely enough, they gave me a passport to come out here as a visitor."

The late Adolph Menjou, one of America's best-dressed men, modestly admitted that he was an authority on Marxism and had published a list of thirty-five books that everyone should read in order to be informed about the menace. He was questioned by Richard M. Nixon (R., Calif.):

NIXON: Have you any other tests which you would apply which would indicate to you that people are acting like Communists?
MENJOU: Well, I think attending any meetings at which Mr. Paul Robeson appeared and applauding or listening to his Communist songs. . . . I would be ashamed to be seen in the audience doing that kind of thing.

Mrs. Lela Rogers omitted any reference in her testimony to a film written by Dalton Trumbo called *Tender Comrade,* which she had attacked earlier as Communist propaganda because her daughter, Ginger, was forced to say, "Share and share alike, that's democracy." (Perhaps someone had told her the title came from Alfred Lord Tennyson, or maybe her philosophic mind had convinced her that share and share alike was not democracy after all, but Utopia.)

But she did attack *None But the Lonely Heart,* an adaptation of Richard Llewellyn's novel, which was written and directed by Clifford Odets. It was Red propaganda, she said, for many reasons, among them being the fact that the *Hollywood Reporter,* one of the trade papers of The Industry, had said that it was "pitched in a low key, is moody and somber throughout in the Russian manner."

RANKIN: Is it true that they eat human bodies there in Russia?
BULLITT: I did see a picture of a skeleton of a child eaten by its parents.
RANKIN: Then they're just like human slaves in Russia?
BULLITT: There are more human slaves in Russia than ever existed anywhere in the world.
RANKIN: You said before that sixty percent of the Communist Party here are aliens? Now what percentage of these aliens are Jews? . . . Is it true, Mr. Bullitt, that the Communists went into the Southern states and picked up niggers and sent them to Moscow to study revolution?

"We [she and Ginger] turned down *Sister Carrie* by Theodore Dreiser," she said, "because it was just as open propaganda as *None But the Lonely Heart*."

As a handful of film geniuses from Chaplin to Giulietta Masina have demonstrated, great comedy and high tragedy are inseparable. The investigation of 1947 was therefore at once a farce and a tragedy. It was a farce because of the kind of assistance the Committee refused to accept—either from the producers or from the "unfriendly" witnesses—and because of the nature of the testimony that the Committee, lavishing praise upon its friendly witnesses, solicited and eagerly swallowed.

For while the trained seals were treated by the stumblebum members of the Committee with deference and respect and were permitted to indulge in wholesale gossip, innuendo, and uninformed "opinion" about everyone and anything under the sun for hours at a time, the atmosphere shifted rapidly the moment John Howard Lawson was called to the stand on October 27: *

LAWSON: Mr. Chairman, I have a statement here which I wish to make—

THOMAS: Well, all right; let me see your statement.

(pause)

I don't care to read any more of the statement. The statement will not be read. I read the first line.

LAWSON: You have spent one week vilifying me before the American public—

THOMAS: Just a minute—

LAWSON:—and you refuse to allow me to make a statement on my rights as an American citizen.

(when the first question on "membership" was raised by Thomas)

LAWSON: The raising of any question here in regard to membership, political beliefs, or affiliation—

STRIPLING: Mr. Chairman—

LAWSON:—is absolutely beyond the powers of this committee.

STRIPLING: Mr. Chairman—

* *Hearings, op. cit.,* pp. 290 ff.

LAWSON: But—

(Chairman pounds gavel.)

LAWSON: It is a matter of public record that I am a member of the Screen Writers' Guild.

STRIPLING: I ask—

(Applause.)

THOMAS: I want to caution the people in the audience: you are the guests of this committee, and you will have to maintain order at all times. I do not care for any applause or demonstrations of one kind or another. . . .

LAWSON: Mr. Chairman, you permitted—

THOMAS (pounding gavel): Never mind—

LAWSON (continuing):—witnesses in this room to make answers of three or four or five hundred words to questions here.

THOMAS: Mr. Lawson, you will please be responsive to these questions and not continue to try to disrupt these hearings.

LAWSON: I am not on trial here, Mr. Chairman. This committee is on trial here before the American people. Let us get that straight.

Lawson was eventually removed, forcibly, from the witness stand, to mixed applause and booing, and a committee investigator and former FBI man named Louis J. Russell then testified for nine pages (of agate type in the printed record) on the allegedly subversive activities of Jack Lawson—one of America's most distinguished playwrights and screenwriters. The quality of this testimony should be examined carefully by anyone interested in the lengths to which the Committee and its like-minded incarnations will go to make publicity—for purposes of gaining appropriations and discouraging nonconformist ideas.

Although Lawson was not permitted to read a statement, the very next witness was not only permitted but *urged* to read his. This was Eric Johnston, former president of the U.S. Chamber of Commerce and then president of the Motion Picture Association of America, which, if it is anything at all, is the trade union of the film producers.

Johnston made a fairly spirited defense of The Industry, insisted that the Committee was smearing it, and offered again (and in vain) to screen "any or all of the pictures which stand accused so that you can see for yourselves what's in them." He told the Committee that he was not going to permit it to dictate what sort of films The Industry should make. He defended the right of free speech—and then turned around and urged the Committee to continue its work of "exposing" Communists: "Expose them, but expose them in the traditional American way." (Of course, he did not make any reference to the verbal guarantees he had given our attorneys in that private conference in the Shoreham Hotel a day or so before the hearings began.) Stripling promptly tried to go to town on Johnston, but Thomas bailed him out and inadvertently made a liar of Johnston (before the "unfriendly" witnesses and their lawyers) when he complained bitterly that the MPAA head had promised that "we would get the full cooperation from you and your organization" (Johnston nodded his head affirmatively), but, said Thomas, "I just wouldn't want to tell the kind of cooperation that we have been getting."

He told Johnston that several critical remarks attributed to the MPAA president made him "boil a little bit," and by the time he got through with him Eric was cooperating like a good little boy, especially when Stripling brought out that one of Johnston's top assistants (Edward Cheyfitz) had once been a member of the Communist Party himself.

When Dalton Trumbo came to the stand the next morning, the Committee reversed itself again and refused to allow him to make a statement, ruling that it was not "pertinent" to the inquiry:

TRUMBO: The Chair has considered a statement from Gerald L. K. Smith to be pertinent to its inquiries.

THOMAS: That statement is out of order.

TRUMBO: And where is mine different from that, sir?

THOMAS: As a witness, if you conduct yourself like the first witness yesterday [Lawson], you won't be given the privilege of being a witness before a committee of Congress, before this committee of Congress. Go ahead, Mr. Stripling.

STRIPLING: Mr. Trumbo—

TRUMBO: I would like to know what it is that is in my statement

[205]

that this committee fears to be read to the American people?
THOMAS: Go ahead, Mr. Stripling, ask a question—
TRUMBO: I have some evidence to introduce—
THOMAS (pounding gavel): Ask one question, Mr. Stripling—
TRUMBO: I should like to introduce evidence—
THOMAS: (pounding gavel): You are out of order.

Trumbo was trying to introduce evidence of the nature of his work: he wanted his screenplays inserted in the record. "Too many pages," said Thomas. Then he tried to introduce comments about his work by General (Hap) Arnold of the Army Air Force, by judges of the juvenile courts, by the head of the Motion Picture Division of UNRRA, by the chaplain in charge of motion-picture projects for the Navy—all in vain.

The Committee was intent on finding out whether Dalton was a member of the Screen Writers' Guild, and several attempts were made:

TRUMBO: Mr. Stripling, the rights of American labor to inviolably secret membership lists have been won in this country by a great cost of blood and a great cost in terms of hunger. . . . You asked me a question which would permit you to haul every union member in the United States up here to identify himself as a union member, to subject him to future intimidation and coercion. This, I believe, is an unconstitutional question.
THOMAS: Well, can't you answer "Are you a member of the Screen Writers' Guild?" by saying, "Yes" or "No" or "I think so" or "maybe"—or something like that?
TRUMBO: Mr. Chairman, I should like to accommodate you. May I try to answer the question again?
THOMAS: Well, we would certainly like to have you accommodate us.
TRUMBO: If there were a committee of Congress, all the members of which had voted in favor of the Taft-Hartley Bill—
MCDOWELL (of Pennsylvania): Oh, that isn't answering the question.
(Thomas pounds gavel.)

[206]

TRUMBO:—it might be considered that committee was hostile to labor.

(The question about membership in the Screen Writers' Guild is asked again.)

TRUMBO: Mr. Chairman, this question is designed to a specific purpose. First—

THOMAS (pounding gavel): Do you—?

TRUMBO:—first, to identify me with the Screen Writers' Guild; secondly, to seek to identify me with the Communist Party and thereby destroy that guild.

Trumbo was also removed forcibly from the witness stand—shouting, "This is the beginning . . . of American concentration camps!"—and the pattern was reestablished: "unfriendly" witness, followed by an investigator who read an endless dossier on the witness's (in this case, Trumbo's) activities, in and out of the motion-picture industry, for the previous ten years.

But the scorn to which the Committee had been held up in the daily newspapers during the first week of the hearings * and the manifest displeasure of the majority of the people in the audience when statements were suppressed by the Committee resulted in an about-face when Albert Maltz was called to the stand the next afternoon.

Albert had apologized to me a few nights earlier, for we had had an argument about our former employer, Jack L. Warner (before he testified), and I had said some very uncomplimentary things about the man. Albert had defended him, saying that he wasn't a bad fellow at all and insisting that my bitter remarks sprang from what he called an "antiproducer attitude." After Warner testified, Albert agreed that the epithet I had applied to the man was scientifically accurate.

* Two examples will suffice, but there were hundreds: "The most un-American activity in the United States today is the conduct of the congressional committee on un-American activities" (*Detroit Free Press*), and, "The beliefs of men and women who write for the screen are, like the beliefs of any ordinary men and women, nobody's business but their own as the Bill of Rights mentions. Neither Mr. Thomas nor the Congress is empowered to dictate what Americans shall think" (*New York Herald Tribune*).

And Albert—to everyone's surprise—was permitted to read his statement in full, and the surprise was augmented by the passionate denunciation of the Committee and all its works that the statement contained. He castigated the Committee for refusing to give the "unfriendly" witnesses "the opportunity that any pickpocket receives in a magistrate's court—the right to cross-examine these witnesses, to refute their testimony, to reveal their motives, their history, and who, exactly, they are. Furthermore, it grants these witnesses congressional immunity, so that we may not sue them for libel for their slanders." *

Albert quoted Jefferson on the right to hold and maintain an opinion, which "shall never be a crime in my view; nor bring injury to an individual." He quoted Thomas as equating the New Deal with the Communist Party; he cited the opposition of Thomas and Congressman Rankin to an antilynching bill; he quoted the Committee's opinion of the Ku Klux Klan as "an acceptable American institution." He wound up with:

"If I were a spokesman for General Franco, I would not be here today. I would rather be here. I would rather die than be a shabby American, groveling before men whose names are Thomas and Rankin, but who now carry out activities in America like those carried out in Germany by Goebbels and Himmler."

The Committee took this bitter dose in complete silence.

Eight more questions were asked by Stripling before Albert said, "I have answered the question, Mr. Quisling," and was excused by Thomas, who promptly put our chief counsel, Robert W. Kenny, on the stand:

THOMAS: Mr. Kenny, will you please take the stand? Raise your right hand, please.

---

* It is a simple, if maddeningly frustrating, fact that no one can be sued for anything he says either on the floor of the Congress or under oath before a congressional committee, because his testimony is "privileged." This privilege originally had an excellent purpose: to prevent witnesses before such committees (and speakers in the halls of Congress) from being intimidated and withholding the truth. It still serves that original purpose, but it has developed what doctors call a side effect. It also *prevents* anyone from having grounds for action when he is libeled, unless he can induce the original liar to repeat his statements outside the privileged sanctuary of the Congress.

STRIPLING: Your right hand.

THOMAS: Your right hand.

CRUM: He cannot raise his right hand.

THOMAS: He cannot?

CRUM: No; he is crippled.

Bob's right hand might have been almost useless, but there was certainly nothing wrong with his mind, as was demonstrated when Thomas attempted to browbeat and blackmail him for a newspaper story that purported to quote Kenny.

Kenny had been quoted as saying (Washington *Times-Herald*) that "he would advise all his clients to invite prosecution by refusing to say whether they are Communists. . . . Hollywood attorney Robert W. Kenny said he would also advise the other 18 'to walk the plank.'"

It did not take Bob more than a moment or two to put Thomas on the defensive for attempting to attribute to him a statement that he did not make and for attempting to invade the sanctity of the lawyer-client relationship:

KENNY: I'm sure you didn't intend to invade that.

THOMAS: I appreciate that. I am not a lawyer; I admit that.

Bob then reiterated his determination not to permit the Committee to find out how he had advised his clients, stated that he had not said he would advise his clients to invite prosecution, and continued:

KENNY: . . . what I undoubtedly did say is that they are probably going to be invited to walk the plank. I don't advise anybody to walk any plank. I am not that bad a lawyer.

THOMAS: I will tell you, Mr. Kenny, as chairman, I want to let you know that you squirmed out of this one temporarily, but if the Committee should determine that is a violation of this Conspiracy Act, then the Committee will take under consideration referring the matter to the United States attorney.

KENNY: That is right, Mr. Thomas. I might say that the Committee has squirmed out of one too, because I am sure that the

Committee did not intend to invade the sacred province of relationship between attorney and client.

THOMAS: Oh, no; and neither would you want to commit conspiracy.

KENNY: Neither one of us is intimidated; is that right, Mr. Chairman?

In reply, and after getting the dossier of Albert Maltz into the record in some thirteen printed pages, the Chair called for the next witness—Alvah Bessie.

When your name is called, you are immediately afflicted by sensations you have experienced before: they are physiological in nature, and if you have ever tried to be an actor—or a soldier in action—you have experienced them often enough. They involve a suddenly stepped-up heartbeat, dryness of the mouth and throat, shaking hands, sharp pain in the intestinal region. And if you have ever tried to be a soldier (or an actor), you will immediately remember the next phenomenon: the moment you step upon the stage—or into the field of fire—the symptoms seem to disappear immediately, and you are just as suddenly at ease and in sharp command of all your faculties—such as they may be.

Actually, the symptoms do not disappear at all; they merely lie directly below the surface, waiting to pop up at any untoward moment and rattle you.

The request to read a statement was met by a curious compromise:

THOMAS: Mr. Bessie, while there is some doubt that your statement is pertinent to the inquiry, as will be very evident when you read it—

NARRATOR: I would still like to have permission to read it—

THOMAS: Just a minute. Nevertheless, the Committee is willing that you read the statement. We were just wondering, in order to save time, if you couldn't read the first couple paragraphs and then let us put it in the record. . . .

NARRATOR: In accordance with your request, I will read the first two paragraphs and the last two. . . .

"It is my understanding of the First Amendment to our Constitution that it expressly forbids Congress to pass any law which shall abridge freedom of speech or opinion. And it is my understanding of the function of congressional committees that they are set up by the Congress for the express purpose of inquiring into matters that may lead to the initiation of legislation in the Congress.

"Now either the Constitution and its Bill of Rights mean what they say or they do not mean what they say. Either the First Amendment is binding upon Congress and all legislative bodies of our government or it means nothing at all. I cannot agree with this so-called committee in its implied belief that the Bill of Rights means whatever this body chooses it to mean or is applicable only to those with whose opinions this committee is in agreement. . . ." Those are the first two paragraphs. Now, the last two:

"In calling me from my home, this body hopes also to rake over the smoldering embers of the war that was fought in Spain from 1936 to 1939. This body, and all its previous manifestations, is on record as believing that support of the Spanish Republic was and is subversive, un-American, and Communist-inspired. That lie was originally spawned by Hitler and Franco, and the majority of the American people—in fact, the majority of the people of the world—never believed it. And I want it on the record at this point that I not only supported the Spanish Republic but that it was my high privilege and the greatest honor I have ever enjoyed to have been a volunteer soldier in the ranks of its International Brigades throughout 1938. And I shall continue to support the Spanish Republic until the Spanish people in their majesty and power remove Francisco Franco and all his supporters and reestablish the legal government Franco and his Nazi and Italian Fascist soldiers overthrew.

"The understanding that led me to fight in Spain for that republic, and my experience in that war, teaches me that this committee is engaged in precisely the identical activities engaged in by un-Spanish committees, un-German committees, and un-Italian committees which preceded it in every country which eventually succumbed to fascism. I will never aid or abet such a committee in its patent attempt to foster the sort of intimidation and terror that is the inevitable precursor of a Fascist regime. And I therefore restate my conviction that this body has no legal authority to pry into the mind or activities of any American who believes, as I do, in the Constitution and who is willing at any time to fight to preserve it—as I fought to preserve it in Spain." *

After the usual identifying questions, Stripling, whom I had begun to think of as the Southern Accent, got right to the point:

STRIPLING: Are you a member of the Screen Writers' Guild?
NARRATOR: This is the same sort of question that was asked of other witnesses. It involves a question of my associations.
STRIPLING: Do you refuse to answer the question?
NARRATOR: I have not refused to answer the question, but I must answer the question in the only way in which I know how, and

* The direct and sinister connection between the House Un-American Activities Committee and the Franco regime has been demonstrated many times. Two outstanding examples come to mind. Early in 1947, the Committee investigated the Joint Anti-Fascist Refugee Committee, headed by Dr. Edward K. Barsky, and sent its executive board to prison for short terms for contempt. (They had refused to turn over to the Committee lists of their contributors and/or members.) At one of these hearings, which was held in executive session—with no reporters present—the Committee grilled the late Dr. Joseph Auslander, and an account of his testimony appeared within two weeks in Madrid newspapers before any American newspaper had access to it. The second example occurred the week this page was written. The Veterans of the Abraham Lincoln Brigade had been engaged for many years in raising money, food, and clothing for the families of thousands of Franco's political prisoners. Such an appeal appeared in *The New York Times* as a paid advertisement in the spring of 1963. On July 29 of the same year, the Committee had the VALB executive secretary, Moe Fishman, on its griddle. It revealed the fact that it had (pseudonymously) sought from the VALB the names of families to "help" and had then turned those names over to the Franco police for "investigation," who promptly informed the House Un-American Activities Committee that they were all Communists. Any objective reporter—even a *New York Times* man—will swiftly testify that *all* opposition to the Franco regime and its policies is immediately labeled both communistic and criminal, thus permitting the opponent, whether a militant trade unionist or a housewife, to be jailed on two counts—without appeal.

that is that I believe that such a question violates my right of association and is not properly falling—[*ah! those symptoms!*] —I do not believe it falls properly within the scope of this committee's inquiry.

STRIPLING: We will move on to the $64 question, Mr. Bessie. Are you now, or have you ever been, a member of the Communist * Party?

NARRATOR: Mr. Stripling and gentlemen of the Committee, unless it has been changed since yesterday, in our country we have a secret ballot; and I do not believe this committee has any more right to inquire into my political affiliations than I believe an election official has the right to go into the voting booth and examine the ballot which has been marked by the voter. General Eisenhower himself has refused to reveal his political affiliations, and what is good enough for General Eisenhower is good enough for me.

There was considerable laughter, applause—and some booing—at this point, but the printed transcript does not reflect it. This was in 1947; since that time, Eisenhower has made his political affiliations—and opinions—more than amply apparent—though scarcely under duress.

STRIPLING: Mr. Bessie, this committee has officially found that the Communist Party in the United States is not a political party but is, in fact, the agent of a foreign government. I will ask you again: Are you now, or have you ever been, a member of the Communist Party?

NARRATOR: Mr. Stripling, if you did not understand my answer to your question—

STRIPLING: I understood your answer.

NARRATOR: I suggest you have the secretary read it back to you.

STRIPLING: Mr. Bessie, there have been charges made before this committee that you are a Communist. I didn't notice any-

* For some peculiar, no doubt snobbish reason, it annoyed me that neither Stripling, Thomas, nor the majority of the Committee members could ever seem to pronounce this word. They invariably said "Commonist."

where in your statement that you denied that charge. You are now being given an opportunity to deny whether or not you are a member of the Communist Party. You have not answered whether or not you are a member of the Communist Party.*

NARRATOR: In the statement which you were kind enough to permit me to read, I stated I stand on the Bill of Rights on this issue; and I think either the Bill of Rights means something or it doesn't; and if it doesn't mean anything, it is news to me, and I think it would be great news to the majority of the American people.

Stripling then requested Thomas to order the witness to answer the question, and Thomas attempted to clarify matters for the witness, who obviously did not understand the question:

THOMAS: Mr. Bessie, in order to save a lot of time, we would like to know whether you are or have ever been a member of the Communist Party. We would like a very frank answer. You can answer it "yes" or "no"; or if you don't care to answer it, just say so.

NARRATOR: Mr. Thomas, with whatever respect is due this Committee, I now state I have given you my answer to this question. I have not attempted to evade the question. I have given

---

* In the House debate on the question of whether or not the "unfriendly" witnesses were to be cited for contempt, the following remarks were made by Jacob Javits of New York concerning this significant statement by Stripling:

JAVITS: . . . Now it is basic in American justice and in Anglo-Saxon justice that a man must be proved guilty of something before he can be called upon to deny it, and you cannot by implication—by saying, "You did not deny it"—convict the man of something that you are charging against him. . . .

I think the whole functioning and the whole existence of the Committee on Un-American Activities has to be reviewed. . . .

Whereupon Javits announced that he was introducing two resolutions: (1) to dissolve the Committee, since "it is not a committee of the House dealing with legislative matters . . ." and (2) to recommend that a joint House-Senate committee should be formed "to investigate all such situations as those which now are within the jurisdiction" of the House Un-American Activities Committee. The resolutions got nowhere.

you the answer to the question, according to my understanding of what protections are offered the American people, and I object violently to the procedure this Committee engages in, in an attempt to make people state what they think, believe, with whom they associate, whom they go to dinner with, or what have you.

THOMAS: The only part of your answer I can remember is that part about General Eisenhower, and I don't think that is a—

NARRATOR: May I ask if you would have General Eisenhower here and ask him—

STRIPLING: Just a minute.

THOMAS: Just a minute.

NARRATOR: —ask him whether he is a member of the Republican or Democratic Party?

THOMAS: I don't think that was a responsive answer to the question. What we are attempting to do—what this Committee of Congress is attempting to do—is to ascertain the extent of Communist infiltration in the moving-picture industry.

NARRATOR: I don't believe that that is what the Committee is trying to do.

THOMAS: Just a minute—

NARRATOR: I believe what this Committee is trying to do—

(Thomas pounds gavel.)

NARRATOR: —is to do exactly the same thing—

THOMAS: I am telling you what the Committee is trying to do. We know exactly what the Committee is trying to do.

NARRATOR: I have my own opinion of it.

THOMAS: That is all right; you can have any opinion you want.

NARRATOR: Thank you.

THOMAS: The Committee would like to know whether you have ever been a member of the Communist Party or whether you are a member of the Communist Party now?

NARRATOR: I have given you several answers to that question, and that is the best I can do for you, Mr. Chairman.

THOMAS: Then do you—

NARRATOR: Because I believe you are violating my rights as an American citizen.

THOMAS: So you refuse?

NARRATOR: I am not refusing. I have told you that is the answer I have given you. The answer is now recorded several times. I don't believe you have the right to ask this question of anybody.

THOMAS: It is very apparent that you are following the same line of these other witnesses.

NARRATOR: I am following no line—

THOMAS: Which is definitely the Communist line.

NARRATOR: —I am using my own head, which I am privileged to do.

THOMAS: You are excused. If you want to make a speech, go out there under a big tree.

NARRATOR: Thank you.

The printed transcript reads "Laughter" at this point, which does not jibe with my total recollection, because the next line reads: "CHAIRMAN (pounding gavel): May we have order, please?" and if there had been laughter at my expense, I doubt that the Chairman would have called for order.

In any event I was accorded the privilege of only five and a half printed pages of dossier, which can only mean one of two things: either the Committee's investigators were not as diligent in researching my history as they had been with the three previous witnesses or I was only (roughly) half as subversive as Lawson, Trumbo, or Maltz.

But some of the items in that dossier continue to fascinate me to this day. They include:

Item: "The *People's World* of October 11, 1939, which is the official Communist organ of the West Coast of the United States, devotes an article in praise of the writings of Alvah Bessie. . . ." (*Comment*: There *is* no official Communist organ on the West Coast, and the *People's World* has also praised the writings of Mark Twain, John Steinbeck, Maxim Gorky, Romain Rolland, William Shakespeare, and the authors of the Old Testament, which puts me in pretty good company.)

Item: "The *People's World* of November 10, 1942, lists Alvah

Bessie as the coauthor of a pamphlet issued by the International Workers Order in connection with its frontline fighters' campaign." (*Comment:* This was a pamphlet entitled "This Is Your Enemy" and had no other author than myself. It detailed Nazi atrocities on the Soviet front and was sent by the IWO to every head of state in the Allied world and to nearly every so-called opinion-maker in the U.S.A. My files contain letters praising the pamphlet from such dignitaries as Ambassador Litvinov's secretary; the private secretary of British Minister of Labour Ernest Bevin; Lord Halifax's secretary; the secretaries of the Australian ambassador, the Polish ambassador; the Netherlands ambassador (himself, for a change); the Belgian, Canadian, and Nicaraguan ambassadors; the secretary (a colonel) of the Chief of Staff, War Department, U.S.A.; the secretary to Jan Masaryk, Czech ambassador; Grace Tully, FDR's secretary; Admiral E. J. King, commander in chief, U.S. Navy; and—though this probably should not be mentioned—the commander in chief of something called the 18th Group Army, then operating out of Yenan, Shensi, China, who wrote quite a long typewritten letter on excellent rice paper and in excellent English—by name, Chu Teh.)

Item: "Alvah Bessie was also sponsor of the organization known as the Artists' Front to Win the War. . . ." (*No comment.*)

Item: "Alvah Bessie . . . made an eloquent plea for money, stating . . . that a $60,000 hospital was to be built in Mexico and that the money was to be used to take care of Loyalists wherever they might be. During the taking of the collection, Bessie took off his necktie and said he would auction it off to the highest bidder. He stated that the tie had a history, that when he was in Spain . . . he had purchased the tie at Barcelona. . . ." (*Comment:* He did, at a shop called *L'Adam.* It brought $100 and was then redonated and brought another $50 and was then returned to him—as a present.)

Item: "On December 16, 1945, a 'welcome home, Joe' dinner was given as a 'tribute to America's young fighting men and women on the occasion of the second anniversary of American Youth for Democracy.' This organization was formerly known as the Young Communist League. . . . Alvah Bessie's name appeared on the program, along with the names of John Howard Lawson and Paul Robeson. . . ." (*Comment:* Both Lawson and Robeson spoke, together with Major General Evans Carlson of the U.S. Marine Corps, and Ingrid Bergman, all of whom sat at the speakers' table, together with the consuls of all the Allied nations in Los Angeles at the time. Said Carlson to Bessie after Robeson's speech, "I wish I could make a speech like Paul's." Bessie, scarcely original, said, "You will, General, you will." Carlson said, "Not as long as I'm wearing this uniform, I won't.")

Item: "Alvah Bessie, writer, New York, N.Y., appeared on a list captioned 'I hereby join in signing the January, 1943, "Message to the House of Representatives" opposing renewal of the Dies Committee.'" (*No comment.*)

There was one extremely damaging item that the Committee's investigators overlooked, but it was picked up for them by Jack Moffitt, screenwriter and *Esquire* movie critic, who had testified a few days earlier and had done a considerable amount of independent research himself. This was the same fellow whose office in the writers' building at Warner Brothers, when I was in residence, had been redecorated at his own expense with Chinese furniture lacquered in black, gold, and red. There were also at least fifteen drawings, sketches, caricatures, and photographs on the walls—of Jack Moffitt.

It seems that the *Hollywood Citizen-News* had covered a meeting of putative writers at which I spoke, and Moffitt read from the newspaper: "The principal talk was given by Alvah Bessie, veteran screenwriter, who was introduced as a hero of the Spanish Civil War, in which he served with the International Brigades. Bessie assured the writers that 'there are never two sides to any question.'"

(*Comment:* He didn't. He said there are never two sides to any really *important* question. There is a difference.)

DISSOLVE TO

BEVERLY HILLS. November, 1947, *et seq.*
The nineteen "unfriendly" witnesses returned to Los Angeles as heroes to the radical, liberal, or merely decent citizens of that

two-hundred-square-mile small town, if caviar (red, of course) to the general. A mass meeting was held in a stadium that was only about half-full (which was disappointing, although there were several thousand people present), and the "unfriendly," made individual entrances across an empty football-baseball field as their names were called (which was embarrassing).

My wife had a present for me from one of my most intimate friends, the fine actor Lee J. Cobb: a kosher salami and a bottle of Courvoisier, which have always been among my favorite comestibles and potables. I had known Lee in New York, had met him in a sort of reverse-English way: I had reviewed his performance as Max, the German Communist, in Hemingway's only play, *The Fifth Column* (1940), and said in *New Masses:* "With such material into which to get his teeth, and with his own great gifts, young Mr. Cobb was able to achieve a performance that is pure, stunning, dignified, and heartbreaking. For this truly creative piece of work *alone,* plus what is left of an intended pro-Loyalist, pro-democratic, anti-Fascist play, you should spend your money. . . ."

To my astonishment, a critic received a fan letter from an actor, who said, in effect, that he would like to meet me because I was the only critic who had ever properly evaluated what he was trying to do. Call it a mutual-admiration society if you will, but our friendship continued in Hollywood, and Lee became one of my latter-day heroes; for until ten years ago, I always had to have a hero of some sort or other, as well as several heroines, both contemporary and historical.

Lee not only was one of the finest actors in America but was also an excellent pilot, with commercial, instrument, and instructor's ratings, and once he had even permitted me to fly his Beechcraft Bonanza part of the way from Los Angeles through Cajon Pass to Barstow, where we visited my ex-chorusman-pilot friend, Paul Pierce, who operated the field there. (He would not let me land the thing.)

The way he got the Bonanza—according to his story—represents a case history in the mores of Hollywood. He had wanted to buy one when they were first manufactured, right after the war, and we had gone out to Lockheed Air Terminal together and taken a demonstration ride (piloted by a girl salesman). There was one small problem: the plane was priced at $7,000 at the time, and Lee did not have that much money. He did, however, put a small down payment on one, and by the time it was ready for delivery, almost a year later, he still did not have the money to spare. But luck or chance (plus his own talents and the corruption of The Industry) brought him this particular bonanza, which cost him little more than the down payment and a one-way plane ticket to Wichita to pick up his ship at the factory. The story, as he told it to me, is offered here as instructive advice to the acquisitive.

Lee's studio had no assignment for him the week word came that he could take delivery on the aircraft. He learned, however, that another studio did want him, so he had his agent tell the second studio that, having read the proffered script, he did not care to do the job. This immediately whetted the studio's appetite, and it replied, in effect, that it would rather have Lee, who did *not* want to play the role, than any other actor in the land who did.

"Sorry," said the agent, "not interested."

"But," said the studio, "there must be something he would like to have—a new car, perhaps?"

"No," said the agent, "he has a new car."

"An extra five grand under the table?" asked the studio.

"Sorry," said the agent, "no deal."

"*But*," said the baffled studio, "there must be *something* he wants." (This is another way of saying that "every man has his price.")

"As a matter of fact," said the agent, "there is. He wants an airplane."

"How much?" said the studio.

"Seven grand."

"Well," said the studio, "all right."

"Another thing," said the agent, "he wants the plane as a present—and licensed in the studio's name so he doesn't have to pay any tax on it."

"Well," said the studio, "we'll have to think about that."

Later, the studio called back and said, "Our lawyers tell us that it would look rather peculiar for us to give the man a present before he has even played the role, so the best we can do is to give him a check for the seven grand, and he'll have to pay the tax. Sorry."

Lee's acting and flying talents, however, were not the only attributes to qualify him as one of my contemporary heroes. He was also a dedicated Socialist—or so he seemed to me—and he not only displayed what seemed to be a profound understanding of Marxist philosophy, but also combined theory and practice in the way that it has to be combined: he had guts. He had the guts—during that difficult period—to accept a layoff from his studio rather than play a leading role in one of the first frankly anti-Soviet films Hollywood made in slavish response to the un-American Committee's "suggestion" that it was about time it made some.

What is more, when he was called into the office of the studio's executive producer, he told him why he would not play the role and suggested that they cancel his contract on the spot. "I could no more play such a role [a brutish and sadistic Soviet Army officer] than I could be an anti-Semite," said Lee, "and I'm a Jew. What's more, I consider the script un-American, fascistic, and dangerous to the peace and well-being of my fellow Americans."

"Okay," said the executive producer, "forget it." And they found another role for Lee and took him off suspension.

There was a lot of courage displayed in the days immediately following the inquisition, which had come to a grinding halt in the face of mounting national opposition and ridicule, with only eleven of the nineteen subpoenaed witnesses "investigated." That was just before the producers, whom Eric Johnston swore would never institute a blacklist, were called into the Waldorf-Astoria Hotel in New York by the boys who really run The Industry (the financiers) and were told where to head in.

The delegation from the Committee for the First Amendment had broadcast two one-hour radio surveys (on October 26 and November 2), which were produced by Norman Corwin and had national hookups and featured live statements from more than sixty top stars, directors, producers, and writers in the motion-picture industry (and out of it).* Typical of these statements was one by Thomas Mann, who said:

"I have the honor to expose myself as a hostile witness.

"I testify that I am very much interested in the moving-picture industry and that, since my arrival in the United States nine years ago, I've seen a great many Hollywood films. If Communist propaganda had been smuggled into any of them, it must have been most thoroughly hidden. I, for one, never noticed anything of the sort.

"I testify, moreover, that to my mind the ignorant and super-stitious persecution of the believers in a political and economic doctrine which is, after all, the creation of great minds and great thinkers—I testify that this persecution is not only degrading for the persecutors themselves but also very harmful to the cultural reputation of this country.

"As an American citizen of German birth, I finally testify that I am painfully familiar with certain political trends. Spiritual in-tolerance, political inquisitions, and declining legal security, and all this in the name of an alleged 'state of emergency' . . . that is how it started in Germany. What followed was fascism, and what followed fascism was war."

On October 29, twenty-eight members of the Committee for the First Amendment presented a petition to Congress "for re-dress of our grievances." It was a courageous declaration of prin-ciples (and facts), but it laid an egg on the Hill, and one of its

* Under the title "Hollywood Fights Back," the program presented the following personalities, who spoke their piece: Charles Boyer, Judy Garland, Lauren Bacall, Joseph Cotton, James Gleason, June Havoc, Peter Lorre, John Huston, Danny Kaye, Walter Wanger, Melvyn Douglas, Burt Lan-caster, Paul Henreid, William Holden, Robert Ryan, Robert Young, Margaret Sullavan, Van Heflin, Humphrey Bogart, Edward G. Robinson, Paulette Goddard, Lucille Ball, William Wyler, Fredric March, John Garfield, Frank Sinatra, Deems Taylor, Harlow Shapley, Artie Shaw, Arthur Garfield Hays, Archibald MacLeish, Vincent Price, Rita Hayworth, Senators Albert Thomas, Harvey Kilgore, Claude Pepper, and Glen Taylor, Myrna Loy, Douglas Fair-banks, Jr., Groucho Marx, Keenan Wynn, Jane Wyatt, Thurman Arnold, Governor Lehman of New York, Leland Stowe, George S. Kaufman, Moss Hart, Richard Rogers, Leonard Bernstein, and many others.

principal signers, Humphrey Bogart, almost immediately repudiated it, accused himself of being a dupe (and a dope), and—by this action (which was obviously the result of having the screws put to him by the producers)—provoked a panic that rapidly destroyed the Committee for the First Amendment itself.*

On November 20, Spyros Skouras, president of 20th Century-Fox, made public a resolution of his board of directors promising "to dispense with the services of any acknowledged Communist or of any employee who refuses to answer a question with respect thereto by any committee of the Congress of the United States and is cited for contempt by reason thereof." (Ring Lardner, Jr., was the only member of "The Ten" then employed there.)

On November 24, a secret meeting of Eric Johnston's organization, the Motion Picture Association of America, was held in the Waldorf-Astoria Hotel. By some odd coincidence, that same day J. Parnell Thomas won citations for contempt of Congress from the House of Representatives of all ten "unfriendly" witnesses, with one hour of debate on this basic constitutional issue allowed. Typical of the voting was that citing Albert Maltz: 346 "yeas" to 17 "nays" ** ("not voting," 68; "present," 1).

The next day, the MPAA issued a statement in behalf of all the major studios that read in part: "We will forthwith discharge or suspend without compensation those [of the ten Hollywood men] in our employ, and we will not re-employ any of the ten until such time as he is acquitted, or has purged himself of contempt, and declared under oath that he is not a Communist. . . ."

Then, in a contemptible and ludicrous attempt to put a better face on the first open blacklist ever drawn up by an American

* The original list of five hundred is, today, still a touchstone of decency—and cowardice. Some, like Bogart, were quickly intimidated and issued public retractions; many were later investigated themselves and were "proved" to be authentic witches; some had at one time or another been sympathetic to radical ideas but—upon investigation—"cleared" themselves; a few became outright stool pigeons; some were blacklisted; most were ultimately silenced; a few are still, if discreetly, active in promoting democratic causes; one—hounded by the investigators—died of a heart attack: Canada Lee.

** These seventeen Congressmen deserve to be remembered. Their names: Bakewell, Blatnik, Bloom, Carroll, Celler, Douglas, Eberharter, Havenner, Holifield, Huber, Karsten, Klein, Marcantonio, Morgan, Pfeifer, Powell, and Sadowsky.

industry, the producers added: "We are frank to recognize that such a policy involves dangers and risks. There is the danger of creating an atmosphere of fear. Creative work at its best cannot be carried on in an atmosphere of fear. To this end we will invite the Hollywood talent guilds to work with us to eliminate any subversives, to protect the innocent, and to safeguard free speech and a free screen wherever threatened. . . .

"Nothing subversive or un-American has appeared on the screen. . . ." *

It was no surprise to read on this document the signatures of such dignitaries as Eric Johnston, James F. Byrnes and Paul V. McNutt (counsels for the producers), Barney Balaban, Nicholas Schenck, Harry Cohn, Joe Schenck, Walter Wanger (despite his appearance on the Committee for the First Amendment's broadcasts), Samuel Goldwyn, Y. Frank Freeman, Albert Warner, Spyros Skouras, Louis B. Mayer, and William Goetz.

But there was one other signature—that of a producer who had been a witness before the Committee and had staunchly defended his right to employ any writer, actor, director, or composer, irrespective of his political opinions—Dore Schary of RKO. His name was also on a telegram, two days later (November 27), to the Screen Writers' Guild, whose board of directors (on the very day that the citations were passed in Congress) had voted to resist the impending blacklist and support the Sabath Bill then before Congress, which called for the abolition of the Committee. This telegram (which was also addressed to the Screen Actors' and Screen Directors' Guilds) urged them to meet with the producers: "We seek to acquaint you with the intent of the producers' statement and to reassure you that our action is designed to protect the industry and all those engaged in it and to disavow any intention of a witch-hunt."

* On this capitulation to the House Un-American Activities Committee, which had been discredited before the entire nation by a barrage of newspaper criticism ranging from mild to venomous, Bosley Crowther, film critic for *The New York Times*, had this to say (December 7, 1947): "It should be fully realized that this action was engineered by the major New York executives, the industry's overlords, and not by the 'Hollywood producers,' who form a different and subordinate group."

One day later, RKO fired Adrian Scott, producer, and Edward Dmytryk, director, of *Crossfire;* two days later, 2oth Century-Fox fired Lardner; on December 1, Lester Cole, writer-producer, and Dalton Trumbo were "suspended" without pay by MGM—that is, fired. The other five, Bessie, Biberman, Lawson, Maltz, and Ornitz, were not under contract at the time, so there was no need to fire them.

Dore Schary appeared before a full-membership meeting of the Screen Writers' Guild, of which he had once been a member. Before the Committee, he had said, "Up until the time it is proved that a Communist is a man dedicated to the overthrow of the government by force and violence, or by any illegal methods, I cannot make a determination of his employment on any other basis except whether he is qualified best to do the job I want him to do."

(Schary was on safe ground, for no court of competent jurisdiction has ever found that a Communist is so dedicated, no Communist has ever been so charged, let alone convicted, and the only convictions of Communists won by the U.S. Department of Justice under the Smith Act—in the total absence of the sort of evidence so many people take for granted as existing—had to rely on "*conspiracy* [my emphasis] to teach and advocate" the overthrow, etc. Not even "teach and advocate," at that.)

Accompanied to the guild meeting by producer Walter Wanger and executive E. J. Mannix (neither of whom said a word), Schary attempted to sell the guild on the Waldorf-Astoria manifesto. He said that he had not agreed with the decision of the New York meeting. He left the impression that the producers hated, loathed, and contemned the House Committee and were terribly sorry that they had to fire anybody for any reason whatsoever— especially such honest, talented people. But despite the opposition of Schary and "other producers," a "unanimous" decision had been reached by the assembled executives—to do exactly what the Committee had asked them to do.

The proposed program of the producers, which Schary wanted the writers to support, had three parts. First, the producers would fire and blacklist the ten witnesses. "We do not ask you to condone this," he said. Secondly, the producers would not hire anyone *believed* to be a Communist. "We do not ask you to condone this," he repeated. The third plank called for a vast industry public-relations campaign (which eventually gave birth to that brilliant slogan "Movies Are Better Than Ever"), a campaign to restore and refurbish the good name of Hollywood by convincing the public that the first two points were justified. This, said Schary, he was confident the writers would condone *and* support.

As this unholy trio left the hall, each paused at a chair in the front row and touched Dalton Trumbo on the shoulder in an amiable gesture.

Trumbo's fighting, delightfully obscene extemporaneous speech, following their exit, cannot, unfortunately, be recorded here, but I would give almost anything to own a tape of it. And the members of the guild were so impressed by Schary's implied assurances that if they would only accept ten martyrs, no one else would ever be hurt that more than four hundred men and women voted (with eight dissenting voices) to reaffirm their demand for an end to the blacklist, which had not only engulfed "The Ten," but already included all the other witnesses who had *not* testified, as well as a "gray list" of more than a hundred others who had merely been "named" by the friendly witnesses.*

At small private meetings throughout the area, any number of people had sagely informed us that, "What the hell! A contempt citation doesn't mean the attorney general will ask for an indictment. The Department of Justice surely has more sense than to truckle to those troglodytes on the Committee. The whole thing is patently absurd!" But on December 5, 1947—less than two months after the hearings ended—a grand jury in Washington indicted "The Ten" for contempt of Congress, and though this may have come as a shock to the community at large, we had

---

* On December 4, Dore Schary received a "Humanitarian Award" for being executive producer of the film *Crossfire*. (Adrian Scott was its actual producer.) Schary did not appear to accept the award; Eric Johnston accepted it for him and stated blandly that "job boycott is a cancer in the economic body of the nation" that "drags down the whole economic level." In a sort of *Alice in Wonderland* remark that was equaled only by the action of the Supreme Court in 1950, Johnston added that the motion-picture industry "knows no such thing as discrimination. . . . In Hollywood it's ability that counts."

half-expected it, while hoping quixotically that a grand jury composed largely of government employees (themselves subject to
a "loyalty check") would rise above their personal situations and
toss the whole thing out.

My wife and child and I were still eating regularly (on what
was left of our savings) at the time, but that situation rapidly
changed. On December 10, "The Ten" "surrendered" to the U.S.
marshal in downtown Los Angeles, and in a display of gentle-
manly courtesy that certainly has few counterparts in the gaudy
annals of crime, we were booked and fingerprinted (but not
mugged) and released on $1,000 bail each, supplied by an ac-
commodating bondsman.

Our attorneys therefore took it for granted that since we had
been booked in Los Angeles, the government would allow us to be
arraigned and plead to the indictments in our hometown. The
attorneys were wrong, for the government took the logical position that since our crime had been committed in the District of
Columbia, we would have to return to the scene of the crime for
subsequent formalities.

On the night of January 11, 1948, we all took off for Washington again, appeared in court the next morning, were arraigned,
pleaded not guilty, and caught the next plane home, at a total
cost of X thousands of dollars and fifty thousand miles of travel
at our own expense. (The X refers to the cost of round-trip cross-
country flights made in 1947 for the investigation, in 1948 for the
arraignment, in 1948—again—to waive trial by jury, and in 1950
for actual trial and imprisonment.)

But the month of the indictment, "The Ten" began to strike
back—in the form of several lawsuits: the first was filed by Dalton Trumbo against MGM and demanded reinstatement and
damages; other suits were filed by Lardner, Cole, Dmytryk, and
Scott against their respective studios; and on March 2, 1948, we
filed a collective suit against all the studios for damages resulting
from the blacklist.

During the litigation one of our attorneys, Charles J. Katz,
made a valiant effort to get Jack Warner to indicate those screenplays in which I had attempted to inject ideas which Warner had

deleted and for which he had fired me. Mr. Warner's deposition was taken in my presence, and I had the dubious pleasure of watching a "privileged" congressional witness squirm when he was caught out in the open.[*]

Q.: What that was written by Alvah Bessie, whose name you mentioned in that context, did you ever remove because you felt it to be un-American by any standard?

A.: I would have to look to see what scripts and pictures he had worked on.

Q.: Prior to the time that you testified in May, 1947, had you actually made an examination of the scripts of Alvah Bessie to determine what you had deleted therefrom?

A.: I not only made—I made mostly the examination of the scripts sometimes and many times what we call the assembled film.

Q.: Is it your statement under oath at this time that you have, in fact, removed anything written by Alvah Bessie from either a screenplay or from a daily—

A. (interrupting):—film itself.

Q. (continuing):—film itself?

A: Yes.

Q.: Because you decided or considered that content to be un-American?

A.: Yes, that is the reason. I personally— Yes, I removed things that I considered—

Q. (interrupting): Things that were written by Alvah Bessie?

A.: I did, yes, sir.

Q.: You are sure of that?

A.: If I said it, I undoubtedly—two years back. . . .

Later in the testimony, Warner was asked:

Q.: Then it was Alvah Bessie whose lines or whose scenes you removed because you considered them to be such as to make

[*] In the Superior Court of the State of California, in and for the County of Los Angeles. Deposition of J. L. Warner, taken on behalf of the plaintiffs, April 21, 1949, at 4000 West Olive Avenue, Burbank, California, pursuant to notice.

Mr. Bessie unworthy of employment at Warner Brothers because of the content of his writing? Is it Bessie to whom you refer?

A.: Yes. I think the testimony given here and in Washington—Here is the name of the picture, *The Very Thought of You.* That is correct.

Q.: Then you will, sir, insert in the deposition that portion of the material written by Mr. Bessie in the picture *The Very Thought of You* which you deleted because you considered it to be subversive or un-American or harmful in some way to the motion-picture industry? You will do that, will you?

A.: Not exactly harmful to the motion-picture industry and all that but harmful to the American public.

Q.: Well?

A. (interrupting): Yes, I will be glad to do that. I said I would.

Of course, he has neither inserted in the deposition nor cited "that portion" at any time since, any more than he fired me in 1943, for he kept me on contract for another year and a half, raising my salary at regular intervals and even rewriting the contract at one point to provide more money than it originally called for, because my agent told him I was "unhappy."

The damages demanded in this collective suit amounted to many millions of dollars.* But this bonanza, if it were ever to be realized, would take years of delay and litigation, and in the meantime, my personal savings were melting in the Southern California winter sun and the bills mounted by the week.

Then, to my relative astonishment, help (or so it seemed) came from an unlikely quarter. For though the "Hollywood big shots," as J. Parnell Thomas put it in an interview with the Associated Press, "were pretty high and mighty at first . . . they got off their high horses, all right"—and promptly instituted the blacklist—my little producer Hal proved that his word was

* In all, suits demanding some $47,000,000 on behalf of "The Ten" were filed against the studios for breach of contract, conspiracy to blacklist, and damages for loss of employment. In January, 1952, four of the "majors" (MGM, Universal, Columbia, and Warners) made out-of-court settlements to the sum of $107,500.

as good as his bond. He refused to be intimidated by the Waldorf-Astoria manifesto; he produced a job for me. In fact, he produced three of them during 1948.

He expressed his hatred of the Committee, his contempt for the cowardice of the "majors," his admiration for "The Ten"—and then he said, "Of course, I can't pay you $600 a week."

"Why not?"

"Well, I—"

He never produced a satisfactory answer to this simple question, but he did produce fragments of several answers, all having to do with the fact that now he would be hiring me *sub rosa;* that he would have to be extremely careful; that he was getting married and would have a wife to support; that if his studio found out he was hiring me, he would be fired too; that he had to set up a "cover" or series of covers for the jobs I would do for him—all of which seemed reasonably reasonable, if scarcely cogent. (The "covers" would also have to get a cut of the fee to compensate them for the additional taxes they would, presumably, have to pay.)

The first job didn't come through until July; it involved "polishing" a screenplay and lasted one and a half weeks at $500 a week. The second job, a brand-new screenplay, involved a "flat deal" of $750 for four weeks' work—or a reduction in pay from my "established" salary of $600 to $187. The third job, which he had told me was a little "brushup" of a screenplay that would take only five days' work, turned out to be far more interesting, for the moment I read this chef d'oeuvre I discovered that it did not even have a story.

When I called this to Hal's attention, he said, "Yeah, it needs a little work." It needed a story and a new screenplay, from scratch, for which I had foolishly agreed to a flat deal of $400 and which I therefore completed in the five days allotted me. (He had a shooting date.)

Events around the *cause célèbre* moved fairly rapidly after that. John Howard Lawson went to trial in Washington on April 14 and was convicted five days later. Trumbo went to trial on April 26 and was found guilty on May 5. The two juries, composed mainly of government employees, showed no more courage or independence than the grand jury that had indicted us and did not seem to be the least perturbed by the fact that virtually all pertinent evidence was excluded by the court—and in Lawson's case, the jury itself was excluded from all but two hours of argument and testimony! Witnesses who came from all over the country at the expense of "The Ten" were not permitted to testify on the issues for which they had been subpoenaed; agreement was reached between prosecution and defense, with the permission of the court, to hold the other eight trials in abeyance pending the Lawson-Trumbo appeals.

Between November, 1948, and June, 1950, when the Supreme Court's refusal to review the case upheld the convictions of Lawson and Trumbo—and brought the rest of us to trial and instant conviction—I managed to earn $4,200, which was scarcely enough to support three people and contribute to the support of two children by my previous marriage.

I started to compile an anthology about the Spanish Civil War and outlined two novels, one to be called *The Summer Soldier* and one to be called *The Winter Soldier,* but the money I earned came from unexpected sources: I got $1,000 for writing—under an assumed name—a treatment of one of Jack London's less interesting novels, for an independent producer. He had offered the job to one of the other blacklisted men, who didn't care to take it on but guaranteed that he would personally supervise my handling of the story. The film was never made. Another job, for another $1,000, came through a writer—still not blacklisted—who had excellent connections with an independent and was working on a script for him. He induced the producer to give me a job, too, and he even suggested a story—an original idea he had found in an old guidebook of California—for I did not seem to have an original idea in my head.*

---

* This story was sold for $5,000 a few months before we went to prison, through a typical black-market operation: another writer put his name on it; my agent took it to still another writer who had an "in" with a minor independent; the second writer pitched it to the producer; the agent came in to close the deal. The $5,000 was split as follows: $1,000 to the original independent, who had commissioned it but didn't want to make it; $500 to the agent; $300 to the writer whose name was on it; the balance to pay bills that had accumulated. The film was made while we were in prison.

I was so barren of ideas that I spent hours sitting at the window of the duplex apartment on South Crescent Drive in Beverly Hills that we rented from Edward Dmytryk and staring at the few people who walked up and down the street. The novel outlines, submitted to a publisher in the East, came back with comment to the effect that it was a good idea—an important idea—but that the publisher would have to see at least a hundred pages (and an outline of the balance) before he could advance any money.

I knew that I could not write a hundred pages of a novel at that time; I doubted that I could even write ten. How could a man concentrate on a major piece of work when the future was not only uncertain but (to his mind at least) impossible?

Across the street, there lived a friend who was a psychoanalyst with whom we occasionally had dinner, and one night I decided to tell him about my dream:

I had dreamed that I was in New York with my wife, in a hotel room where there was a meeting of the Central Committee of the Communist Party (no less), not one of whose members I had ever met in my life, if you except that brief encounter on the *Santa Fe Chief* with Earl Browder, its former general secretary.

Two of these gentlemen took me aside—suddenly it seemed to be a cocktail party, not a meeting—and told me confidentially that my wife was having a love affair with an FBI agent.

Looking at her over their shoulders, I could see that she was gay and chatting brightly with some of the other guests and seemed to have a clear conscience (as though anyone could tell).

Appalled, I said, "Are you *sure*?"

Sadly, they said, "We're sure," and had the good grace to add, "We're sorry."

In the dream, I remember saying grimly to myself, "I'll have to divorce her." (In spite of our eventual separation and divorce, there was no pleasurable feeling associated with this decision.)

"*Don't* tell me your dream," our psychoanalyst friend said. "This is a family dinner." He indicated his wife and children, my wife and daughter.

But I persisted—when I got him alone later—and when I had told him the dream, he said, "Who's the FBI man in your life?"

"Huh?"

"The man who watched you and approved—or, more likely, disapproved—of you?"

"Who?"

"The man who slept with your mother," he replied. "Your father. You told me once before that you never got along with him."

I recall using—or, more likely, wanting to use—a four-letter expletive in reply, but instead I decided then and there that if this doctor, who was a Freudian and said he was also a Marxist, could come up with an interpretation like that, then psychoanalysis was really for the birds.

My wife, Helen Clare, who was *really* perceptive, dismissed the doctor's remark and said simply, "It's a wish-fulfillment dream." I pondered this statement, and although I never told her so, I was inclined to agree with her.

The pressures on the marriage were enormous. There was never enough money, and there did not seem any likelihood of any coming in. We were strapped and bound to Hollywood, at least until the case had been resolved, and it was my personal conviction that we would all wind up in prison anyhow. There was therefore a persistent sensation of being engulfed in molasses, of doing no more than treading viscidly, just to keep my nose in the air.

But if the dream vanished temporarily from my conscious mind, the depression did not. During the investigation itself, my wife had written a brilliant satirical article, titled "The Case of the Contemptuous Wife," which was immediately snapped up by a radical magazine called *Mainstream* and almost as swiftly published in Paris in translation.

It had found its springboard in an intercepted telephone conversation (we were on a party line with the lady downstairs), when Helen Clare picked up the phone to make a call and overheard our neighbor talking to an FBI man and informing him—as though he needed such information—that she lived right underneath "that Hollywood writer who is being investigated in Washington right now." If the FBI man was baffled by the call, he must have been utterly confounded when my wife broke into the conversation and tried to explain to the man what our neighbor was struggling to tell him.

The article detailed, in a lighthearted and light-handed manner, what had happened to Helen Clare during the two weeks that we were in Washington: how not only the woman downstairs but people in the neighborhood with whom we'd been friendly for more than a year had cut her dead on the street or made idiotic comments when she and Eva went for their daily walk; how only one child on the block was permitted to play with our four-year-old, whereas she had formerly been welcome in every home between Olympic and Wilshire Boulevards.

There is no doubt in my mind that I was jealous of that article, the ease with which it seemed to have been written, the scintillating wit of which I have never been capable, its ready acceptance by the same magazine that had turned down an article that I had been *asked*—by its editor—to write.

What I interpreted as jealousy—in reverse—also appeared in my wife, who accused me of having an affair with a handsome young woman we had met at a party. I had not had an affair with her, but I had wanted to (" . . . whosoever looketh on a woman to lust after her hath committed adultery with her already in his heart"), and the situation was not alleviated when this young lady, who was fairly well to do, gave us a turkey for Thanksgiving and was instrumental in getting us a loan in the bargain.

So after watching me sitting at the window for three weeks, my wife suggested that I see a psychiatrist. And though I resisted the idea (certainly I flatly refused to consult our friend across the street), the time came when I could not seem to cope with the enormity of our problems, and I finally did make an appointment with a highly recommended man (who was also guaranteed to be a Marxist with no Freudian nonsense about him) and spent fifty minutes spilling my guts, to all of which he made no reply except, "Um."

Then he informed me that he would like me to start writing my autobiography: "Writers work better that way," he said, and he said that he would refer me to another man, as he was too busy to take me on.

"Obviously," he said solemnly, "you need deep analysis, and it may take several years."

For some reason or other, I temporarily accepted this prognosis and started the next day to write my autobiography from scratch (*and* the age of one). I worked furiously on it for five days, until I became so disgusted with myself that I refused to go any further.

The recommended man, I found out (about two years later), had worked with a great many Hollywood writers and actors, and it was a matter of some astonishment to discover that at least six of his patients turned up at subsequent investigations of The Industry (in 1950 and 1951)—and every one of them was a stool pigeon. It also appeared that the man was not a psychiatrist at all; he was not even a psychologist—but apparently he *was* an FBI man (if not the one who had slept with my mother).

In all justice, however, it must be said that the task that the so-called Marxist psychiatrist set me to must have acted as a form of self-therapy that lasted several years, for the depression disappeared and my ability to work returned. But it did not solve the economic problem that was, together with the domestic, at the root of my depression. This problem was never adequately solved, but stabs were made at it—first in attempts to find work and finally, in desperation, through borrowing money.

An idea occurred to me that seemed positively inspired. It involved the producer of *Northern Pursuit*, Jack, who had left Warner Brothers and, according to the trade papers, had set himself up as a producer of commercial and television films on La Cienega Boulevard. His voice echoed in my memory: "We'll make pictures together from now on in. We'll go around the world together making pictures. You want to go to Russia? I'll go *with* you."

With my heart in my throat, I looked up his number, called, asked for him, and got him immediately. I told him that I would like to see him and was agreeably surprised to hear him say, "Come right over."

DISSOLVE TO

INTERIOR. JACK'S OFFICE

—an unpretentious but successful-looking place overlooking the swanky steak houses of La Cienega Boulevard. NARRATOR looks in vain for the autographed photograph of Henry Wallace that he associates with Jack, then thinks, Of course, it's at home over his desk. He has just told his former producer what a desperate plight he and his family are in, and he has asked for work. JACK rarely sits during this scene, but PACES BACK AND FORTH, swinging the gold key chain that spells J-A-C-K and his last name.

JACK

I wish I could do something for you, but I can't.

NARRATOR

(presuming on their old friendship)

Why not?

JACK

Because I've got a wife and family to support myself, and if it got out that I'd hired you, I'd be finished.

NARRATOR

Who would know?

There is a long PAUSE, as JACK STOPS pacing, TURNS TO NARRATOR.

JACK

Besides, I don't approve of the position you took in Washington.

NARRATOR

What's that got to do with it? I'm a good writer; I can do a job for you; nobody needs to know about it—and I'll work cheap.

(Jack shakes head)

Look, man, it's going to be a question of eating pretty soon.

JACK

You should have thought of that before you got messed up in all this stuff.

[236]

NARRATOR is amazed. This is his old pal Jack talking. JACK notices his astonishment, now TURNS, SPEAKS vehemently.

JACK

Look, I know you. I'm a good friend of J. Edgar Hoover. I've got so much confidence in you that if you want me to, I'll call him up right now and say, "Look, Edgar, this is a friend of mine. He may have some screwy ideas, but I *know* he's not a traitor to his country, I'll vouch for him and I'm asking you to go easy on him."

NARRATOR

Save your nickel.

NARRATOR GETS UP, STARTS toward door of office.

JACK

(stung)

What's more, I wouldn't give you a job even if I could!

(Narrator turns to stare)

I make commercial films promoting the American way of life—capitalism, if you please. Would you write *that* kind of film?

NARRATOR

(hot)

You pay me to write a film showing what marvelous technical processes are involved in making whatever the hell it is you're promoting and I'd be delighted. Who do you work for, anyhow?

JACK

DuPont, among others.

NARRATOR

Shame on you!

JACK

(amazed)

Why shame on me?

NARRATOR

You're a Jew too, aren't you?

JACK

Of course.

DuPont has subsidized some of the most vicious anti-Semitic outfits in the country. You *like* that?

JACK

I don't believe you.

NARRATOR

I'll bring you the documentation tomorrow—from the Black Committee of the Senate.

JACK

Don't bother. I *know* a couple of the DuPonts, and finer gentlemen you'll never meet. I've never seen any signs of anti-Semitism in *any* of them.

NARRATOR

You wouldn't. You're making money for them. You're one of their *white* Jews.

NARRATOR PUTS HAND on door knob, and JACK APPROACHES him, PUTS HAND on his shoulder.

JACK

No hard feelings. I know you're an honest man and—
(an inspiration!)
—I'll *tell* you how much confidence I have in you. You *go* to Russia and you come back and tell me it's *good* and I'll believe you.

NARRATOR OPENS door, EXITS.

DISSOLVE

Finally the time came when there was, literally, nothing in the house to eat (this was late in 1949). And there were bills that simply could not be paid. And there were no jobs to be had, either on the black market or in any other market.

We had had worldwide publicity; our names and faces were well known. Aside from writing, although I had personally held jobs (in my youth) that ranged from managing a bookstore to teaching boy scouts about snakes, lizards, frogs, toads, and salamanders, there was very little that I was qualified to do. Hollywood was a company town, and I was not a factory worker or even a carpenter—in fact, I did not have a single useful trade.

Other blacklisted writers either were more resourceful and more creative or had better contacts. Some sold insurance; others, who had money put away, backed their wives in small dress or cosmetic shops; one sold wallpaper; one started a bar; others moved to New York and tried to break into television (*sub rosa*).

I was still submitting the outlines of the two novels to various publishers in New York, who reacted "favorably" but offered no advance. The anthology of writings on the Spanish war contained more than ninety authors, many with worldwide reputations, but it was being handled by the Veterans of the Abraham Lincoln Brigade, and their executive secretary reported that the table of contents evoked favorable reactions from several publishers—but no firm offer.

It was all too easy to borrow money, I'm afraid, from people who were generally sympathetic to our situation or from those who felt guilty because they were not in the same predicament. One big star, who insisted on giving it to me in cash, said, with enormous originality, "Hell, man, there but for the Grace of God . . ."

But I was determined not to borrow any more money if it could be avoided. I had another brilliant idea—a story idea, at least—and I approached the Biggest Star of Them All. I had met him several times in various places: at the swanky home of Clifford Odets, where we all listened to excellent recorded music when we were not listening to a strange, little man named Lewis Browne, who had written a book called *How Odd of God* (to choose the Jews). I had also met him at the Soviet consulate on the anniversaries of the October Revolution and/or Red Army Day, and he had even attended a private party to help launch the Marxist magazine *Mainstream*.

So I called Chaplin and asked for an appointment and drove up at the appointed time with a dry throat and a pounding heart. He was seated at an organ in the entrance to the house when I arrived, playing very well indeed, and he was courtesy personified. We went onto the semienclosed porch of his house, and he dismissed his secretary, who was seated at a typewriter. I found myself tongue-tied. He was, after all, the second great artist I had ever met in my life, and I scarcely knew him. But I remembered my businessman father's advice about how to "sell yourself" to a man, and I was determined to do it. I told him that I had a story idea that I wanted to sell to him and that all I wanted was to write a treatment of it and he could take it from there.

The great Walter Huston was still alive, and my idea involved a modern version of *Don Quixote,* with Huston playing the Knight of La Mancha and Chaplin as Sancho Panza. The locale would be modern Spain under Franco, and what would drive Quixote mad, instead of the romances of chivalry of the sixteenth century, would be his belief in the clichés of the now worldwide American credo, which I had learned at my father's knee: "A man is judged by the appearance he makes"; "Woman's place is in the home"; "Work hard enough and you will succeed"; "It's not who you are but who you know"—etc., etc., *ad nauseam.*

Chaplin was an excellent listener. He watched me as I spoke, one hand at his cheek, and seemed to be considering the idea. His eyes even lit up at one point, and my heart—which had not stopped pounding since I arrived at the portico of his house—was racing unbearably. The fantasy on which I was operating was out of hand—I could see it all: a good story that he would make into a great film. Whether or not my name was on it would not matter a damn, for *I* would know that I had supplied the original idea and worked out the treatment and that a genius had done the rest.

When I had finished (and no fee or amount of money had even been mentioned), he said, "It's a good idea. But there are two things about it that bother me. For one, I've been under attack so long for so many things that if I were to tamper with a great classic like that, they'd crucify me. For another, I like the things I do to be my *own.*"

My heart stopped racing instantly. In fact, I thought for a moment that it had stopped completely, and I knew that I had lost. Feebly, I said, "By the time you're through with it, it *will* be your own," but he shook his head.

I could hear my father's voice in my ear—another of the clichés of the American credo: "Never take no for an answer." *Sell* yourself! Put your foot in the door and don't take it out! But

I knew that while my father had been a superb salesman, I had none of the attributes of the breed. I had even found it impossible to distribute ten thousand free leaflets advertising a cheap fire extinguisher he had invented—and had floated them down the Hudson River instead.

Chaplin ordered tea and, without preamble, began to read to me sections of the *Limelight* screenplay, which he was completing; it was much more bitter in its attitude toward the public than the version that ultimately appeared on the screen. We also got into a discussion of *Crossfire*, which, to my astonishment, he insisted was an anti-Semitic film.

I couldn't get enthusiastic about the argument, for I kept thinking, You will leave here empty-handed and without a job, and what will you do tomorrow? But I asked him why he felt that way, and he said, "You remember Sam Levene, the way he played the part."

Then he stood up and *became* Sam Levene: his face changed; he assumed the stance; and he gestured, "washing" his hands. Inventing words to illustrate what he felt Levene's interpretation of the role of the Jewish victim implied, he said obsequiously, "Why're you picking on me? I'm a nice feller; really, I'm a nice feller. . . ."

It was a shattering performance, and it convinced me at the time; though when I thought about it later, I could not agree with him at all.

"That's funny," I said. "I'm a Jew too, and I don't know why I wasn't aware of this."

He smiled at me and said, "I'm not a Jew."

"I always thought you were."

"Many people do," he said, "and I've never bothered to deny it. But I'm not."

His young wife, Oona, appeared at that moment, dressed in a sunsuit, and her eyes were the eyes of her father, Eugene O'Neill, whom I had seen many time in Greenwich Village speakeasies during Prohibition and later at rehearsals of *Marco Millions* at the Guild Theatre. They were eyes that were so compelling that you wanted to dive into them immediately and drown.

Chaplin introduced us, though we had met before. He patted

her behind and said, "Why don't you join us for tea, child?" but she said that she was going to play tennis with Bill Tilden and would see us later.

I was becoming restless and was wondering why I did not excuse myself and leave. He would not buy the Cervantes idea and he was a busy man, and I should have been grateful for small favors and got out of his affluent life and driven down the hill in the old Hudson. But I remained, partly out of the fascination of watching a man who was obviously far more interested in himself than he was in anybody else—and was therefore disappointing one of his greatest admirers; for the only other great artist and human being I had met up to that time—Paul Robeson—was just the opposite: *he* was interested in the person he was talking to; and when he first played *Othello* at Princeton, I watched him autographing programs for young college students and directing on each one, as he or she approached his dressing room, the sort of concentration that he devoted to his role onstage.

Chaplin began to talk of Big Bill Tilden, who had recently been released from prison after almost a year's confinement for committing a homosexual offense. He said that when Tilden had been picked up, he, Chaplin, had gone to the judge and pleaded for him, telling the judge that if the court would release the man this once, he would guarantee that Tilden would leave the States. "I own a place in the south of France," he told the jurist, "and Bill can start a tennis club there. I'd be happy to let him live there rent-free till he's earning a living again."

I was listening to him and talking to myself, silently. I want to go home, I was saying; why don't I go? This man is going to be no help at all, and why should I sit and listen to him talk about himself?

The judge, said Chaplin, was amenable. Then Chaplin started to laugh and said, "You know, I told Bill we could get him out of this one if he'd go abroad and live on my place, but he said, no, he had committed a crime and he wanted to be punished for it! Can you imagine that!"

So Tilden did his time on the honor farm; and when he was released, Chaplin let him use the tennis court on his place to teach private pupils.

Chaplin suggested that we go down and watch, as he had a date to play too. So we walked down to the tennis court, and I watched Chaplin play doubles with Tilden and two other men. There was another fellow watching from the roof of the building that housed the dressing rooms; he was very young and very pretty, and he pouted through two sets.

Chaplin, at sixty, was fantastic on the court and, with his partner, held Tilden and his partner to a love game. Then Big Bill came up to the roof of the dressing-room house and said to the pretty young man, "I'm sorry it took so long. I'll walk you to the car."

"I can walk by my-*self*," the young man said, but he accepted Tilden's company.

Chaplin came up after showering, wearing a dressing gown, and walked *me* to my ancient car and said that he was sorry that he couldn't use the Quixote idea, but you know how it is.

I climbed in the Hudson, and he shook hands with me and turned and walked rapidly away. I looked into my hand; there was a bill folded up in it—a $100 bill.

The $100 didn't last more than three weeks, and the situation was just as desperate as before, so finally I went to see Lee Cobb, who was on his way up, in spite of having always been a character straight out of Dostoevski—or maybe because of it. He had a studio contract at that time that paid him $1,500 every single week. He had just bought a new house with wall-to-wall carpeting. He had a Capehart that covered half the wall of the living room and a record library that covered the other half. His convertible was still brand-new, and he still had his personal Beechcraft, in which he not only flew to New York when the mood struck him, but used weekends to hop to Las Vegas, where he regularly lost anywhere from one to several thousand dollars at the gaming tables; for, like Dostoevski himself, he was a compulsive gambler at the time.

He was an emotional man. During the hearings, he and his then wife had sent a wire reading: "You've raised our spirits and filled our hearts with pride by the magnificent stand you have taken for the preservation of our freedom. Please convey these sentiments to Albert and the others. Love." He was capable of bottomless moods of depression that put my own to shame, for he did not emerge from them for days; and during those days, he would not say a word to anyone, including his wife and child. I had even flown with him when he was in these moods and had touched earth again with a shattering sense of liberation from certain death. He was, and is, I imagine, a manic-depressive type who rarely goes through the manic phase. But he was *kind*.

I told him my predicament and asked for a loan of $500.

CAMERA COMES TO
INTERIOR. LEE'S LIVING ROOM. MED. TWO SHOT. LEE. NARRATOR
—as Lee's solemn face grows even more solemn.

LEE

I'm not solvent.

NARRATOR
(smiling)
Look, you could pick up the phone and get me $500 in less than five minutes.

LEE
(reasonably)
That won't solve your problem.
(pause)
What you need is a job.

NARRATOR
Right. Can you give me one?
(LEE SHAKES HEAD.)
Do you know where I can get one?
(no answer—warmly)
It's a matter of eating. There's nothing in the house to *eat*— and I have half a dollar in my pocket.

LEE
(sadly)
If that's the way it is, why don't you send Helen and Eva up here? We can always give them a meal—
(suddenly)
—or you can buy groceries and send the bills to me.

(getting hot)

You don't get the *point*! I need $500. Now!

LEE

(melancholy)

I can't give it to you.

The NARRATOR STANDS UP. He is unreasonably angry and wonders why he is feeling that way. He listens in amazement and horror to the SOUND of his own voice as he calls his friend a filthy name. LEE's Dostoevskian face is filled with sadness as he STANDS, in turn.

LEE

(pontifical)

I forgive you.

As NARRATOR looks startled, LEE CONTINUES swiftly.

LEE

I can understand how a man like you, who's been through what you've been through and who's going to prison, can say a thing like that to an old friend.

NARRATOR, remembering his interview with Jack, his old producer, STARTS for door. LEE FOLLOWS him.

LEE

I hope you'll come to see me again.

NARRATOR does not reply, REACHES for doorknob.

LEE

(watching him)

You're a revolutionary, you know.

(NARRATOR OPENS door)

Go *on* being a revolutionary.

(pause)

Go on being an example to me.

DISSOLVE TO

WASHINGTON, D.C. June, 1950.

The *Alice in Wonderland* aspects of the 1947 investigation of Hollywood were not confined to the totally unbelievable facets of the witch-hunt already touched upon: the blacklisting and

[245]

ostracism of almost two hundred motion-picture workers; the imprisonment of ten for a misdemeanor that had never before drawn down on its perpetrators more than a minimal fine; the momentary courage of hundreds of other Hollywood workers—who ran for cover the moment the whip was cracked; the power wielded by a congressional committee that had been held in wide contempt ever since it was first set up under the chairmanship of Martin Dies and that has yet to produce a piece of solid legislation; the wholesale betrayal of friends, wives, husbands, and former lovers by people anxious to preserve their paychecks and their real or symbolical swimming pools; the rationales concocted to make such betrayals even momentarily palatable to the betrayers.

The high comedy started in 1948 and came out of the mouth and activities of Chairman J. Parnell Thomas, *né* Feeney. Having expressed a sort of *rosé* indignation (which was edited out of the printed transcript of the hearings) that anyone could be so subversive and dishonest as to create motion-picture characters who were venal judges, stingy bankers, and corrupt Congressmen in order (as friendly witnesses insisted) to downgrade the American way of life, Thomas found himself in prison before any of "The Ten" got there.

He was exposed in 1948 by Drew Pearson and brought to trial, where he pleaded *nolo contendere* (no defense) to charges of having put some of his relatives on the public payroll and permitting them to kick back to his personal bank account. In 1949, he was sent to the Federal Correctional Institution in Danbury, Connecticut, where he later enjoyed the company of Lester Cole and Ring Lardner, Jr., and it is too convenient (but pleasant) to believe that poetic justice assigned such a chicken-shit personality to the work he did in prison: cleaning out the chicken run.

Though he was sentenced to six to eighteen months, only eight passed before he made parole; and President Truman, as one of his last acts in office, granted him a full pardon, along with another solon and a general who had done nothing, really, but pile up a little loot during the war by peddling their influence to munitions makers.*

The characters involved in this farce and the sequence of events would make a marvelous situation for a motion picture that (1) never could be made and (2) never would be believed if it were, for it is simply too pat.

And while Thomas' predicament was greeted in Hollywood with hilarious laughter, no one was optimistic enough to believe that his fate presaged any amelioration of the imminent fate of "The Ten"—for that would have been fantasy indeed.

But the fantasy *did* extend even into the sacrosanct halls of the Supreme Court of the United States, which, since the *West Virginia v. Barnett* decision of 1943, had sedulously sidestepped any reaffirmation of those rights which adhere to the American people under the First Amendment. It is not that the Supreme Court was not *asked* to make such a reaffirmation. In the case of "The Hollywood Ten," more than thirty briefs *amicus curiae,* representing scores of organizations and several million individuals, prayed the court to grant certiorari (that is, grant a hearing to the case)**—the largest number of such briefs ever filed up to that time except in the "restrictive covenant" cases that had come before the Court.

Two examples of this *Alice* (or perhaps it should be *Through the Looking-Glass*) quality attached to the name and personality of former Associate Justice Felix Frankfurter. A friend of mine, angered by the Supreme Court's June, 1950, refusal to review our case (a five-to-four decision), wrote to Mr. Justice Frankfurter to express his disappointment that Frankfurter himself had

* General Bennett Myers, imprisoned for subornation of perjury during an investigation of influence peddling; Congressman Andrew May, convicted for selling his influence to contractors seeking war contracts.

** Such organizations and individuals as the American Civil Liberties Union, the Unitarian Fellowship for Social Justice, the NAACP, the American Jewish Congress, Methodist Federation for Social Action, Fur and Leather Workers Union, United Furniture Workers, National Lawyers Guild, thirty-two leading publishers, writers, and playwrights, the American Labor Party, the Progressive Party, United Public Workers, Wives of the Hollywood Ten (this brief was written by my then wife).

been in the majority. Saying that he had followed the jurist's career for many decades, admired him greatly since the days when he defended Sacco and Vanzetti, and thought of him always as a liberal, my friend stated that he could not understand why Frankfurter and a majority of the Court refused to rule upon the important constitutional questions at issue.

To his astonishment, he received a reply from Frankfurter, which, alas, cannot be quoted verbatim, since my friend's outrage negated his sense of history and he tore up the letter and flushed it down the toilet. What the distinguished jurist said, in effect, was this: he did not usually answer such letters, not because he did not respect the people who wrote to him, but because it was obvious from my friend's letter that he was a layman who simply did not understand the law. The point, said Mr. Justice Frankfurter, was that in refusing certiorari, the Court was not making any determination of the merits of the case. All that the Court was doing was saying, in effect, that at the present time, it did not care to grant a hearing. (No reason need be given.) It could be, wrote Frankfurter, that at some future time, another case might come before the Court that would raise the same or similar issues, at which time the Court might be disposed to hear it.

Verbum sap.

In the last month before we went to prison, an associate of our New York attorneys was assigned to hang around the halls of the Supreme Court and try to get wind of which way the Court was going: was it going to grant certiorari or was it not?

He had been a clerk for Justice Frankfurter some years before, and he ran into the jurist in the corridor one day. The conversation is said to have gone something like this:

FRANKFURTER: Joe (call him Joe)! What are *you* doing down here?

JOE: I'm here on the Hollywood cases.

FRANKFURTER: So, you're associated with the Hollywood cases! Well, you tell your colleagues that rarely in my life have I had the pleasure of reading such brilliant and erudite briefs. Especially Judge Kenny's brief on "The Right of Silence." Wonderful! You tell them that it's a pleasure to read such cogent arguments.

He told them.

But the arguments apparently were not cogent enough. Nor was the appeal for a rehearing. Nor was the international excitement and indignation that the case had aroused, indignation that brought protests and/or resolutions from such individuals and organizations as the Author's Guild, the Association of Cinematograph and Allied Technicians (England), Vittorio De Sica and Roberto Rossellini, the International Congress of Cinematography (Perugia and Rome), George Bernard Shaw, Pablo Picasso, Martin Andersen Nexö, a Hollywood film-industry group numbering 209 writers, actors, directors, and producers, the Union of Technicians of the Cinema (France), the British Film Academy, Frédéric Joliot-Curie, the All India Progressive Writers Association, Gwyn Thomas, Union of French Film Workers, and the British Screen Writers Association.

Since John Howard Lawson and Dalton Trumbo had already been convicted, they left for jail; Adrian Scott was in the hospital recovering from an operation; the seven who remained to be tried left from Los Angeles International Airport, which was jammed with three thousand people (kept in order by police reinforcements).

To my astonishment, I saw the melancholy face of my former friend Lee Cobb; he was standing in the front row behind the police lines as I kissed my weeping wife and two sons good-bye (Eva had been left at a friend's house on the way). And as I walked across the apron to the plane, I remember saying something to him, to which he did not reply, but I cannot (oddly enough) recall what it was—or perhaps I don't want to remember it.

The seven were tried in one morning, before three separate judges (we had waived trial by jury), who gave five of us the maximum—one year and $1,000—and Biberman and Dmytryk half as much.

But although *Alice* and *Through the Looking-Glass* seem to be fantasy and nonsense, they are both among the most dialectical works ever created, for they were written by a mathematician, and if you examine the nonsense and fantasy carefully, you will discover that their logic is impeccable and that cause and effect are inextricably interrelated.

The same holds true for what happened to us—in reverse. Samuel Ornitz, Albert Maltz, and I appeared before Judge David A. Pine, and if we thought for a moment that a *Landsmann* might be inclined toward sympathetic understanding—not to mention leniency—we were swiftly disabused of that notion.

If Judge Pine can wait until I operate Warner Brothers Burbank studio (and give Jack Warner a job commensurate with his ability), I will be glad to cast him in a film as an American judge (*ca.* 1950), for he could have been type-cast by Hollywood itself. He was poised; his hair was white; his demeanor was judicial; he listened carefully and even smiled on occasion when our attorneys made cogent arguments; and he retired to his chambers for all of ten minutes to read a supplementary brief and letters urging probation in view of the fact that we were all first offenders and respectable citizens who had never so much as spat on the sidewalk.

Several hundred such letters, in fact, had been submitted to the three judges, as well as petitions with thousands of signatures. But Judge Pine (like the other two judges) found all three of us guilty as charged, and like the judges in the Lawson and Trumbo cases, he ruled out every "irrelevant" issue that our attorneys attempted to present.

These "irrelevant" issues included offers of proof:

1. That the question of political affiliation was an incriminating question that we could not be compelled to answer, since the Committee had made it plain that it considered the Communist Party an international criminal conspiracy;

2. That the question concerning trade-union affiliation was a link in a chain of questions to establish Communist membership and activities believed by the Committee to be criminal;

3. That the purpose of the Committee hearings was to inflict

penalties on those it believed to be Communists, including criminal sanctions, discharge from employment, and destruction of their careers;

4. That the hearings were specifically directed against each of the defendants;

5. That there was no waiver of the privilege against self-incrimination in any of the cases, whether the defendant invoked the First or the Fifth Amendments;

6. That the Committee failed to conduct its interrogations in such a way as to establish a refusal to answer.

In both the Trumbo and Lawson cases, the district and appellate courts and the Supreme Court itself, the latter by its refusal to hear the case, had brushed aside more important constitutional issues and matters of fact and law; for example:

1. That the Committee's utilization of congressional power to compel disclosure of private political opinion and association is forbidden by the First, Fourth, and Fifth Amendments, as well as by the Ninth and Tenth;

2. That this particular inquiry into the motion-picture industry lay entirely outside the lawful bounds of the power of the House Committee, because it constituted a censorship of the content of motion pictures (First Amendment);

3. That the Committee in its attempts to impose a blacklist had placed itself above the Constitution and had disregarded the elementary requirements of due process of law;

4. That the statute creating the Committee itself was on its face unconstitutional;

5. That the trial courts committed innumerable prejudicial errors and denied petitioners a fair trial.

In the trial courts themselves, the following offers of proof were brushed aside as irrelevant:

• An analysis of thirty-nine years of research into the content of American motion pictures, by Richard Griffith, executive director of the National Board of Review of Motion Pictures, Inc., to demonstrate that no American motion picture had ever contained "material which by any standard could be considered to be subversive to . . . our system of government . . ." and to demonstrate the impossibility of screenwriters' subverting the motion-picture screen and establish that they therefore represent no potential or actual threat;

• Cross-examination of Chairman J. Parnell Thomas and other committee members to demonstrate the actual purpose of the hearings: to inflict penalties on those believed to be Communists;

• Demonstration of the fact that the questions asked were not pertinent to the inquiry, were an illegal invasion of the defendants' right of privacy, and were not necessary to aid the Committee in any way in obtaining information for any lawful legislative purpose;

• Demonstration of the historic acceptance under American law of the privacy of union membership lists;

• Disclosure of the history of the Screen Writers' Guild and the early attempts to prevent its growth and development by many of the friendly witnesses before the Committee (James K. McGuinness, Rupert Hughes, Fred Niblo, Jr., Richard Macauley, and others), who, at the time, took the position of the motion-picture industry and supported its attempt to prevent the organization of screenwriters into an effective union.

The only questions that were relevant, apparently, were these:

1. Was there an investigation?
2. Was the man subpoenaed?
3. Did he appear?
4. Did he "refuse" to answer the questions?

Judge Pine smiled at me after he had pronounced me guilty as charged and asked whether I had anything I would like to say.

This is, of course *pro forma*, and while I was strongly tempted to say nothing, the obligation of a man who saw himself in the position of opposing the government when he thinks the government is wrong * dictated that something should be said.

My wife could not afford to make the trip from Los Angeles to Washington to witness this relatively unimportant moment. I thought briefly of Nazim Hikmet, the fine Turkish poet and

* See Twain's *A Connecticut Yankee in King Arthur's Court*, Thoreau on "Civil Disobedience," and the writings of other notable subversives.

revolutionary, who was doing thirty years in prison, of thousands of others who had been tortured to death in Nazi Germany for lesser crimes, and I hoped I did not sound too pretentious. Judge Pine smiled several times during the three minutes I spoke and nodded in agreement (?) once or twice, and then he pronounced sentence: ". . . twelve months in a common jail and that he pay a fine of $1,000."

It was a small courtroom, but it was impressive, as all American Federal courtrooms are impressive. It was paneled in oak and marble; the American flag stood behind the judge and to his right; the atmosphere was solemn, if not oppressive; the officers of the court—judges, attorneys, attendants—were soft-spoken, courteous, correct; the small audience was attentive; the place was clean and well lighted.

After all three of us had been convicted and sentenced, we were handcuffed and led by the U.S. marshal out of the courtroom and down the marble corridor to the elevator; and within the space of two minutes and two stories of a building, the dialectical opposite of the decorous judicial process was revealed: the bullpen was filthy and crowded with men; the paint was peeling off the walls; the open latrine in the corner stank; the men—mostly Negroes—sat on battered wooden benches around the walls, for the most part apathetic, depressed, and disinclined even to ask each other, "What're *you* in for?"

The gears began to mesh, to roll. The fingerprints were taken (again); the papers were filled out; the minutes dragged as we waited for a sandwich, which one of the cops eventually supplied, drank warm water from the fountain in the other corner, waited for transport to the Washington District Jail.

Some Negro prisoners who were being booked shouted through the screening at us, "Hiya, Hollywood kids!" Our attorneys made brief appearances on the other side of the wire, their faces distraught. Biberman and Dmytryk were brought in to be booked and held up their hands with six fingers extended, to indicate that they had each drawn six months instead of twelve.

We waited about two hours, then we were led, handcuffed two by two, through a narrow corridor and out into the brilliant

[253]

Washington sunlight, made more brilliant momentarily by the flashbulbs of a battery of newspaper photographers.

We rode through the streets of our capital city in a van, screened with heavy wire, to the District Jail, where the van was admitted through double doors and the process of finger-printing and mugging (with a number hung around your neck) began again, followed by stripping, showering, and the issuance, temporarily, of prison clothing. We were shaken down on our entrance into the central well of the prison, and what cigarettes we had managed to secrete were confiscated, with stern words of admonition not to try *that* again.

The strangest moment of all came shortly thereafter. We were directed to individual cells on various tiers of the prison; the doors of these cells opened, apparently automatically; we entered and the doors clanged shut.

In my cell there were two cots, double-deck; a toilet without a wooden seat; a washbasin; steel walls painted a dull green—nothing else. Later, a cellmate came in from a court hearing, but we could not make contact because he spoke a foreign language that I did not understand.

I stood at the entrance to the cell and automatically grasped the bars. It was almost instinctive behavior, although there is no doubt that it originated in my memory of countless prison films.

A trusty came to the cell and slipped me two packs of cigarettes. "Lawson and Trumbo bought these for you," he said.

"Where are they?"

"Shipped out—a couple days ago."

I tore open the pack and lit one with trembling hands. Can I *do* this? I thought; can I do this for a whole *year*?

FADE OUT

FADE IN

TEXARKANA. April, 1951.

Said Brother Hikmet, in "Advice to a Fellow Prisoner" (and he had spent fifteen years of a thirty-year term at the time):

Just because you did not give up your hopes
for the world, for your country, and for humanity,
they either send you to the gallows
or put you in jail
for ten years, for fifteen years
or, who cares, for even longer.
Never say,
"I wish I were swinging
at the end of a rope like a flag."
You must keep on living.
Perhaps living is not a pleasure any more
but it is your duty
to spite the enemy,
to live one more day.
In your jail one part of yourself may be all alone
like a stone at the bottom of the well,
but the other part of you
should mingle so with the crowds of the world
that in your jail you will tremble
with every rustling leaf forty days away from you.
It is sweet but dangerous
to wait for letters,
and to sing sad songs,
to keep awake till morning
with your eyes fixed on the ceiling.
Look at your face whenever you shave,
forget your age,
protect yourself from lice
and from the spring evenings.
And then you should never forget
how to eat your bread to the last crumb
and how to laugh heartily.
And who knows,
maybe your woman doesn't love you any more
(don't say it is a small matter;
to the man in jail
it is like a young limb broken off the tree).
It is bad to dream about the rose and the garden;

and good to dream of the mountains and the seas.
I would advise you
to read and write without any rest,
to take up weaving
and to cast mirrors.
So it is not impossible to spend
ten, fifteen years in a cell
or even more;
it can be done—
provided under your left breast
that precious gem
the jewelled heart stays bright.

When I thought of Hikmet, who was released by the Turkish government that same year after worldwide protest (and died the week these words were written), I was ashamed. Ten years? Fifteen years? How could a man live *five*? Yet all around me there were prisoners (such as the pimp who was puzzled by characters like me) who did "easier" time. As I *should* have, they considered a stretch in prison an occupational hazard. They could say, with the Polish cultural attaché I had met at the Hollywood party (with Hikmet), "I am a man who, in my time, has spent fifteen years in prison." (He had also said, quite casually, and I remembered it many times, "I was first arrested when I was seventeen. A student demonstration. During that first interrogation I lost all my teeth.")

A fellow prisoner had admonished me many times, passing my cell and seeing me sitting on the cot and staring at the wall, "Uh-uh! You'll never make it that way!" (*It is . . . dangerous . . . to keep awake till morning/with your eyes fixed on the ceiling.*)

They called me Short-Timer because I *was* a short-timer, but they also called men with long terms Short-Timer too, and these short-timers did not seem to be making "hard" time. They had the poise and the "adjustment" I had hoped to discover in myself, and I was certain that they had not developed those psychosomatic symptoms from which I suffered during that last month:

sleeplessness, daydreams of liberty, fear, mounting pains (mysteriously only in the right thigh), facial tics, flatulence and belching, loss of appetite.

But it is true that the time does pass—in time. It is true that the day of your release finally comes, and you go through the prison routine that final day in a state of anxiety that has no counterpart outside a psychiatric hospital.

For you are remembering the past and the present, and you are wondering about the future. You see—as you saw it so many years before—that wonderful moment in *The Life of Emile Zola* (made by Warner Brothers, no less) in which the prisoner Dreyfus (old Rudolph Schildkraut's son Joseph) is released from his cell on Devil's Island and *tries* to walk through the open door of his cell into the sunlight.

You are remembering the anthology you found in the prison library, called *The Great Prisoners,* in which you read a score of Dreyfus' letters and discovered, to your horror, that he was not the admirable and courageous man you had always thought, but a man whose pity for himself was so outrageous that you could almost hear him snivel as he wrote.

You are remembering the advice of the prison screws: "When you get out and're waiting for the bus in Texarkana, *stay* in the bus station. Nothing these Hoosier cops like better than to pick up a released con an' toss him in the hoosegow."

You are wondering how in hell you will make a living in a town—and in an industry and in a country—that has rejected you and made of you a social outcast, so that even your wife's neighbors, having read about you in the papers, refuse to speak to her and do not let their children play with your seven-year-old daughter.

You are remembering what your younger son, David, who was all of fifteen when you went to jail, said at the airport, "Don't let them push you around, Pop." And you remember your older son's tears (he was eighteen), and you remember what you were told by your wife when she visited: how Dan had hitchhiked to New York that first summer—looking for a substitute father in your older brother; how David was continually embroiled in fistfights because the other kids told him that his father was a traitor to his country.

But the day finally comes. And the night comes. And after supper, you are told to sit in your cell until they send for you. You sit. And four or five of the twenty men in your cellblock come to say good-bye (so few?). The whistle blows for lights out at ten, and you sit there for another hour, smoking and saying to yourself, I will go to sleep till they send for me, but you cannot go to sleep.

And just before eleven, you hear a slight sound, and the big man, Bob, the one built like a bear, the man who had gone AWOL from the Army and to whom you had lent James Aldridge's novel *The Diplomat,* tiptoes into the cell—the room lit by the floodlights outside—and he says, "I don' know what I'm gonna do without you here; I don' know *what* I'm gonna do," and there are tears in his eyes, and he grasps your hand briefly and moves rapidly out of the cell.

Then a screw comes (not Griffin this time) who tells you to go to the room where you will be dressed out, and he accompanies you through the sleeping cellblock and down the empty corridors and down the stairs to a small room, where you find another screw on duty, who hands you the suitcase your wife has sent.

There is the "good" suit you used to wear at home, but it is somewhat too large for you; and there is a white shirt and a tie and shoes, all of which feel uncomfortable when you have put them on; and since it is cold out that night, the screw insists on giving you a cheap felt hat, though you never wear hats.

Then you are told to sit on a bench in the hall outside the control room; and the hands of the big clock on the wall never move, but the time passes until midnight, when the man on duty in the office comes out and calls your name. You go into the office, and he hands you a number of articles, naming each one as he hands it over: "Your books. Your papers. The plane ticket your wife sent. The balance of your money," and you sign a receipt for these articles and go back to the bench and sit. (You wonder about the bus ticket to Dallas.)

You were supposed to be released at midnight, but it is past midnight now. You are going into town in a light pickup truck driven by one of the hacks who is delivering milk to the railroad station in Texarkana.

And at 12:25 (the bus leaves at 1 A.M.), the hack beckons to you, and you go through the barred gate, which is locked behind you, and walk to the truck in front of the administration building, where you used to mow the lawn, and climb in next to the driver. He waves one arm at the guy in the control tower (with a rifle?), and you move out of the prison grounds and onto the highway.

Far down the highway, past the officers' village, where everyone seems to be asleep, there is a standpipe you had noticed ten months earlier when you were driven to the prison: natural gas is flaming bright blue from the top of the pipe in a jet ten feet tall. You ask the driver, "How long has that been burning?" and he says, "Long's I can remember, an' I been here eight years come August," and you think, What a waste!

Then you are in the town, and across the street from the bus station, the driver pulls on his brake and says, "I'll get your ticket; stay here," and he crosses the street.

He is back in a few minutes and hands you the ticket and says, "Go into the waiting room and wait here. The bus's late." He puts out his hand and says, "Good luck."

So you cross the street with your suitcase (the packages of books, papers, letters—unopened—are now inside it) and walk into the lighted waiting room with your heart in your mouth.

Do they know I am a convict, released? Are they looking at me? (They glance at you.) You go to the counter and say, "When is the bus for Dallas due?" and the woman who looks as though she knows who you are, all right, says, "It's late."

You want to say, "How late?" but are afraid of attracting attention to yourself. You remember Dreyfus-Schildkraut walking tentatively out of his cell and turning and walking back inside again, twice, three times, before he walks into the sunlight, his entire body hunched—as though he expected a blow on the head.

So you ask for change of $5 and go to the phone booth and

place a call to Los Angeles, collect. It is 12:45 A.M. in Texarkana; it is 10:45 P.M. in Los Angeles.

The voice is familiar, and you say, "I'm waiting for the bus to Dallas, but it's late. How are you?"

"Fine," she says.

"How's Eva?"

"Asleep."

"See you tomorrow at eleven."

"Yes, yes," she says. "How do you *feel?*"

"Fine, fine."

Then you hang up, and noticing the lunch counter, you approach it and ask the sleepy waitress whether you can have a steak. A steak! A *real* steak that you can *pay* for. "Rare."

"Sure thing," she says, so you order the most expensive steak on the greasy, fly-specked menu ($1.50); it comes in short order, and it is tougher than the burro you ate in Spain.

And the bus, which was supposed to leave at one, does not leave until three.

DISSOLVE TO

"I assume that I am speaking to an honest man."

All this is ancient history, and history never really repeats itself, in spite of Karl Marx, who wrote, "Hegel remarks somewhere that all great, world historical facts and personages occur, as it were, twice. He has forgotten to add: the first time as tragedy, the second as farce." Men and institutions change, growing out of themselves into something new and different, good, bad, or *in*different.

Although the Supreme Court has yet to tackle a First Amendment case head on, it has shown the courage to make an oblique attack. It happened in 1957, when John T. Watkins' appeal from a contempt of Congress conviction was heard by the Court—and reversed. On the same day, it set free five West Coast leaders of the Communist Party who had been convicted under the Smith Act and ordered new trials for nine others.

Both reversals were made on technicalities that need not concern us here, but in his majority decision in *Watkins*, Chief

[*260*]

Justice Earl Warren went out of his way to reaffirm the viability of the First Amendment:

"There is no general authority," he wrote, "to expose the private affairs of individuals without justification in terms of the functions of Congress. . . . Nor is the Congress a law enforcement or trial agency. . . . No inquiry is an end in itself; it must be related to and in furtherance of a legitimate task of the Congress. Investigations conducted solely for the personal aggrandizement of the investigators or to 'punish' those investigated are indefensible. . . . The Bill of Rights is applicable to investigations as to all forms of governmental action. . . ."

And, even more pertinently: "Who can define the meaning of 'un-American'?" asked Warren.

The Washington *Post* (June 20, 1957) picked up the question and drew the logical conclusion: "However 'un-American' it might seem, peaceful advocacy of change to a parliamentary system or even to a Socialist system is certainly as permissible as, say, advocacy of an income tax or suffrage for women or the abolition of slavery."

Watkins had testified about his past political associations and activities but had refused to give the names of persons who might have been Communist party members but were so no longer.

The fourteen California Communist leaders had been convicted of "conspiring to teach and advocate" the violent overthrow of the government. The Supreme Court held that no one can be convicted of so nebulous a crime. *The New York Times* put it this way in its lead editorial (June 23, 1957): "It [the government] will have to prove that the prisoners at the bar actually intended to overthrow the Government by violence or to persuade others to attempt to do so."

Yet the House un-Americans (this free translation, and more appropriate version, of the group's formal name is, the Committee has stated, *proof* of Communist subversion) continues to operate at the same old stand and gets enormous appropriations every time it asks for them, with scarcely a dissenting vote in the House. (At the moment of writing, it is engaged in harassing a number of college students who deliberately challenged the State Department's illegal ban on travel to Cuba and visited that dangerous little island "ninety miles from home.")

And Hollywood itself has moved, in this particular area, if only an inch or two—and under enormous pressure. Eight of "The Hollywood Ten" are alive: Dmytryk "recanted"; on March 10, 1957, at the age of 66, Sam Ornitz died of cancer in the Motion Picture Country Home; and two of "The Ten" are writing under their own names again: Dalton Trumbo and Ring Lardner, Jr.

The blacklisted actors have never returned to the screen, with the exception of two or three who have appeared in independently made and exhibited films. A few have managed to work their way back onto the Broadway stage and into television programs, but scores of literary and dramatic artists are still indifferent salesmen of real estate, insurance, cosmetics, ladies' lingerie, toy models, and building materials. Some have gone to Europe, but few have made it there in film.

In the last five years, it has seemed that the blacklist—whose existence the producers have always denied—is on its way out.*
In 1959, the Academy of Motion Picture Arts and Sciences rescinded its inane bylaw (instituted in 1956 under Committee pressure) that precluded even the nomination of anyone who had refused to cooperate with the un-Americans.

By that time, it was common knowledge that writers who were reportedly on the list had been responsible for such films as *Friendly Persuasion* (Michael Wilson), which had been denied nomination for an Oscar under the bylaw; *The Bridge on the River Kwai* (Wilson and Carl Foreman), which won; *The Brave One* ("Robert Rich"), which won; *The Defiant Ones* ("Nathan E. Douglas"), which won; and others of like stature.

* So far as is known, the first commercial TV program dealing with this subject was CBS's series *The Defenders*, on January 18, 1964. It was written by Ernest Kinoy, was called "Blacklist," and was an honest and uncompromising attack on the blacklisting of people for holding unorthodox political opinions. The actor-hero of the story had appeared for and supported Republican Spain and had the guts to say he still felt he had done the right thing. The program, appropriately, won several Emmy awards for its creators.

Following the revelation that Ned Young, blacklisted actor-writer, was the "Douglas" who, with coauthor Harold Jacob Smith, had won the Oscar in 1958 for *The Defiant Ones,* Dalton Trumbo modestly admitted that he was the "Robert Rich" who had not appeared to claim his award for *The Brave One* the year before. He also revealed, on June 15, 1960, in a front-page interview in *Variety* that he had written thirty screenplays for money in the thirteen years since the ax fell. He said, "Everybody used to say: 'Why don't you spill everything and end all this trouble?' I haven't heard that recently. As a matter of fact, it hasn't happened in quite a while."

Earlier that year, independent producer Otto Preminger had publicly announced the hiring of Trumbo to do the screenplay from Leon Uris' *Exodus;* and on August 8 of the same year, *The New York Times* broke the news that he was also the writer of the film version of Howard Fast's *Spartacus* and that he would receive solo credit on the screen.*

Trumbo's success in breaking the blacklist is due, of course, to several factors: he had important credits and a big reputation long before 1947, and he is probably one of the best screenwriters Hollywood ever developed. In addition, he is a consummate public-relations artist, with a magnificent sense of timing and a mordant wit.

When the news was out about *Exodus*—and when the film was released—the American Legion and the Motion Picture Alliance for the Preservation of American Ideals passed protest resolutions and a handful of pickets appeared in front of a handful of theaters. The same thing happened when news of *Spartacus* ** and the film itself were released. But the sky did not fall, the earth did not burn—and both pictures made millions of dol-

---

* This is surely the cream of the jest, for when Fast wrote his novel, he was an avowed Communist, and he had to print it himself. When he recanted, the book was reprinted and sold in millions of copies; it was reviewed in ecstatic terms by the commercial press for the first time and sold to the movies.

** *Exodus* was distributed by United Artists, not a member of the MPAA, which formulated the blacklist; *Spartacus* by Universal-International, which at the time had withdrawn from the MPAA.

lars; and Trumbo is now reputed to be the highest-paid screen-writer in Hollywood history.

But the bulk of the blacklisted writers do not have his credits or prestige—or his talent—and so they remain "nonexistent" in their former field. Their cause was also set back a few years by an incident in 1960 involving Frank Sinatra, who announced the hiring of Albert Maltz to write the screenplay for William Bradford Huie's novel *The Execution of Private Slovik*.

Maltz and Sinatra had been friendly since World War II when Albert did a short screenplay starring the singer, called *The House I Live In* (from Earl Robinson's famous song of the period). But Sinatra apparently made a few miscalculations: he chose a book about the only American to be executed as a deserter during the war; he announced the hiring of Maltz before the film was in work; and he forgot for a moment that as an entertainer (no matter how wealthy), he was far more vulnerable to pressure than an independent producer or director.

The attack on him was swift and relentless, and within a few weeks he knuckled under to Hedda Hopper, the Hearst press, the Legion, and—so the rumor went—the Kennedy machine.

". . . the American public," Sinatra announced, "has indicated it feels the morality of hiring Albert Maltz is the more crucial matter,* and I will accept this majority opinion." **

If the Maltz hiring-firing was a setback to those fighting the blacklist, the announcement by Otto Preminger (again) that he had signed Ring Lardner, Jr., who had written *Forever Amber* for Preminger in 1947, to write a screenplay from the Patrick Dennis' novel *Genius* was distinctly heartening.

Lardner paid tribute to Preminger for being the first to hire Trumbo openly and said that it was "the most important individual step" against the blacklist, but he insisted that "the blacklist still exists. There's a general delusion that it's in the dim past,

* More crucial, that is, than Maltz's "pro-American approach to the story," which Sinatra praised.
** The decisive pressure, it is said, came from the Pentagon, which unequivocally told Sinatra's representatives that it did not want the picture made, period. But Huie's book has since been purchased by an independent producer.

[264]

but it is still in operation in both motion pictures and television"
(*The New York Times*, November 27, 1962). More than three
hundred motion-picture artists still say amen to that.*

In addition to permanent exclusion from one's chosen field of
employment, social ostracism, divorce, and voluntary exile (a list
that numbers many hundreds if not thousands), there have been
even greater tragedies that cannot be forgotten. For in the roll
call of victims of the proliferating local, state, and national witch-
hunting committees, there are many who cannot answer. Their
premature deaths from "natural" causes and from suicide may be
laid directly or indirectly at the doors of these inquisitorial outfits.

Number among them: John Garfield, heart attack preceding
his second scheduled appearance before the un-Americans; Harry
Dexter White, assistant to the Secretary of the Treasury, heart
attack following appearance before the Committee, where he
denied Whittaker Chambers' accusations that he had headed an
espionage ring; Mady Christians, actress, died following blacklisting, which followed Committee testimony; John Brown, actor,
died following blacklisting by all media after decades of perform-
ing on radio; Edwin Rolfe, poet, blacklisted, unemployable, heart
attack.

Also, Frances Young, blacklisted actress-wife of blacklisted
actor-writer, suicide; Madelyn Dmytryk, former wife of then-
blacklisted director, suicide; Philip Loeb, blacklisted actor, suicide; E. Herbert Norman, Canadian ambassador to Egypt,
accused by a Senate committee of having been a Communist, suicide; Lawrence Duggan, State Department official, suicide following charges before the un-Americans that he had been a
courier for Whittaker Chambers; Abraham Feller, UN general
counsel, suicide following appearance before the Senate Internal
Security Committee; Raymond Kaplan, Voice of America engineer, suicide following attack by Senator McCarthy's committee.

Also, Francis O. Matthieson, Harvard professor and renowned

* On January 26, 1964, in the *New York Herald Tribune*, Joe Hyams
wrote that Albert Maltz had finally broken through the Hollywood ice jam:
"He has been hired by an independent producer to write under his own
name a screenplay of a film. No publicity has been released. 'We don't want
to take any chances with the lunatic fringe at this time,' said the producer."

critic, suicide following accusation by J. B. Matthews before a Massachusetts legislative committee that he was a Communist-front member; Walter Marvin Smith, Justice Department attorney, suicide after being mentioned as a notary in a transaction involving Alger Hiss; Morton E. Kent, former State Department official, suicide following FBI hounding; John Winant, U.S. ambassador to Britain under FDR, suicide following charges that he had failed to facilitate entry of U.S. troops into Berlin; William K. Sherwood, brilliant young Stanford University research scientist, suicide by poison two days before his scheduled appearance before the un-Americans in San Francisco.

Sherwood's widow, Barbara, attempted to read a statement before the Committee in June of 1957. She was thrown out of the hearing room. This is her statement:

"Members of the Un-American Activities Committee:

"You have helped kill my husband and make my four children fatherless.

"That is our personal tragedy.

"It is as nothing to the crime you have committed against the children of America and the children of the world.

"For when you drove my husband to his death, you destroyed a man of bright promise, a talented fighter in the army of devoted men who are warring against disease.

"My husband thought that he had found an important clue to the understanding of cancer and schizophrenia. Perhaps he was mistaken. Only time, and the opportunity to continue his researches, could have supplied the answer.

"This opportunity your committee has denied him, and the loss is not only mine.

"Throughout his lifetime, my husband had but one goal: to ease the suffering of mankind.

"It was this goal that drew him to support the Loyalists in the Spanish Civil War, that inspired his youthful identification with radical causes.

"It was this goal that led him, when greater maturity had mellowed and deepened his understanding, to abandon politics completely and devote himself single-mindedly to science.

"Is it a crime for a young man in his twenties to dream of a bright new world?

"Must the children of our country leave their idealism in the cradle so that their future careers will not be blighted by the Un-American Activities Committee?

"And is it fitting, now that he is dead, that you insinuate he was a traitor to his country?

"Is not his death enough for you?

"Must you also besmirch his honor, now that he is no longer able to answer you?

"Members of the Committee, what you have done and what you are doing is an evil thing. Do not persist in it. Go away, go home, bow your heads in prayer and ask forgiveness of your God."

Requiescat.

DISSOLVE

For those of us who have survived, there are many gratifications to be found in our particular forms of "nonexistence," though I still cannot believe that there are any extenuations to be found in poverty.

For one: in my last interview before leaving Texarkana to re-enter the *free* world, one of the prison officials said, "Bessie, I've read your testimony and the others'; I've looked up the Supreme Court decisions in similar cases and I've studied a lot of American history since you came here. And I want to tell you this: I understand you're some sort of radical—and I don't hold with such ideas—but from what I understand of the American democratic tradition, you *are* here on a bum rap."

For another: ever since I rejected the idea (at twenty) that if I could not write a novel as great as *War and Peace,* there would be no point in writing at all, I have been compelled to put words on paper. So there is a new novel going the rounds; there is a television play I made from my novel *The un-Americans* that is being produced this year in two Socialist countries and a ninety-minute radio version of the same un-American story that the British Broadcasting Corporation will produce. It is bittersweet (if not too remunerative) to know that the novel itself has sold twenty times as well in foreign countries as it did in my own.

There was even a recent offer (black market, of course) from an independent producer to write a screenplay about a celebrated American radical who has been safely dead for thirty-seven years and may therefore be considered sanctified: Eugene V. Debs.

And there is my job in a San Francisco nightclub.

I have been in and around the theater all my life; I like and understand show people and can get along with them. And my boss, while totally unpredictable and erratic in most areas, is basically a kind man and doesn't give a hoot in hell what I believe in or what I've done in the past. In this gin mill, where I am employed as a sort of combination stage manager, light man, and disembodied voice announcing the acts over an off-stage mike, not a night passes but some lush in the showroom applauds loudly when I come onstage to adjust the microphone. Not a week passes but someone at the bar says, "Aren't you Sir Cedric Hardwicke?" And for seven years, I have scrupulously denied the allegation.

But one week a man said, "Your face's familiar."

"Hardwicke," I said, not even taking the trouble to practice my phony British accent.

The fellow reached in his pocket for pen and paper, then thought better of it. He said, "Are you up here to make a movie?"

"Just the weekend," I replied.

"I've enjoyed your pictures so much."

"Thank you."

He bought his ticket and went into the showroom, and I've been wondering ever since what he felt when I came out on the stage between the acts with the comedian's props, laid them on the piano, and raised the mike to the right height.*

FADE OUT

* I *should* have said, "And there *was* my job in a San Francisco nightclub." For it ended the week I wrote those very words, seven years and six days after it began, when a new manager decided to replace a number of the staff with his own stooges. So what began in 1947 as a personal "tragedy" seems to have ended in 1963 as a farce. Could it be that Marx was right?

index

Abraham Lincoln Brigade, 13, 212, 239; *see also* Lincoln Battalion
Academy of Motion Picture Arts and Sciences, 262; Awards, 140–142, 144, 186, 262–263
Action in the North Atlantic (film), 65–67, 136
Adler, Larry, 195
"Advice to a Fellow Prisoner" (poem), 254–256
Agriculture, Department of, 165–166
Aherne, Brian, 167
Aldington, Richard, 34
Aldridge, James, 146, 258
All India Progressive Writers Association, 249
Allied Artists, 164, 167–172
Amazing Dr. Clitterhouse, The (film), 106–111
American Civil Liberties Union, 247
American Jewish Congress, 247
American Labor Party, 247
American Legion, 263, 264
American Youth for Democracy, 217
Anders, Glenn, 2
Animal Kingdom (film), 197
Anti-Semitism, 164–165, 167, 237–238
A & P, 12
Ardrey, Robert, 195
Arnold, General Henry (Hap), 206
Arnold, Thurman, 222
Artists' Front to Win the War, 217
A. & S. Lyons, 159–163
Association of Cinematography and Allied Technicians, 249

Atkinson, Brooks, 16
Auslander, Dr. Joseph, 212
Authors' Guild, 24, 249

Bacall, Lauren, 189, 195, 222
"Baker," 82–87, 88
Baker, Mary, 32–33
Bakewell, Claude Ignatius, 223
Balaban, Barney, 224
Ball, Lucille, 222
Barsky, Dr. Edward K., 212
Bastille Day, 164, 184
Bates, Ralph, 12
Baum, Vicki, 96, 99
Baxter, Alan, 159, 163
Beechcraft Bonanza, 219–221, 243
Benjamin, Maurice, 193
Bennett, Constance, 2, 167–170, 171, 182–183, 200
Bennett, Richard, 16, 167
Bergman, Ingrid, 102–103, 104, 218
Bernstein, Leonard, 189–190, 222
Bess, Demaree, 72
Bessie, Alvah: as Academy Award nominee, 136, 140–142, 144; at Allied Artists, 164, 166–172; autobiography of, 235; blamed for CSU strike, 138–139; at Columbia, 164; described, 1; dream of, 232–233; early career of, 11–24, 33, 92–93, 238; edits anthology on Spanish Civil War, 231, 239; and "Hal," 167, 182–183, 229–230; and HUAC, 172, 182–183, 195–196, 210–217; illness of, 78–79; interviews stars, 101–105, 142–

Eberharter, Herman Peter, 223
Eisenhower, General Dwight D.,
213, 215
Emerson, Faye, 74, 97
Endore, Guy, 20, 198
Epstein, Julius and Philip (the
Twins), 36, 197
Erskine, John, 11
Execution of Private Slovik, The
(novel), 264
Esquire (magazine), 199, 218
Executive Order 9835, 166
Exodus (film), 186, 263

Fair Employment Practices Com-
mittee, 165
Fairbanks, Douglas, Jr., 222
Fascism, 11, 212, 221, 222; in
American organizations, 164,
167, 208; as seen by Holly-
wood, 79, 104, 128, 131, 136;
of E. F. Sullivan, 164; and J.
Warner, 79, 131
Fast, Howard, 263
Faulkner, William, 1, 30–31, 34;
as script writer, 126–127
Faust (play), 20, 44
Federal Bureau of Investigation
(FBI), 2, 204, 266; agents of,
72, 232–235
Federal Correctional Institution
(Danbury, Conn.), 42, 246
Federal Correctional Institution
(Texarkana, Tex.), 2, 9, 111–
118, 154–158, 172–182, 254–
259; captain at, 117–118; description of, 3–5, 9, 57–58;
garage at, 57–58; inmates at,
39–40, 46, 58–62, 112, 144–
154, 174–177, 256, 258;
journey to, 42–46; officers at,
87–88; officials at, 146–149,
267; poems written in, 81–82,
117–118, 120–121, 145, 153,
177–179; warden at, 1, 87, 118,
120–125
Federal prison system, described,
122–123, 125
Feeney, J. Parnell; *see* Thomas, J.
Parnell
Feller, Abraham, 265
Feuchtwanger, Lion, 68, 96
Fifth Amendment, 188, 251

Fifth Column, The (play), 219
First Amendment, 156, 189, 211,
247, 251, 260–261; text of, 6
Fishman, Moe, 212
Flynn, Errol, 2, 36, 80, 81; and
Helen Clare Bessie, 91–92; trial
of, 52–53; in *Northern Pursuit*,
51, 53–54
Fonda, Henry, 189–190
For Whom the Bell Tolls (film),
103–105
Foreman, Carl, 262
Forever Amber (film), 264
Fountainhead, The (novel), 201
France (ship), 10
Franco, General Francisco, 208, 211,
212
Frank, Leonhard, 1; described, 96;
life and character of, 96–99,
111; writing *Dr. Clitterhouse*,
106–111
Frankfurter, Felix, 247–248
Freeman, Y. Frank, 224
Friendly Persuasion (film), 262
Fritchman, the Reverend Stephen
H., 179–180
Fuchs, Daniel, 1, 20; in Hollywood,
29, 33, 34–35, 47, 48, 93
Fur and Leather Workers Union,
247

Gage, Arthur, 73, 76
Gallo, Luigi, 133–134
Garfield, John, 2, 36, 64, 222, 265;
films of, 65–66, 127
Garland, Judy, 222
Geller, James, 18–19, 20, 105; inter-
view with, 32–33
Genius (novel), 264
Gentlewoman (play), 93
Gershwin, Ira, 195
Ghosts of Berchtesgaden, The (film),
128
Gleason, James, 222
Goddard, Paulette, 189–190, 222
Goetz, William, 224
Goldwyn, Samuel, 68, 224
Goodman, Benny, 189–190
Grand Hotel (film), 96
Grant, Cary, 127
Grapes of Wrath, The (novel), 55,
88
Grauman's Chinese Theater, 141

United Artists, 263
United Electrical and Machine Workers' Union, 132, 135
United Furniture Workers, 247
United Jewish Appeal, 64
United Public Workers, 247
Universal-International, 229, 263
UNRRA, 206
Uris, Leon, 263

Vail, Richard B., 195
Vane, Sutton, 73
Variety (trade paper), 25–26, 263
Very Thought of You, The (film), 73–75, 80–81, 131, 196, 229
Veterans of the Abraham Lincoln Brigade (VALB), 17, 212, 239
"Vince" (director), 1, 47–48, 64
Volpone (play), 20
Volunteer for Liberty (newspaper), 15, 29

Wald, Jerry, 1, 31, 49, 64, 66, 67, 128, 190; Alvah Bessie's first meeting with, 33–34; helps write a story, 76–78, 79–80, 130–131, 140; and *The Very Thought of You*, 73, 80
Waldorf-Astoria Hotel meeting and manifesto, 221, 223, 225, 230
Wallace, Henry A., 54
Walsh, Raoul, 1, 53–54
Wanger, Walter, 222, 224, 225
Warner, Albert, 224
Warner Brothers, 198, 229; Alvah Bessie's contract with, 27, 29, 75, 139, 229; engages Alvah Bessie, 19–24; pool of writers at, 36, 46–48, 105–106, 125–127
Warner, Harry, 63–64, 131
Warner, Jack L., 2, 22, 23–24, 63–64, 65, 102, 108; deposition of, 227–229; and Fascism, 79, 131; and HUAC, 64–65, 166, 195–

Warner, Jack L. (*cont.*)
198, 200, 207; meeting with, 80–81; releases Alvah Bessie, 136, 138–139, 227–228
Warren, Earl, 260–261
Washington (D.C.) District Jail, 2, 253–254; described, 36–42; poem written in, 39, 40–41
Washington *Post* (newspaper), 261
Washington *Times-Herald* (newspaper), 209
Watkins, John T., 260, 261
Webster, Ben, 163
Weiskopf, Franz, 96
West Virginia v. *Barnett*, 9, 247
White, David McKelvey, 13
White, Harry D., 265
Whitty, Dame May, 163
Wiggam, Lionel, 73
Wilk, Jake, 27; interviews with, 19, 20–22, 24
Williams, Esther, 146–147
Williamson, Thames, 138
Wilson, Michael, 262
Winant, John, 266
Winter Soldier, The (novel), 231
Without Fear or Favor (screenplay), 76–78, 79, 130–131
Wives of the Hollywood Ten, 247
Wood, Sam, 104, 200
World War II, as seen by Hollywood, 63–65, 127
WQXR, 23
Wyatt, Jane, 195, 222
Wyler, William, 200, 222
Wynn, Keenan, 222

Young Communist League, 132, 217
Young, Frances, 265
Young, Ned, 262–263
Young, Robert, 222
Young, Stark, 2

Zanville, Bernard, 66–67, 74
Zina, 68–70
Zweig, Stefan, 96